Juliett Platoon worked as a team, the way we were trained. One for all and all for one. All the men of Juliett Platoon have their own stories to tell. Some may be more accurate, some may not be. This is my story as seen through my eyes from my position within the platoon.

I owe my getting back to the States alive to the professionalism of the officers and enlisted men of Juliett Platoon. What a lucky man I am to be alive.

DARRYL YOUNG

THE ELEMENT OF SURPRISE:

Navy SEALs in Vietnam

Darryl Young

IVY BOOKS • NEW YORK

Ivy Books
Published by Ballantine Books
Copyright © 1990 by Darryl L. Young

Library of Congress Catalog Card Number: 89-92452

ISBN-0-8041-0581-2

Manufactured in the United States of America

First Edition: May 1990

Maps by Bob Rosenburgh

DEDICATION

To my wife of sixteen years, Sandy; to my son, Jamie; to my daughter, Jennifer—the most valuable people in my life.

To my mother and father—thanks for saving all my letters, movies, photos, notes, maps, and my UDT swim fins.

To the officers and enlisted men of Juliett Platoon and all Navy SEALs and Underwater Demolition Team members who served, lived, and died in Vietnam.

ACKNOWLEDGMENTS

I am deeply appreciative and grateful for the support and help of the following people. Without them this book would have been a hard obstacle to complete.

UDT/SEAL teammates: Nicolas E. Walsh, M.D. Timothy R. Reeves, Barry E. Strausbaugh, Lloyd "Doc" Schrier, John A. Shannon, Lt. Ronald R. Weber, Frank "Fronk" Schroeder, John Passyka, Sr. Chief Petty Officer Jim Berta, Michael Emerson, Greg Burham, Tom Boyhan, Craig Banfield, Dan Blocker, Brian Curle, Pete Remillard, Gary "Abe" Abrahamson, and Darryl "Willie" Wilson.

I would also like to thank Lt. Commander (ret.) John Keuter for information and support, John Jadwinski for a history of the light SEAL support craft, Roger Joy for friendship and support, Pete Schroeder for marine recon information, and Jack Green for literary coaching. Thanks also to Verna Brown, typist, James Reeves, author of MEKONG, Owen Lock, Editor, Ivy Books, and Ellen Key Harris, editorial assistant.

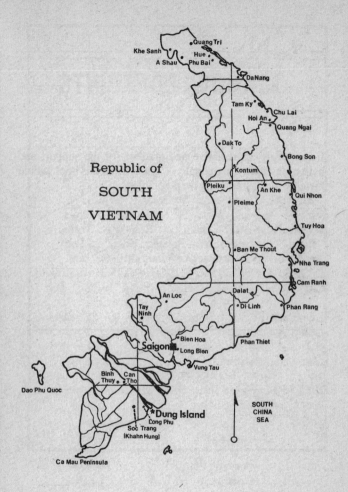

Republic of
SOUTH
VIETNAM

Quang Tri
Khe Sanh
Hue
A Shau
Phu Bai
Da Nang
Tam Ky
Chu Lai
Hoi An
Quang Ngai
Dak To
Bong Son
Kontum
Pleiku
An Khe
Qui Nhon
Pleime
Tuy Hoa
Ban Me Thout
Nha Trang
Cam Ranh
An Loc
Dalat
Di Linh
Phan Rang
Tay
Ninh
Bien Hoa
Phan Thiet
Saigon
Long Bien
Vung Tau
Binh
Thuy
Can
Tho
Dao Phu Quoc
★ Dung Island
Long Phu
Soc Trang
(Khahn Hung)
Ca Mau Peninsula
SOUTH
CHINA
SEA

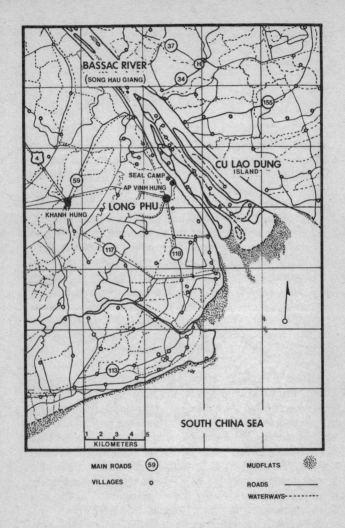

BASSAC RIVER
(SONG HAU GIANG)

37

H

34

155

CU LAO DUNG
ISLAND

4

59

SEAL CAMP

AP VINH HUNG

LONG PHU

KHANH HUNG

117

118

113

SOUTH CHINA SEA

1 2 3 4 5
KILOMETERS

MAIN ROADS   59

VILLAGES   o

MUDFLATS

ROADS ————

WATERWAYS - - - - - -

"Courage is
almost a contradiction in terms.
It means a strong desire to live
taking the form of a readiness to die."
                              G.A. CHESTERSON

I arrived at Coronado Naval Amphibious Base in San Diego California in August of 1969 as a brand new naval ensign. Like the rest of the officers and men in my Underwater Demolition Team (UDT) training class, I wanted to become part of the best of the best, the United States Navy SEAL (*Sea Air Land*) Teams. For officers and chief petty officers, UDT training was preceded by a two-week indoctrination course which introduced us to the handling of the "inflatable boat, small" (IBS), tried to prepare our bodies for the coming physical assault—which no one *could* truly prepare for—and to provide leadership during the stress of training to come. Each day started with two hours of calisthenics, followed by IBS work, running in the sand, or ocean swims. The two weeks passed quickly and soon all 204 of us, officers and enlisted, were assembled as a training class, Class 54.

No one is forced to undergo UDT training; all must volunteer. Prior to assignment to the training, each of us had been screened to insure that we were physically, mentally, and psychologically ready to withstand the onslaught of the next six months. Even with the screening, historically about three-fourths of those who start UDT training fail to complete it. To quit, an individual merely had to throw his helmet down and say, "I quit." With that, he was quickly removed from the training class and returned to the unit from which he came with no stigma attached.

The training brochure stated, "UDT training requires extremely high personal commitment and dedication to complete the course of instruction." If there was ever an understatement, that was it. We soon realized the only easy day was yesterday. The minimum physical requirements for completion of training were to run the obstacle course in 10 minutes, swim 2 miles in the ocean with fins in 70 minutes, run 4 miles in 30 minutes, and 14 miles in 110 minutes on the beach in fatigues and combat boots.

Underwater demolition training was supervised by Naval Special Warfare officers but carried out by Special Warfare enlisted personnel who had ample combat experience in Vietnam and other wars. Among their other duties the enlisted instructors were to insure that the officers who completed UDT training were competent and that they themselves would be willing to serve under them in a combat environment. This was one of the unique aspects of the UDT and SEAL team training: officers were trained *with* the enlisted, by the enlisted, and were expected to perform in a manner superior to the enlisted personnel. Unlike other military units, where the officers were trained separately or were present merely to provide administrative support, the prospective UDT/SEAL officer went through every hurdle with the enlisted personnel. The officers were harassed, intimidated, and made examples of with apparent maliciousness. The instructors looked for even the slightest hint of resentment or anger, as these reactions have no place during a combat mission. A SEAL officer had to earn the right to command, it was not given to him.

The first four weeks of UDT/SEAL training were spent in physical conditioning, two hours in calisthenics every day, running on the beach in the sand wearing combat boots and fatigues for hours every day, and rowing the "inflatable boat, small" (IBS) with seven man crews of six enlisted and one officer. Every morning started with a spit and polish inspection with the most minute defect resulting in the offending individual's "hitting the bay," which meant jumping into 55-degree water fully clothed. This resulted in a lot of brass and boots to polish for the next day. If too many trainees failed the inspection, the entire class hit the bay, which was a common event. We ran everyplace we went. We ran over from the Bachelor Officer's Quarters in the morning, ran in the training area, ran to lunch, ran every-where. My jungle boots became custom molded to the bot-toms of my feet.

The morning calisthenics were grueling: hundreds of sit-ups, push-ups, miles of duck walks, deep knee-bends, and more pull-ups than one could count. When the enlisted instructors thought you weren't doing the pull-ups satisfac-torily, you repeated them all. When they thought you weren't meeting the requirements for sit-ups, they'd start off by standing on your stomach and if that didn't improve things, they resorted to the side of a boot into your ribs. However, the harassment was always two-sided; you could always verbalize your thoughts—unless the instructors could figure out who had said what, then you'd duck walk for miles.

Every day we thought our weary bodies wouldn't go any further. Evenings were spent shining brass and boots, get-ting ready for the next day, and going to sleep as fast as we could. Each day our evolutions were more difficult, the physical requirements increased, each at a faster pace with the instructors tolerating no errors. Physical and mental harassment were combined to maximize the stress on each individual. On one hand, the instructors would say, "If you want the pain to stop, then just quit." On the other hand they continued to tell you, "You can do it, it's merely mind over matter." Every day the training increased and every day there were fewer in our class, which meant more in-dividualized harassment for those of us who were left. One of the worst days was the triple threat: two hours of calis-thenics in the morning, a mile jog in formation to the ob-stacle course, completion of the obstacle course, followed by a four mile timed run on the beach.

The obstacle course was a challenge for upper body strength. It began with tiered parallel bars that you had to hop along to the top and jump down three steps (arms only), jump off, over the top of an eight-foot wall, run forward to a fifteen-foot wall with a rope, swing over the top, run up a zigzag of timbers till you were fifteen feet in the air, then swing along on monkey bars, a few of which were intentionally loose. If you happened to hit those with the wrong grip, you fell off and had to start over again.

After that, one continued across multiple obstacles which included a tripod that rose thirty feet in the air and had two ropes extending down and out in two different directions, secured to two poles approximately seventy feet from the tripod. The object was to climb up metal steps, grab a rope, swing free of the tower and go for the bottom as fast as you could, kick a pole, drop to the ground, and run to the next obstacle.

The cargo net rose fifty feet into the air. We had to climb up one side and down the other, crawl under barbed wire on our stomachs and on our backs, run through zigzags over logs, swing on ropes to clear pits, then finish off with a final set of jungle-gym bars that routinely ripped the callouses from our hands. All this had to be done in the space of five to ten minutes.

Following the obstacle course came the timed four-mile run in combat boots and fatigues in the soft sand. Four miles in thirty minutes was the slowest allowable time. At the end of the run, we ran to the chow hall for lunch. After lunch, we put 350-pound IBSs on our heads, walked them a mile and a half to the ocean, rowed them through the waves, rowed for miles and miles, and then landed them on the rocks in front of the Hotel del Coronado. There's nothing that quite compares with surfing an IBS into a rock wall! If anybody made a mistake, we ended up like a box of toothpicks slammed by the ocean into the rocks.

The fifth week of training was hell week, of which it was said, if you lasted to see the sunrise on Wednesday morning, you'd probably make it. Hell week was basically a five day continuous triathalon performed without sleep. During hell week, we always had our paddles, our IBS, a kapok life jacket, and boots with us. We never went anywhere without them.

For Class 54, hell week started in late October on a Sunday night after our lockers were carefully inspected (officers and enlisted were all in the same barracks). The uniform of the night was combat boots, swimming trunks, kapok life jackets, and a helmet. Our class was assembled and equipment laid out on the lawn as the sprinklers were turned on to get us wet and cold from the very start. After an hour, we were briefed on the night's mission, which was to row the IBSs to the Hotel del Coronado boat house (two miles), portage to the North Island Navel Air Station fence (one mile), row a mile back to the Hotel del Coronado rocks, land at night on a flashlight signal, portage over the rocks, row four miles south, portage across the highway, then row ten miles back to the Naval Amphibious Base for mid rats (midnight rations), which would be served at midnight. The week's activities were all evolutions competing against each boat crew with points awarded. The boat crew with the most points got to retire early, on Friday afternoon; the rest of us would continue until Saturday morning. Obviously, there was a lot of incentive to come in first. That first night we rowed all night, arriving back at the UDT area at six A.M. We changed into clean fatigues, went out for inspection, and all had to hit the bay. Calisthenics were as usual for the next two hours, then we deflated our IBSs, put them in a truck, and were taken to the Imperial Beach mudflats, which was more likely part of the Imperial Beach sewage treatment plant. For the remainder of the day we held races in the mud, using telephone poles that had lain in the mud for years and were waterlogged and heavy. Each team had to lift a pole from one side, up over our heads and down the other side. It took all the strength we had to lift the pole. At lunch we ate in the mud; the box lunches ended up being part mud and part food. The remainder of the afternoon was a repeat of the morning. At the end of the day we got back in our IBSs and rowed to Coronado, six miles away. The rowing would not have been bad except that the instructors kept trying to run over the inflatable boats with a high speed UDT/SEAL delivery craft. We constantly had to dump boat, stop, turn the IBS upside down, let the water drain out, flip it back over, get back in the boat, and start rowing again, just in time to nearly be run over again. We got to the UTD training area in time for dinner. We ate dinner, ran four miles, then had an operations briefing, the same as the night before. Again we rowed to the Hotel del Coronado, portaged across the highway and north to the North Island fence, then rowed to the Hotel del Coronado rocks again. During the landing one of my crew got between the boat and the rocks. The next wave crushed him, resulting in four fractured ribs. The injured crewman was taken to the dispensary and "rolled back" to the following class. The remaining six of us portaged down the beach, back into the ocean, stopped for dinner at midnight, and rowed until morning.

Tuesday was explosives day. After morning calisthenics, we deflated the IBSs, then rode in trucks to the demolition range for explosive ordnance qualification. We crawled, crawled, and crawled while quarter-pound blocks of TNT blew up around our heads; walked across a rope bridge while an instructor on one end tried to shake us off into the mudpit below while the TNT continued to detonate around us. The noise from the explosions was terrible. As the concussion hit, we felt the pressure waves against our bodies. The smoke, mud, and sand flying through the air made it impossible to see, and the smell of the TNT was horrible. Our orders were "don't stop, don't hold your breath, keep your head and face down, and keep moving." When this was finished, we got back in the IBSs and rowed north. As luck would have it, the wind was blowing south and it took the remainder of the day to row the boats back to the training area. We had dinner, ran four miles, and once again had night evolutions, carrying the IBSs and rowing until dawn. As always, we tried as hard as we could so we could get more points than the other boat crews. Thinking back on it, it's amazing how close the scores stayed despite the fact that the instructors would offer bonus points if you finished each evolution just a little faster or did this or that, requiring more and more exertion from a body that hadn't had any sleep since Sunday night.

The all-night evolutions on Tuesday night were shorter than usual. We arrived back at 4:00 A.M. for the next evolution. We assembled for inspection in new dry uniforms, wet kapok life jackets, swimming trunks, and combat boots. Then, one by one, officers first, we snapped our life jackets onto a quarter-inch rope, and jumped into the 55-degree water of San Diego Bay. The instructor said if we could kick hard enough to straighten out the line at the end of the pier they'd let us out of the cold water and into the hot showers. The only problem was, the current at the end of the pier was faster than anyone could swim, so straightening the line was impossible. A couple of times the instructor said, "Okay, I'll let you get out and see if you can get organized. You have three minutes." Only the first half of the men on the line could get out of the water before the three minutes was up, and they had to get back in. An hour and a half later, as the sun rose, the drill was over. Now I knew why if you saw sunrise on Wednesday morning, you'd probably make it through hell week.

We had five minutes to shower, dress, and report back dry for inspection for our next evolution. After inspection we were told to hit the bay again, and we started Wednesday. Calisthenics, IBSs on the head over to the beach where we participated in sand calisthenics, sand races, sand fights, everything we had done at the mudflats, but this time in sand.

That afternoon we took our IBSs to the pool. We swam races while holding towels in our hands, and held every other kind of race the instructors could think of, climaxing with a game of king of the mountain played on an IBS turned over in the middle of the pool. The instructor awarded maximum points for whichever boat crew ended up as King of the Mountain.

After dinner we had another evolution, the Big Dance— Chief Jones playing the radio with everybody dancing with each other in kapok life jackets. He'd stop the music and read the advertisements from a magazine, including prices and manufacturing details; when he finished reading the advertisement he'd ask questions about it. As long as we could answer the questions correctly we didn't have to hit the bay. As soon as one person made a mistake everybody went into the bay one foot. If we got the answers right, we got to come out one foot. If we got the answer wrong, we went another foot deeper in the water. Another answer wrong, three feet into the water. Another answer wrong, and we were four feet into the water. Another answer wrong, and then we were floating. Needless to say, there was a lot of incentive to pay attention, and we stayed dry.

Wednesday night's evolution was Treasure Hunt night—the treasure hunt consisted of solving riddles to find treasure. When your boat crew solved the riddle, you carried the boat on your heads to find the treasure. Of course the more treasure your team could find, the more points you received. We probably walked 25 miles that night. We were still walking at sunrise on Thursday morning. Next we did calisthenics, deflated the IBSs, packed them up into trucks, and went back to the mudflats—the same fun as before, but enjoyed by a lot fewer people. By this time, less than two-thirds of Class 54 was left. As people were injured or quit, boat crews were combined so each boat had five to seven people. When we finished in the mudflats that afternoon, the instructors were back out in their boats trying to run us over as we rowed back to the base.

When we arrived, we were told to get cleaned up, we were going to have a walk and then a rest. One of the instructors took off walking so that everybody had to run to keep up with him. We were tired and he could walk fast! We finished a four-mile walk around the base, and were then told we could grab a blanket and lie down in the athletic field as long as we didn't close our eyes. If we closed our eyes—we'd end up in the bay, singing. Of course, everybody ended up hitting the bay singing! After that we rowed down to the mudflats, had mid rats at midnight, and rowed back. The row back was the most unsettling time of the entire hell week because by this time we were hallucinating from lack of sleep. People thought they were in the surf zone instead of in the bay, they thought they saw the San Diego Ferry off-loading cars directly in front of them, and threw the paddles out of the boat thinking they were snakes. When we arrived back at the UDT training area Friday morning, I swore that it had snowed in the bay. The rest of the morning we again spent in the sand with the IBSs. After lunch we again had IBS races in the pool and another game of King of the Mountain. At four that afternoon, the winning boat crew got to retire. The rest of us went to dinner and got ready for that night's evolutions of races and rowing. We were told if we could row the mile to the Hotel del Coronado boat house and back in a set period of time we would be released from hell week—but *all* of us had to make the time to be released. On the first try we missed the time by a few minutes. On the second, we missed by a few minutes. The third we ran across the Coronado's golf course, took every short cut we could, and still got back a few minutes late. At midnight we were standing in the UDT training area beleaguered to say the least, when it was announced that it was all over—we'd made it through hell week!

That night we were locked in the barracks with a guard at our door. It was feared that disorientation from exposure and sleep deprivation would endanger us. In the morning we had a medical examination. All of us had swollen hands and feet from cellulitis.

Looking back on it, hell week is part of what makes SEALS who they are. It's been part of UDT/SEAL training from the beginning, during the Second World War at Ft. Pierce, Florida. The purpose of the week is to push individuals past their physical and psychological limits. If you could withstand this challenge, nothing in the future would appear impossible. Many times in Vietnam when faced with what appeared to be overwhelming odds, I knew that my men and I could complete the task because we'd already been through worse: hell week.

Following hell week, the second phase started with two weeks of weapons training. We were all too beat up to do much of anything else; however, calisthenics didn't change at all. The instructors were there to remind us that we had just started training and had a long way to go. Things would get more difficult every day. During the two weeks of weapons training, our hands and shoulders were sore from firing more rounds than I thought any human being would shoot in a lifetime. We shot the weapons, cleaned them, disassembled them, reassembled them, and shot them again until we knew every weapon like the backs of our hands.

As things progressed during the second phase, we started traditional underwater hydrographic reconnaissance. We learned how to survey a beach in every possible manner; by day, by night, in plain view and clandestine. The best part of this phase was "cast and recovery." Wearing diving masks, fins, and UDT life jackets, we rolled off an inflatable boat attached to a moving LCPL (Landing Craft Personnel Launch) into the water, so that everyone was spread out at different intervals in a long thin line and could swim towards the beach on reconnaissance. We moved all the way up to the high-water recording everything with a pencil on a plexi-glass slate and then would swim back out to form a recovery line. The LCPL would then return snatching each man up into the IBS. Holding a rubber hoop in his arm, one student would kneel in the IBS. As it approached, we'd kick our swim fins hard, bringing our upper bodies high out of the water, hook an arm and he'd catch it with the rubber hoop. We would grab our hooked arm with the other arm and be flipped up on to the IBS, then scramble into the LCPL so that the recovery man could grab the next person in the recovery line.

In addition to the traditional UDT cast and recovery, we learned helo swimmer cast, in which we swung through the "hell-hole" on a CH56 Sea Knight helicopter and dropped ten to fifteen feet at ten to fifteen miles per hour. These are the techniques utilized in combat situations to enable UDT/SEALs to complete reconnaissance and locate any mines in enemy waters and remove underwater obstacles, before an amphibious assault or scouting a beach position.

As we became proficient in conducting hydrographic surveys, we started learning demolition and commando reconnaissance tactics. First we learned land navigation and how to move rapidly over rough terrain. We then moved on to small-unit tactics, which included basic reconnaissance, patrolling, and ambush techniques. Daytime patrols and navigation were followed by night exercises, with us stumbling through the backyards and running away from the barking dogs of Cardiff by the Sea, a small town north of San Diego.

We practiced navigation and raiding problems near the Imperial Beach Naval Air Station and the Mexican Border. Each day seemed longer and each day the calisthenics grew harder. By Thanksgiving, we were climbing thirty-foot ropes using two ropes, one in each hand, to the top then back down again. We would hang on the pull-up bars while the instructors tried to dislodge us using quick punches to the abdomen from six inches away, counting how many times you'd swing on the bar. We never stopped running the obstacle courses, running in the sand, or swimming in the ocean. The currents became stronger and the water was cold for those two-mile swims. The day after Thanksgiving we left for San Clemente Island sixty miles off the coast of Los Angeles for three weeks of demolition/explosive training.

The training on San Clemente Island was different because everything was "real." Real bullets, real dynamite, and real plastic explosives were used. We started with double daylight savings times, which meant all watches were turned back two hours to allow more daylight time for training. This meant calisthenics began at 5:30 A.M., actual time, in the dark. Calisthenics lasted for two hours, followed by breakfast then application training with explosives and weapons. Each day the practical training was mixed with distance runs and swims—ocean swims up to six miles. Each evening we were back in the classroom learning more about explosives, demolition, and small-unit tactics. Before every meal we had to do 25 pull-ups and 25 dips on the parallel bars just to get through the door of the chow hall. If we didn't, we got to fly "the butterfly," a wooden shipping pallet with a butterfly painted on it. One flight meant holding the pallet on your back above your head, and running up the side of a 200 foot cliff and back to the training area.

Throughout training, the physical and psychological stresses increased, more was demanded and more was expected. The reason for such intense training was to test the students' physical, emotional and mental abilities under adverse conditions. Because we were continually being pushed, we didn't realize we were getting stronger physically and growing more proficient in our skills. The instructors for the San Clemente portion of the training were all experienced SEALs with recent tours in Vietnam. They taught us what they knew we would need to know to stay alive and accomplish our missions in Vietnam.

The eighteenth week of training was hell week in another form. The physical and mental demands were great, but this time we were required to think in addition to just performing physically. Simulated combat conditions were maintained throughout the week with selective live fire from numerous machine guns as well as explosive charges simulating enemy fire. During each 24-hour period, we received 4 to 6 hours of rest with all other time devoted to preparing and running the full-blown operations. One of the operations was a traditional UDT beach reconnaissance with demolition of an entire underwater obstacle field using multiple forty pound packs of plastic explosives. We had to free dive twenty or thirty feet to set the explosives on the obstacles. The operation went without a hitch. It's amazing what that much plastic explosive blows up—the noise, water and dead fish were incredible! When we rechecked the demolition area, the massive concrete and steel obstacles were gone.

The night inland raids were a different story. The first night we attained the objective without difficulty. Everything went well: Using our IBSs we had a long row to the beach, a long row out, arrived at the target undetected, and escaped without difficulty. The second night went well until we were going back out through the surf. A storm was moving in and the waves were ten to twelve feet high. The last IBS was flipped straight up and over, with a loss of all weapons, and the other boats had to go back to recover the crew. The next day we were back out, diving to retrieve the weapons and salvage the IBS which had been shredded on the rocks.

We returned from San Clemente Island to the Marine Training Center at Camp Pendleton for field exercises in which half of the group fought the other for three days in simulated commando operations. When we were finished, we returned to the Naval Amphibious Base in Coronado, cleaned our weapons and left for Christmas leave. By this time, Class 54's training group had dwindled to below sixty officers and enlisted.

After Christmas leave, we spent six weeks in diving training, learning to use scuba, semi-rebreathing and full rebreathing diving systems. Physical conditioning was harder than ever but by then our bodies were ready to take it. Diving training in the pool went fast. The instructors tried to make things difficult by doing such things as taking our regulators apart while we were at the bottom of the pool so that we had to breathe from the diving bottles to continue a swim. We conducted bounce dives in the ocean to the depths of 200 feet and spent a lot of time on the bottom of San Diego harbor using an attack board which had a depth gauge, watch, and compass secured to it. The dives were always long and cold, whether they were at night or during the day—the 55-degree temperature of the water never changed. On each dive, we were tied to a diving partner by a six foot line and worked as a single unit to accomplish a job. On each combat swim, one swimmer held the attack board and maintained the team on course and time; the other held onto the navigator's elbow, served as a look-out, and counted the number of kicks as a backup for navigation. During night dives, your diving partner always put pressure on your arm to let you know that you weren't alone. Each dive was at a specific depth over a set course, and was evaluated by how close one came to the target. After a while, partners knew how many kicks it would take to swim each one hundred yards, and how long it would take. For my partner and me, it was usually three minutes per one hundred yards.

We continued to endure physical conditioning, obstacle courses, and timed runs right up to graduation. About a quarter of my training class that started UDT training still remained. Just before graduation, everyone received orders for final team assignments. Approximately the top fourth of the class went to SEAL team One, then commissioned, with the remainder being divided between the U/D

Underwater Demolition Teams eleven and twelve.

After reporting to SEAL Team One at Coronado, personnel went to Army parachute school and then returned to cadre SEAL team training: physical conditioning continued. Great attention was paid to ground commando tactics—learning how to operate as a seven-man squad and as a fourteen-man platoon against the Vietcong. There was more weapons training with much attention on foreign weapons, the Stoner weapons system, and other devices utilized by SEAL Team One. The emphasis was on not being seen or heard and the ability to react if discovered.

We practiced rappelling from helicopters, rapid insertion, emergency extraction, and extraction by helicopter, boat, and any other means possible. The training included combat first aid, fire movement and maneuvering, unarmed combat, controlling ambush encounters, ambush techniques, booby traps, and tactics.

Each training exercise was designed to hone the skills necessary for a successful mission behind enemy lines. Proficiency in land warfare skills was obtained by teaching a particular subject in the classroom followed by practical application with hands-on experience in the field under the watchful eyes of the instructors. Each session was followed by a critique of performance with suggestions for improvement. We practiced each skill as a unit against a simulated enemy force first without ammo, then with blanks, and finally with live rounds. There was always a need to improve accuracy, timing, and teamwork. The constant repetition was never boring as we realized that every skill might be needed to stay alive in the very near future.

Throughout this training, we constantly tried to blend in with the undergrowth and move silently towards the target. In tactical training we worked in squads, each squad made up of an officer and six men. Patrols, combat maneuvers, immediate-action drills, and weapons' firing were repeated until each was performed as an innate act with total precision. Always the emphasis was on small unit tactics, team work, and what to expect in Vietnam. During this phase of training, the drop-out rate was low (ten percent), primarily those individuals determined not fit to participate in SEAL operations. During the fourth and final weeks of training we held field exercises near the Salton Sea, the canals of which I later realized looked just like those of Vietnam at night.

SEAL team training was intended to hone one's survival and judgement skills to the cutting edge. We were trained to react and to make split second decisions about a target that could be friend or foe knowing that your judgement meant life or death.

With basic SEAL Team cadre training completed, we were assigned to our platoons. LTJG Joe Quincannon was the officer in charge of Juliett Platoon, I was the assistant platoon commander. SM1 Larry LePage, a first class petty officer, was the ranking enlisted, and HM1 Doc Schrier was the independent-duty corpsman assigned to our platoon.

The platoon began training all over again by reviewing how the two squads functioned within a platoon. It was important for us to know what to expect from each member of the platoon in a combat situation. After going through multiple field operations at the Salton Sea in southern California, our platoon left for Mares Island in Vallejo, California, where the Riverine patrol force trained because of its similarity to the canals in Vietnam. We worked for a week with the river patrol craft—day and night on multiple targets—to practice before deploying to Vietnam.

After Mares Island we returned to Coronado, then spent a week in the desert for familiarization with special equipment, and continued practicing night live-fire operations. When we returned to Coronado again it was almost time to leave for Vietnam. Everyone packed weapons, clothing, and miscellaneous items for deployment to Vietnam, packed up their apartments or rooms, put everything in storage, and departed on leave prior to deployment. When we returned, equipment and supplies were rechecked, and we loaded on the plane at the North Island Naval Air Station for a long trip on a C118 to Vietnam.

In Vietnam the SEALs were known as the men with green faces. The legend of the SEALs among the Vietnamese was that they came out of the swamp and went back into the swamp, they were never tired, they never slept, they never ate, and if they took you with them, you would never return. The Navy SEALs were among the combatants most feared by the Vietcong and North Vietnamese, and were among the most ferocious commandos in the world.

Many have perceived SEALs as clandestine commandos who eagerly volunteered for suicide missions. In fact, very few SEALs were killed in Vietnam, due to their courage and superior training, their awareness of the inevitable danger of the missions they undertook, and their skill at minimizing that danger. Teamwork was an essential element in accomplishing the mission of each operation. A successful mission was one in which the squad or platoon was able to arrive at its target, to complete its task, and leave, without having been detected. The missions of the SEALs in Vietnam included capturing high-level Vietcong for intelligence, reconnaissance, interdiction, ambush, and sabotage.

The SEALs' total strength in South Vietnam never exceeded nine platoons, i.e. was never more than 150 men. In six years this group accounted for 600 Vietcong killed confirmed by direct body count, another 300 "probable" kills (according to intelligence reports), and in excess of 1,000 prisoners. Individual awards for valor were 3 medals of honor, 2 navy crosses, 42 silver stars, 402 bronze stars, 2 legions of merit, 352 Navy commendation medals, 51 Navy achievement medals, and hundreds of purple hearts. The targets were usually intelligence objectives of high value that could not be reached by conventional forces. During the Vietnam conflict, the Navy SEALs lost fewer than twenty men due to VC/NVA action. In addition, Navy SEALs contributed immensely to the intelligence effort, which is not measurable.

Nicolas E. Walsh
Lt., USA (ret.)

CHAPTER ONE

The Navy C-118 left the runway and circled to the north, then to the west, as we gained altitude leaving Guam behind. We were on the last leg of a four-leg flight from Coronado, California, to Tan Son Nhut Air Force Base, Saigon, Republic of Vietnam. The sun was setting as I looked back out the starboard window, watching the shoreline disappear behind a large, reddish, cumulus cloud. Our plane weaved in and out of the large clouds until we gained enough altitude to level out. I couldn't get my mind off our next stop, Vietnam.

The plane landed at Tan Son Nhut at 0230 hours, 29 June 1970. I was one of fourteen men assigned to SEAL Team One, detachment Golf, Juliett Platoon. Out of the two officers and twelve enlisted men, only five had completed one or more tours of duty in Vietnam. The other nine, including myself, would be "in-country" for the first time.

Lt. J.G. Quincannon, "Mr. Q," as we called him, was the officer-in-charge of Juliett Platoon. He had a slight eastern accent; dark, short curly hair; and was about five feet, ten inches tall. He had had a previous tour to Nam with SEAL Team One. He was easygoing, and the men of his platoon looked up to and respected him.

Ensign Walsh was second-in-command of Juliett Platoon. He had graduated with UDT/SEAL Training Class 54 and this would be his first tour to Nam. Mr. Walsh was six feet tall, medium build, dark hair, and even after he had just shaved, his dark beard would be exposed on his face. Mr. Walsh was very easy to get along with, but he was one gung-ho son of a bitch. He was quick-thinking, making

1

wise decisions, and was in control of his men and surround-
ings at all times. He would never ask his men to do anything
he wouldn't do himself.

Signalman First Class Petty Officer LePage, the highest
ranking enlisted man in our platoon, probably had more
experience with SEAL teams in Vietnam than anyone else
in our platoon. He was also the oldest man in our platoon.
He had been shot in the ass twice and creased in the head
by an AK-47 on a previous tour with SEALs. This was at
least his third tour to Nam with SEALs, and maybe he even
had another. LePage was five-ten, wore a crew cut, had
brown hair, and came from New Orleans. He was fun to
be around, on or off duty. He liked his whiskey and beer—
it didn't matter what kind, he drank them all. His nickname
was Leaper, and for a good reason.

Radioman Second Class Petty Officer Bruce was six feet,
two inches tall, brown eyes, brown curly hair, and a big mustache that looked like a set of Navy parachute wings. This was
Bruce's second tour to Nam with SEAL Team One. He was a
good SEAL operator and a great asset to our platoon. Bruce
was from California, and he wore hippie beads—or war
beads, as we called them in Nam—around his neck.

Machinist Mate Second Class Petty Officer Sitter was
another SEAL with Nam experience. At five-ten, he was a
stocky man with light-colored hair. Sitter also enjoyed his
beer on his free time. Sitter was from Oklahoma.

Engineman Baylett went through UDT/SEAL Training
Class 52. This was his first time to Nam. Baylett had light
brown hair, a round face, big ears that stuck out, and always
had a shit-eating grin on his face. He reminded me of Howdy
Doody, except for his Pennsylvania drawl and no freckles.
Though six feet tall and stocky, he acted like Howdy. Maybe it was his Pennsylvania background. He was a great
morale booster for Juliett Platoon.

Aircraft Ordnance Petty Officer Panella was about five-
ten, with curly brown hair. He was from California and
owned a gold Corvette. While back in the States the gas
pedal was always kept to the floor and he couldn't go through
the gears fast enough. Being in Nam for his first time, like

the rest of us new guys in SEALs, he was in for a treat.

Seaman Weber graduated in my UDT/SEAL training class, Class 53. Being from Nebraska, he had never seen the ocean before. He was six feet tall, with dark hair, a medium build, and brown eyes. Weber was a very quiet person, and it really took a lot to piss this guy off. This was his first time in Nam also.

Seaman Reeves was six feet tall with blond hair and blue eyes. His home town was St. Louis. He had also never seen the ocean until he joined the Navy. Reeves graduated in UDT/SEAL Training Class 53 with Weber and me. The three of us had been training together for a long time, and we knew each other pretty well. We would get to know each other even more as our six-month tour to Nam went on day by day. Reeves was a slim man and seemed to be very independent. He was to be second squad's rear security.

Torpedoman Grimes graduated from Class 54. He was six feet tall, with blond curly hair and a thick blond mustache, dark eyes and an intimidating stare. Grimes was from California, and this was his first Vietnam experience. His dad had been a boxer, and he boxed too. That's where he earned his nickname, ''The Dude.''

Radioman Seaman Shannon was the tallest man in Juliett Platoon, close to six-four with dark hair and brown eyes. This guy always had a smile on his face; a man couldn't ask for a better friend. If Shannon said something, he meant it. Like Mr. Q, Shannon had a slight eastern accent. He came from UDT/SEAL Training Class 54, and grew up in Baltimore.

Ship Fitter Pipe Fireman Strausbaugh was also from Class 54. He was the shortest man in our platoon, but a stocky man. At five-nine, he had light brown hair with a thin blond mustache. He was a quiet guy, but absorbed everything around him. His job was point man for second squad.

Hospital Corpsman First Class Petty Officer Schrier was from Oregon. He was six feet tall, a slim man. He had dark hair with a curl in the front and a trimmed dark mustache. Like LePage, he loved his beer and had plenty of Vietnam experience with SEALs. The medals on his chest proved that. Like most corpsmen in the service, he received the nickname "Doc." When Doc spoke, everyone listened. Maybe that's why Doc carried the PRC-77 radio for our platoon. I never could understand why a cowboy would join the Navy. He was always in control of all situations that came up, and was quick-thinking, with sound advice and suggestions, even when he drank too much beer. Everyone in our platoon liked Doc, looked up to him and respected him.

Seaman Young, in Nam for my first time. Nobody made me come here but myself. Blond hair, blue eyes, six feet tall, medium build, thin blond mustache. I was nineteen years old, well-trained, and was ready to do my duties for my country with thirteen of the best men I have ever met in my life. I was to be first squad's rear security.

As we disembarked the plane, Lieutenant Boyhan, the SEAL officer in charge of Charlie Platoon, was waiting to meet us. Charlie was the SEAL platoon we were to relieve. Mr. Boyhan informed our officers that five SEALs were killed the day before in a helo crash. A slick had picked up the five men at a place called Sea Float, down on the Ca Mau Peninsula, for a ride to Saigon. Apparently the helo had been shot up on an operation but had not shut down to check out the damage it sustained. So it fell from over a thousand feet into the jungle below. By the time the other SEALs in the platoon geared up and reached the crash site, all the bodies had been stripped of weapons and usable gear. One of the men on the helo was on his way to Saigon to help Mr. Boyhan orient our platoon and welcome us to Vietnam.

What a welcome. I hadn't even seen the enemy and already I was mad. SEAL-team and underwater-demolition team members are close, no matter which team they are from. I was shocked at the bad news, and I wondered if I would make it through my six-month tour.

We rounded up some transportation and loaded our gear for the trip to the Victoria Hotel, downtown Saigon. This hotel was made of concrete, and the walls were old but still had the marks from the wooden forms used when they were poured. The Victoria was one of the SEALs' favorite hangouts in Saigon. As we checked in, LePage, our leading (senior) petty officer, suggested we meet on the roof of the hotel after getting settled. Weber, Reeves, and I got a room together on the sixth floor. I was surprised at how cheap it was compared to a hotel in the States, the equivalent of six American dollars. After entering our room, we looked under our pillows and beds for booby traps. After a while we decided to see what was up on the roof. Topside we found a swimming pool along with a bar, food, and—of course—bar girls awaited us there. I'd have to be pretty drunk to swim in the green, slimy pool, but LePage had arrived first and the partying was well under way.

Although the drug of the day was alcohol, some of the people in my platoon smoked pot. They were always trying to pull me aside to smoke a little with them, but being in a combat zone for my first time, I wanted to stay straight. Besides, I had never tried it.

As the day wore on and our beer consumption increased, we got rowdier. The bar girls sitting opposite us would stick their legs under the table and massage us with their toes. Being a young kid of nineteen, I wasn't used to that sort of thing. They weren't the best-looking things I ever saw, but I didn't ask them to stop.

The next morning, despite having terrible hangovers, we found ourselves back at the airfield loading our gear on board the twin-engine C-117 that was to fly us south to Binh Thuy, a small town a few miles west of Can Tho on the south bank of the Bassac River. When we were airborne, I looked down and got my first peek at the Mekong Delta. Large rivers meandered through lush, dark green jungle, with man-made and natural canals entering the main rivers like blood vessels and veins. What wasn't jungle was rice paddies or dikes holding out the water from a high tide from the South China Sea. Very few highways or roads could be seen.

We landed on the short runway at the Tactical Air Support

Facility in Binh Thuy a short time later. All our gear was unloaded and stacked alongside the runway, awaiting a helo to take us to our final destination. Mr. Q, our officer-in-charge, and Mr. Walsh, our second-in-command, crossed the highway to the SEAL Quonset hut (the headquarters for all SEAL units in the Delta region), located at the Naval Support Facility. The rest of us waited by our gear. Soon they returned and informed us that a CH-34, a helo left over from the Korean War, was on its way. After landing close to our gear, we loaded up and headed southeast about forty miles down the Bassac River toward the village of Long Phu. The helo flew at a lower altitude than the C-117, and I got a closer look at the rice paddies, jungle, and small villages below. Sunlight reflected off the numerous waterways that flowed through the entire region. It was obvious that the Vietcong and North Vietnamese soldiers had thousands of places to hide and just as many escape routes. Capturing Charlie won't be easy, I thought. A change in the pitch of the rotor blades tore me away from my thoughts.

Our helo started circling a South Vietnamese outpost on the south shore of the Bassac River. Looking down, I saw several plywood shacks resembling something on the outskirts of Tijuana, Mexico. A man down below threw a yellow smoke grenade out by the one-helo helo pad, and the pilot started descending for his landing. Located on the south bank of the Bassac River and the west bank of the Long Phu River, the camp covered about three acres. The two perimeters not along the rivers were protected by barbed wire, claymore mines, trip flares, lights, and sandbagged bunkers with interlocking fields of fire. This was to be my home for the next six months. Coastal Group 36, Advance Team 71. I noticed a thirty-foot tower at the southwest corner of the camp with .50-caliber machine gun mounted on top. Stationed at the camp were fourteen U.S. Navy SEALs, six MST (Mobile Support Team) members who ran our special shallow draft boats, a few Navy Seabees from MCB5 (Mobile Construction Battalion), and a few South Vietnamese sailors who ran the outpost. Three South Vietnamese "junk-type" river patrol boats were anchored in the Bassac just offshore.

We grabbed our gear and carried it over to our hootch. The Seabees had built several plywood hootches with tin roofs. Of course, they occupied the best ones. Our hootch had bunks stacked three high on all four walls, with room for our footlockers lined back to back down the center. This is where the SEALs and MST personnel bunked. I claimed a top rack, just above LePage. I had barely got my mosquito net hung when someone yelled, "Chow time." Hell, that was one of my favorite times. I followed the flow of people to the chow hall, a larger plywood hootch located nearer the river. In the background I could hear a diesel generator that must have powered the camp. Inside, four large picnic tables were arranged on the left, serving counter on the right, all you could eat. After the noon chow I returned to my rack to straighten things out.

Because of our strange duty hours, SEALs didn't have to pull extra duty in camp, like KP or perimeter guard. We did have to take turns burning the shit from the outhouse, but besides that, our free time was ours. Anytime we weren't operating, we were on alert status. SEALs could be used anywhere, anytime, for anything that might come up. If one squad was operating and got into a "world of shit," as LePage used to call it, and needed assistance, the free squad could be there in a matter of minutes. If another unit needed assistance, we were usually available.

That night I had problems trying to sleep. New country, new barracks, new rack, etc. LePage bitched half the night because of my tossing and turning. Next morning, after chow, I looked around for a new rack. All were taken. I borrowed a hammer, nails, some two-by-fours, and some plywood from the Seabees and built my own rack up in the rafters. It was hot as hell up there, but at least I didn't have to listen to LePage bitch.

Five days passed before our platoon started operating, because the entire platoon had diarrhea from the Vietnamese drinking water. My fourth day in Nam I made fourteen trips to the head, a small two-holer on the west side of camp. I kept count by carving notches in the plywood with my K-bar knife as I sat there. My rear end was so sore, I felt I should have received the Purple Heart for my wounds.

On one of these fourteen trips, Mr. Q had beaten me there, so I took the hole next to him. "We have an op tonight, Young," he said. "Mission briefing will be at 2000 hours [eight P.M.]. Man, is my asshole sore."

At 2000 hours, myself, Quan (our Vietnamese interpreter), Mr. Boyhan, and five other SEALs from first squad met Mr. Q in the briefing hootch, an eight-by-fourteen porta tent with plywood floor. Quan was a South Vietnamese civilian who worked with Navy SEALs as an interpreter to keep himself from getting drafted into the South Vietnamese Army. Mr. Boyhan had stayed back with our platoon to go on the first two operations with each of our squads. Mr. Q began the briefing as soon as the door was secured. "Okay, listen up. Tonight's operation will be conducted on Dung Island. We will depart camp at 0200 hours and proceed up the Bassac River. The MSSC [Medium SEAL Support Craft, or "medium"] will move around the west end of Dung Island and insert us in the small canal on the north side." He pointed out the route on a picto map hanging from the wall.

"Our mission is to capture five high-level VC living on the island—" He paused for a moment. "—if capture is possible. If capture is not possible, we are to neutralize the targets. However, our main goal is to take them alive for Intel. Only first squad along with our interpreter Quan will participate in this mission." Quan operated with both squads.

"The sky should be clear, with an air temperature of eighty-five degrees. Water temperature will be seventy-four degrees. There will be a slack tide with river current running seven kilometers per hour. Heavy triple-canopy jungle covers the banks of the canal, with dense brush and rice paddies farther inland.

"No other friendly units, American or South Vietnamese, will be operating on Dung Island. This is a free-fire zone.

Second squad [the remaining seven SEALs] will be on standby in case we run into trouble and need help. We will use the medium for our insertion and extraction. After insertion, we will set up a perimeter while our boat leaves the area. After listening for a while, we will patrol to the village, make the snatch, and return to the extraction point. Our call sign will be Stingray-one. Second squad will be Stingray-two. The medium will be Alpha-one, and the LSSC [Light SEAL Support Craft or "light"] will be Alpha-two. The order of march will be as follows: Grimes, point; Quan, Mr. Q, Mr. Boyhan, Doc Schrier, Bruce, LePage, Strausbaugh, and Young as rear security. Final inspection will be at 2130 [nine-thirty P.M.] hours. Lost communication and emergency extraction will follow standard operating procedures. We have two OV-10 Bronco fixed-wing aircraft as air support from Binh Thuy. They take anywhere from twenty to thirty minutes to fly to our operating area from Binh Thuy. Are there any questions?''

I was being briefed for my first operation in Nam, but Mr. Q and Mr. Boyhan had been working on setting up the operation for two days already. "If there are no questions I'll see all of you at the boat at 0130." There were none, so after sterilizing the briefing hootch by putting away all maps and notes, we left to prepare.

I felt confident as I readied my gear for my first mission in-country. As a SEAL trainee, and while training with the platoon, I had done this many times. But this time it was for real. Depending on the officer-in-charge, SEAL teams are given a great deal of leeway as to what is worn on missions. I wore good old Levi's jeans along with my blue and gold tee-shirt with a standard cammo top. Over the top I wore an inflatable UDT life jacket. Over all that I wore a special nylon vest that had five pockets sewn onto it to hold five plastic Stoner-box ammunition magazines.

Since I was rear security, I chose a Stoner 63-A light machine gun as my main weapon. The Stoner had a maximum rate of fire of one thousand rounds per minute and used disintegrating-link 5.56mm ammo. Depending how you set the Stoner up, it could be belt fed from the right-

or left-hand side, or fed from a plastic box magazine with a 110-round capacity, or a metal aluminum drum with 150 rounds. A three-position gas port just back from the muzzle turned, to adjust the rate of fire from 700 to 1000 rpm. For backup weapons I carried the standard MK-2 K-bar knife with an MK-13 day-and-night flare taped to the knife's sheath, and a mod. 15, .38-caliber revolver. Standard jungle boots were worn without socks. I hated socks. In the wet they would ball up in the bottom of the boots, keeping feet wetter longer. In my special-made nylon vest, given to me by Mr. Boyhan, were four Stoner boxes, a total of 440 rounds of ammo. There was another 110-round box in the Stoner itself. This gave me 110 rounds more than my standard ammo load, in case we got into a world of shit and needed extra ammo. That left me with an empty box magazine pocket at the rear of my vest for two M-26 frag grenades, one incendiary, and one smoke grenade. All equipment was bound with ordnance tape to keep it quiet and painted with flat black spray paint to prevent telltale reflections. I cammied my face, slid into my jungle boots, slung an LAW rocket over my back, grabbed my Stoner, and headed down to the water's edge for inspection at 0130 in the morning.

While waiting for Mr. Q and Mr. Boyhan to arrive, we passed around a roll of olive-drab ordnance tape to seal off the bottom of our pants to keep out leeches. As I looked over the rest of the squad, I saw that they were as ready to operate as I was. Grimes, our point man, was wearing a full set of jungle-green left-pattern cammies. He carried a CAR-15 (a short-barreled M-16) with 300 rounds of 5.56 ammo, and three M-26 frags, one CS (tear gas) grenade, and one smoke grenade hung from the web belt attached to his H-harness. Two MK-3-A2 concussion grenades were also attached to his web belt, along with his K-bar knife. His face, the back of his neck, and his hands were cammied, and his blond, curly hair was hidden under an olive-drab triangular bandage.

Doc, the platoon's corpsman, wore tiger-stripe cammies and a standard H-harness. Doc packed the PRC-77 radio, and two red-star parachute pop flares packaged in aluminum tubes were also taped to his H-harness. The tube contained the rocket motor, flare, and parachute. It could be launched by removing the cap from one end and placing it over the opposite end. While holding the metal cylinder in one hand and pointing it into the sky, the cap could be struck with a sharp blow from the other hand, causing the firing pin in the cap to ignite the rocket motor. This propelled the red-star signal and parachute to a height of 650 to 700 feet. The flares came in different colors and were used to signal an emergency extraction in case our radios were not working. The flares also came in the illuminating type to light up an area. Along with an M-16 rifle, 300 rounds of ammo, his medical gear, and a cammied face, Doc was ready.

Bruce wore Levi's jeans, standard cammo top, and jungle boots. He packed an M-16/XM-148 grenade-launcher combo. He carried twenty high-explosive 40mm grenade rounds along, and 360 rounds of M-16 ammo in thirty-round magazines in his specially made vest. Also attached to his vest were two M-26 frags and two illuminating parachute flares. The firepower from the M-16/XM-148 was unreal. Bruce was a one-man army by himself.

LePage wore standard cammies, top and bottoms, and packed the Stoner, with 550 rounds. He carried two frags, one concussion, and a yellow smoke, along with extra prisoner-handling gear, plastic flex handcuffs, and extra ordnance tape for blindfolding and gagging. It added very little weight.

Wearing jeans and standard cammo top, Strausbaugh was also an automatic-weapons man, humping the M-60 machine gun. With 450 rounds of 7.62mm linked ammo wrapped around his chest and in his weapon, he was ready to go. Our M-60 machine guns had been modified to reduce weight and increase handling capabilities. The standard butt was replaced by the rubber cup used by helicopter door gunners, and the bipod and front and rear sights had been removed. The barrel was shortened and the flash suppresser moved back almost even with the gas piston. Even this small amount of work made the M-60 considerably lighter, being about sixteen pounds instead of its original twenty-three pounds, as well as making it shorter and more maneuverable. A couple of frags completed his armament.

I looked toward the briefing hootch and saw Mr. Q, Mr. Boyhan, and Quan heading in our direction. Boyhan and Quan both carried M-16s with our standard load of ammo. Mr. Q also packed a Smith & Wesson model 39 semi-automatic 9mm pistol in a shoulder holster, and two extra magazines, two frags, two concussion grenades, and a star-light scope. Levi's jeans and standard cammo top seemed to be popular that night. Mr. Boyhan was dressed similar to Mr. Q, who inspected Quan and the rest of our squad to make sure all gear was taped down and all essential equipment was present. From the months of training together, everyone knew his personal job on this patrol. We knew each other's habits and actions, and knew what to expect from each man. Arm and hand signals varied from SEAL platoon to SEAL platoon. Very few words, if any, were spoken throughout a mission. That was standard operating procedure.

The mobile support team (MST) personnel had already squared away our boat and were standing by as we did some last-minute touch up on our cammied faces. A steel-plated deck attached to half-filled 55-gallon drums went down the muddy bank, out into the river, and were T-ed off. The drums helped stabilize the dock, which was hinged in several places to compensate for the tides. The tides from the South China Sea, six or eight miles downriver from us, affected the river for miles inland. A tidal change of several feet was experienced at Long Phu. With the help from some Seabees, Doc Schrier and Sitter had built the dock over the last couple of days. It made boarding the shallow-draft boats much easier than wading through the thick mud. At low tide our dock lay on the muddy bottom several feet from the Bassac River.

Everybody ready, we boarded the medium. First Class Petty Officer Melfa, the MST coxswain, backed the medium out into the Bassac. As the boat turned and headed upstream away from our camp, I watched our perimeter lights disappear in the dark night behind us.

CHAPTER TWO

Heading upriver on step—that is, fast enough for the boat to plane—Melfa switched on the radar to pick up other boat traffic in the area, which was rare at night, and terrain features. Using the radar was the only way to locate our insertion point in the dark. The medium was a shallow draft aluminum-hull boat with a catamaran bottom designed strictly for SEAL use. Powered by twin 427-cubic-inch big-block Chevy engines with 325-horsepower and Mercury outdrives with twenty-inch propellers, that mother had no problems getting us to or extracting us from our areas of operation in a hurry. The medium was thirty-six feet long, twelve feet wide, and nine feet tall from top to bottom. Maximum-load weight was 23,558 pounds, and it usually carried a crew of four to six men plus fourteen SEALs.

Our medium was armed with a minigun mounted on the stern, two .50-caliber machine guns mounted on either side aft, and two fixed M-60 machine guns mounted on both sides forward. Inside the craft, under a canvas top, were two long bench seats down the port and starboard sides. Melfa drove the boat sitting on a padded seat, with Mr. Q and Mr. Boyhan standing beside him watching the radar. The two other MST crew members sat on the benches ready to man the medium's weapons. The rest of us SEALS sat on the benches in our pre-determined insertion order. The butt of my Stoner was resting on the deck with the muzzle pointing safely toward the canvas top. We had not yet locked and loaded our weapons, since we had a long way to go to reach the far side of Dung Island.

We seemed to be the only ones on the river that night.

Not many American boats operated in the area, and anyone traveling the local waterways after curfew had to be Vietcong. I was thinking about how I was ready for the operation as we cruised through the pitch-dark night at top speed toward our objective. The west end of the island was located on our radar. We continued at top speed.

Then, without warning, the medium hit a sandbar barely sticking out of the water, coming to an abrupt stop. All on board flew forward and landed in a big pile on Mr. Q, Mr. Boyhan, and Melfa. Nobody knew what had happened until Mr. Q said, "Fuckin' radar didn't pick up on the sandbar." There we sat, low tide, stuck in the middle of the Bassac River 0200 hours in the morning. Luckily, no one was seriously injured. Two A.M. in the morning, dark as shit, and I was scared. Melfa tried to back us off the sandbar, but that was useless; we were high and dry. The only thing we could do was wait for the tide to come in and float us off. So we sat there, taking turns looking through the starlight scope checking out the river upstream and downstream, to our port and the triple-canopy jungle to our starboard side. Through the starlight scope I could make out the long gouge cut through the mud behind us by the medium. With both engines shut down, everyone got as comfortable as possible and waited for the tide to come in. I expected the Vietcong to set up on us from shore and a B-40 rocket to come slamming into us at any time. Being a sitting duck for Charlie wasn't my idea of a good time.

I was awakened by the sound of the boat's engines starting. I looked at my diving watch. We had been there over an hour. Slowly, the boat maneuvered off the sandbar and backed into the main channel. Even though we were delayed, Mr. Q decided there was enough time left before dawn to complete the mission. We continued on, making our way around the west end of Dung Island and down the north side. The Bassac River was twice as wide and twice as deep—three to four fathoms, depending on the tide—on the north side of the island. The channel was used by large ships taking supplies upriver from the South China Sea. Moving a bit slower, we continued to use radar and the starlight scope to find our way. A smaller canal was soon picked up on the radar, running parallel with the Bassac back into Dung Island.

The signal was given to lock and load. The sounds of our weapons cocking filled the inside of the medium. As we approached the mouth of the canal, shots were fired off the starboard side, Charlie's "jungle telegraph," a quick way to warn his comrades of danger approaching. With individual Vietcong posted along likely approaches throughout the island, the VC leaders could be warned of American or South Vietnamese troops being in the area. Firing back would only give our position away even more and compromise the success of our mission. I crouched down below the gunwale, Stoner on safe and pointed away from my teammates.

Leaving the main stream of the Bassac behind us, we maneuvered down the smaller canal. The triple-canopy jungle quickly moved in on both sides. Mr. Q was glued to the radar, looking for a still smaller canal on the port side we were to use as our insertion point. Soon it showed on the radar.

The medium slowed to just about idle. We began our port turn into the smaller canal, which was only eight feet wide at its mouth, not wide enough for our boat. Melfa pulled it in until the bow ran up onto the muddy bottom. Then, as planned, five of us went over the port bow and the other four went over the starboard bow. Assigned as rear security, I was the last man to leave the boat off the starboard side. When I stepped off the starboard bow, I didn't step far enough to the left, and missed the bank of the canal. Under the weight of all my gear, I went straight to the bottom. The only thing sticking out of the water was my right hand. I tried to push off the bottom, but my feet stuck in the mud. Too heavy to swim, too stuck to walk out. Just as I was ready to ditch all my gear and inflate my life jacket, someone grabbed my hand and pulled me up. Trying to gasp for air quietly, I set up security in my position with the rest of the squad. Bruce had saved my life. Even if I had inflated my life jacket and dropped all the gear, I don't think it would have pulled me out of the mud.

The medium backed out and headed down the canal to make a couple of fake insertions and wait for our radio call for extraction. Listening to the medium's engines fading away into the dark, I looked out into the jungle covering my designated field of fire. With the medium gone, I realized how completely alone we were. I had thought I was scared sittin' in our boat on the sandbar in the middle of the river. But I was really scared now. I wished I was back at camp sittin' on the shitter. We lay low in the mud, listening for enemy movement. But the normal jungle sounds slowly returned.

After twenty minutes or so Mr. Q signaled Grimes to check out the canal ahead. Grimes slipped back down into the canal and started to patrol. Quietly, one by one, we followed. We couldn't get too far apart because of the darkness. Everyone kept an eye on the man in front of him and the man in back of him. For a moment I forgot about being scared. I watched the squad moving silently in front of me. The darkness and camouflage made them almost invisible. I watched behind us as the squad patrolled forward. Looking away from the others gave me the feeling of being completely alone. I turned back several times toward the others, just to make sure they were still there. After moving about forty meters inland, we stopped to listen again. I could hear movement on the canal banks ahead of us. Was it Grimes? The banks rose about three feet above our heads on both sides and were heavily overgrown with vegetation. At this point the canal began to narrow considerably. Was Charlie waiting for us to walk into an ambush? What about the warning shots we heard back by the main river? These thoughts registered in my mind as I crouched in the mud, covering our rear. The noise on the canal banks ahead stopped. We waited, listening.

Soon Grimes began patrolling again. We followed. After moving forward another ten meters we stopped again. The sounds of people, moving on the canal banks ahead of us, were louder this time. What a place to get ambushed, I thought. Word was passed back that Grimes had found booby traps along both sides of the canal and out in front of him. I don't know how he found them in the dark. Since Charlie was aware of our presence in the area, Mr. Q decided to fall back to our insertion point. I received the word to take over point and lead us back out. I started out in the waist-deep mud and water. One step, then another. Stop, listen. One more step, then another. Was I going to be alive after my next step? What was the noise we heard on the canal banks? Ambush? I just knew I was going to trip a wire or step in a punji pit. I stopped again to listen. Was Charlie circling around to meet us at the canal? The fact that our squad had just come through the canal didn't matter, I was being extra careful. We finally made it back to the mouth of the canal. As we set up a perimeter, Doc radioed the medium to extract us. We waited silently, watching and listening for Charlie. Soon I could hear the medium coming up the canal. Using the radio, Doc guided it into our position.

The medium came into our canal as far as it could. One at a time we waded out through the mud and water. Mr. Q and myself being last, we waded through the mud backward, covering our asses. Mr. Q and I were the last ones to climb over the bow of the medium. After a head count to make sure everyone was aboard, the medium was backed into the canal while we all trained our weapons on the banks. We proceeded out the canal and back into the Bassac River. Back around the west end of the island we went, watching for the sandbar on the radar and with the starlight scope. We reached our camp as it was nearing dawn.

We held a short debriefing after unloading the medium of all our gear. Before I washed the cammo off my face and cleaned up, I tore my Stoner apart and cleaned it thoroughly. After cleaning both my weapons and gear, I dumped the wet, muddy ammo into the Bassac then refilled the Stoner boxes with fresh, clean ammo. Not until all my weapons and gear were cleaned and squared away did I clean myself. Face paint was great for making us hard to see in the jungle, but it sure gave you a hard time washing it off. Some of the SEALs on this op were annoyed that we had made no contact with Charlie. I was just glad to get back to the shitter.

CHAPTER THREE

After breakfast I climbed up into my rack in the rafters to rest. But I woke up around noon; the heat beating through the tin roof of our hootch made sleeping impossible. I slid into my UDT swim trunks and went outside. Some of the SEALs and MST personnel were gathered down by the dock. As I approached I saw that the medium was gone. I asked Mr. Q about it. He said, "One of the MST guys left it untied while he went to chow, and it floated downriver with the outgoing tide." I went back to my rack and grabbed my vest and Stoner. After arriving back at the dock, I boarded the light with the MST crew. Down the Bassac River we went in an attempt to recover the medium before the Vietcong. By the time we caught up with it, it had drifted halfway to the South China Sea, but everything was still aboard. With two M-60s, two .50-calibers, and a mini-gun, the Vietcong would have been set up pretty good.

After we returned the two boats to camp, a Seabee took up a collection to buy a pig in the village. It wasn't long before a couple of Seabees and a couple of SEALs took the Seabees' six-by out the gate into the village to bring one back. A short time later the pig came back all dressed out and ready for the fire. The Seabee cook stuck the customary apple in its mouth and placed it over the coals, then Seabees took turns standing two-hour watches turning the spit and keeping the fire going. It was to be completely cooked by noon the next day.

Later that night second squad, along with Mr. Boyhan, gathered at the briefing hootch for a mission briefing. SEALs participated in the "Phoenix Program," capturing high-level political figures for intelligence purposes—which was the main reason for SEALs' operating in the Delta, where little was known about VC activities. Second squad's mission that night was to infiltrate Dung Island and patrol to a small village run by a Vietcong cadre. The squad was to attempt to capture him alive, if possible. Intelligence collected by Juliett platoon or other SEALs was usually fresh and reliable. If we captured high-level Vietcong, we were supposed to turn them over to the Army for interrogation. As soon as Charlie was captured, if conditions permitted, we would do a field interrogation. Hell, he was generally scared shitless anyway, a good time for him to talk. Quan did most of the interrogating with our officers close by. Fresh and accurate intel would result in successful operations.

Second squad was led by Ensign Walsh. He and Mr. Q had gone through the same rigorous training as the rest of us.

Second squad geared up for its mission. I wished them good luck as they started loading into the medium. The next morning, just after sunrise, second squad returned to camp. With them was the hamlet chief. The members of first squad gathered around the medium as the high-level gook, handcuffed, gagged, and blindfolded, was brought ashore. Second squad had sneaked up on him while he was sleeping, killed his guards, and captured the little runt. Then, dragging the gook all the way, they were chased off Dung Island by the Vietcong. The SEALs took no casualties of their own.

The little gook was put in our holding box, a large, oblong plywood box with three prisoner chambers. Each compartment had a door that lifted up to open. I went to our hootch and returned with my 8mm movie camera. The hamlet chief was the first Vietcong I had ever seen, and I wanted him on film. He wore a white tank top with black pajama pants.

His feet were bare. After I shot pictures of him, the door was slammed shut and locked, the gook still handcuffed and blindfolded inside. I listened to second squad's debrief as they stood outside the briefing hootch. White streaks showed through the cammo paint on their faces where rivulets of sweat had washed the paint away. Mud and water dripped from their clothes and weapons.

After the debriefing, second squad cleaned its weapons and gear and hit the chow hall. Mr. Boyhan cleaned up and was packing his gear for the long flight back to the States. After two operations, we had officially relieved Charlie Platoon.

Hoping we might have a chance to use them, our platoon had brought a pair of water skis with us from the States. One of our operating boats was a fiberglass Boston Whaler skimmer. With a forty-horse engine, it would flat-ass move out. We had skis, we had the boat and the Bassac River, but we didn't have a rope, so after chow we made a visit to the good old Seabees. The rope they gave us was heavy, but it worked. Made of nylon, it stretched like a rubber band. Up and down the Bassac River we went, staying way out in the main channel to avoid getting shot by the enemy. As we got closer to camp we got braver, and would ski along the south shore, weaving in and out of the bushes that grew out into the water. Since our camp was in a hostile environment, we packed a Stoner, Bruce's M-16/XM-148 combo, and a few M-26 frags with us. But even out in the middle of the river we were easy targets for the Vietcong.

We skied past one of the South Vietnamese patrol boats, and three of its sailors got wet from the rooster tail. As we made our second pass on them, one of them held up an M-16. He held it as if to say, "Try it again." As we cruised by, not spraying them this time, I held up my Stoner and Bruce held up his M-16/XM-148 combo. The sailor put down his weapon and we continued to ski. Needless to say, we never sprayed another South Vietnamese patrol boat.

Soon after this, Mr. Q signaled us ashore. As we pulled up to the dock, he said, "The pig is done." Do you know what fourteen hungry SEALs can do to a roast pig? Well, the day ended as fast as it started. I walked over to the thirty-foot tower with the .50 caliber mounted on top. A few SEALs were sitting up on the tower with some Seabees. As I climbed up to the top with them, I smelled marijuana. It was passed to me, but I declined. The men on watch had a starlight scope to aid their search of the surrounding jungle and rice paddies for VC. Of course, the watch also looked around the camp to spot the approach of officers or unsympathetic enlisted men so that they could put out their joints.

Looking up the river, I saw the sky light up with two large flashes. The explosions were heard a few seconds later. Then tracers started filling the sky. A South Vietnamese outpost upstream was being attacked by the Vietcong. It wasn't long before air support arrived to help the outpost. Then a doobie was passed to me again. This time I tried a puff. Coughing my lungs out, I passed it back.

Upstream, red tracers started pouring out of the sky in one big red line down to the perimeter of the outpost. It was easy to tell then. It was Spooky, a C-117 armed with miniguns. As it circled in the night, an endless red line of tracers pounded the earth from above. More bright flashes of light were followed by the sound of explosions.

As Spooky circled the outpost, the joints circled the tower. I was soon feeling light-headed. A feeling I had never had before. A good feeling, not like the depression of alcohol. As I sat on the sandbags surrounding the top of the tower, watching the expensive light show, I thought about how much whiskey and beer I had been drinking, and how terrible they made me feel. Maybe pot was an alternative. I was also paranoid about being busted, but continued to accept the doobie as it was passed to me. The light show finally stopped upstream. As I got up from the sandbags, I fell backward and bumped into the bag I'd been sitting on. It fell the thirty feet to the ground. I would have fallen too, but Bruce caught me. Everyone in the tower started laughing, myself included. I climbed down from the tower and walked over to my hootch. The lights were out and most of the SEALs were sleeping, so I climbed the ladder into my rack in the rafters. Damn, it was hot up there. With a

loaded Model 15 on one side, Stoner loaded with 110 rounds
on the other, Stoner vest hanging from the ladder below
with 440 rounds of ammo, two frags, an incendiary, and a
smoke grenade ready to go, I got the best night's sleep I'd
had since entering the combat zone.

The next morning I rolled over and glanced at my diving
watch—1000 hours. And it was hot. I was being baked
alive. I climbed down out of my rack, still surprised at how
well I had slept.

My squad had been on two missions so far, both without
contact with Charlie. Tonight we would be challenged with
our third operation.

Later in the day, first squad was summoned to the briefing
hootch for our early morning mission. Mr. Q said, "We
have received reliable intel from second squad's prisoner
on a VC tax collector. He is living in a hootch on the east
end of Dung Island. He is protected at all times by two to
four heavily armed guards. Our mission is to patrol in,
eliminate his guards, and snatch the tax collector for intel.
Once the snatch is made, we will check the VC hootch for
documents and weapons as the field interrogation is being
conducted, if conditions permit."

Mr. Q used his pointer to show us our insertion, extraction, and patrol routes on the picto map. The picto maps
we used most looked like regular maps but were made from
seamless mosaics of photographs. An awful lot of detail
was visible on those maps: trails, roads, dikes, rice paddies,
canals, rivers, jungle, villages, river depths, banana groves,
mangrove swamps, sandbars, and individual hootches.
Sometimes a white cloud appeared on the maps, just a white
spot with the word "cloud" printed on it. Since the Mekong
Delta was mostly green, so were the maps. The only difference I could find was that the water in the rivers and
canals was printed blue instead of the muddy brown of real
life. Being military, the maps used thousand-meter grid
squares and were printed by the Army Map Service, Corps
of Engineers.

The canal we would use to enter Dung Island ran west
to east, three-quarters of the length of the island. It was the

largest and longest canal that ran through Dung Island. It was very wide at the east end and very narrow at the west. "A sandbar, illustrated on the map here"—he pointed—"blocks the eastern end of the canal at low tide. We will be taking the medium in at high tide. The west end of this canal can also only be navigated at high tide." A perfect place for Charlie to set up an ambush, I thought. We had used the canal from the west end on our last op. It was so narrow, the jungle scraped both sides of the medium as we passed through it. We had nicknamed it Ti Ti Canal, as *ti ti* was Vietnamese for "small."

After the briefing we left the hootch to ready our gear. At 0300 hours we gathered at the dock for inspection, then boarded the medium and headed downstream toward the South China Sea. We had no problems locating Ti Ti Canal's east entrance, as it was more than 1500 meters wide. The medium turned northwest, slowing down so we could spot the sandbar. I cocked my Stoner and put it on safe as the medium moved deeper into enemy-controlled territory. Soon, as we moved slowly upstream, the engines just above idle, warning shots were fired by VC on both sides of the canal. The east end of Dung Island was mostly mangrove swamps. Moving through the swamps by foot was next to impossible. The Vietcong used the area to their advantage—it was a perfect place for them to hide out during the day.

As we neared our insertion area, we made a fake insertion, then another, trying to throw Charlie off, if he was watching and listening. We continued upstream. Mr. Q watched the radar screen for the smaller canal we were to use for our real insertion. Everyone crouched low in the medium, faces and hands camouflaged, weapons held ready. The triple-canopy jungle grew right into the river there, and the small canal we were looking for was hard to pick out from the rest of the shoreline. Then it showed up on the radar. The medium turned ninety degrees into the small canal, and one by one we silently went over the bow into neck-deep muddy water.

We moved up the canal a short distance and set up a perimeter. With all the vines and bushes and vegetation

growing in the water, it was very easy to hide. Doc called
in the radio check by clicking the mike twice. The boat
acknowledged the same way. Radio checks were made every
hour. No words were spoken. Our squad would initiate the
radio check from the jungle first, then get a reply from the
MST crew. Radio checks after that followed the schedule
assigned at the briefing earlier. In case of immediate contact
with Charlie upon inserting, the MST crew was to automatically open fire with the two M-60s, two .50-calibers,
and the minigun at treetop level or forty-five degrees or
higher. They were also to fire at the far flanking banks and
shoot M-79 HE (high explosives) rounds over our heads.
All the fireworks were meant to startle the enemy, giving
us a chance to maneuver back to the boat. This was standard
operating procedure for our support unit, the Mobile-
Support Team personnel.

The medium moved up the channel away from our position to make two more fake insertions. It was a hot, muggy
night. The sweat, some physical, some psychological,
beaded my camouflage paint. I tasted salty sweat as it rolled
over my lips.

After lying silently for what seemed like hours, I pulled
back the black leather cover on my diving watch to check
the time. We had only been there twenty minutes, but the
normal sounds of the jungle had already returned. The mosquitoes enjoyed my blood as I lay there. Wait, don't move,
listen. Maybe on this operation first squad would make
contact with Charlie.

We had about 300 meters to patrol up this overgrown
canal to reach our objective. We used the canals to patrol
in as much as possible. Not only was it quieter sneaking
in, but the Vietcong booby-trapped the canal banks, dikes,
and trails more.

Grimes finally started up the canal, moving slowly while
he looked for booby traps. Right from the start the going
was rough. Vines and tree roots under the water snagged
our gear and wrapped around our legs. Trying to keep it
dry and out of the mud, I carried my Stoner above my head.
The Vietcong used canals like this at night like highways

to reinforce their troops with men, weapons, and food, but it was one hell of a place for a firefight. We slowly moved along, stopping often to listen and check for booby traps. Several times we had to stop and help each other across deeper places in the canal.

The canal began to circle to the left and widen a bit. The going was a little easier there. We stopped again to listen. Grimes had moved out ahead, and we waited for his signal to move up. I noticed a strange odor in the air. Not the normal jungle smell. Then I realized it was mosquito coil, the kind of incenselike repellent that resembled the burner on an electric range. The Vietnamese burned the coils to ward off mosquitoes. I stayed low in the muddy water, looking back down the canal. Then the signal came back to me that we were getting close and to be extra quiet. We moved silently ahead through the water and took up positions along the canal bank directly behind a large nipa palm hootch. Goddamn, it stunk there! Looking up, I saw an overhang made from limbs and pieces of bamboo. I was lying in the muddy water underneath a gook shitter! That was my position until it got light enough to rush the hootch.

I crouched against the bank with only head and Stoner out of the water. I had to take a leak, so I did, right in my jeans. Sweat ran down my cammoed face, dripping into the filthy water. Mosquitoes used my face like a pin cushion. I couldn't move, had to stay quiet.

As the morning sky lightened, I could make out a sampan tied up to the shore on my left. Its bow was pointing in my direction, and a plank led from the stern to the bank. I hoped we would make contact with Charlie here. I didn't want to lay in gook shit for nothing.

Eventually there was some movement and someone coughing in the hootch. It was time. Mr. Q gave the signal, and all eight of us rushed the hootch quietly. I ran toward the near left-front corner of the hootch and flopped down in the mud, covering the left side of the hootch and the canal behind me. The rest of first squad set up a perimeter around the hootch in different places while Quan, Grimes, and Mr. Q busted in the door. Doc stayed outside with his

back toward the door in case Mr. Q needed the radio. Doc
also covered the canal behind us with his M-16. All outside
scanned the surrounding jungle for signs of movement. If
anyone ran out of the hootch on my side, they were dead
meat. Inside the hootch, bodies were hitting the dirt floor
and Quan was barking questions in rapid Vietnamese. Children were crying and a mamasan was begging for her life.
Quan was slapping someone inside. Soon Grimes dragged
a half-naked gook out of the hootch by his hair and laid
him on the ground facedown. His CAR-15 was trained at
the back of the gook's head. His family followed and were
laid out beside him. Quan was asking questions like,
"Where are there any American POWs?" "Where are your
weapons and ammo?" "Where are your leaders?" "How
many Vietcong or NVA are in the area, where are they?
How many weapons? Lead us to them."

The gook wouldn't answer. Shit, I thought, here I am,
wet, muddy, tired, shitty, and practically packed away by
mosquitoes, and the gook won't talk. Mr. Q signaled Bruce
to search the sampan tied up behind us. I moved to a stump
beside the canal and sat down on it, covering Bruce, the
Stoner laid across my lap. A small cabin on the sampan had
two entrances into it, one on the bow and one on the stern,
both covered with burlap. Bruce walked up the plank and
onto the stern of the sampan. In one quick movement he
was through the burlap door and down inside.

All of a sudden Bruce's M-16 was opened up on full auto
and he was yelling, "Gook coming out." I jumped to my
feet thinking Bruce just ate the big one. A Vietcong came
running out the bow cabin door. He spotted me, turned and
took two shots at me with his M-1 carbine, the bullets
cracking past the left side of my head. I lifted the Stoner
waist high and forgot about the three- or four-round burst
I'd been taught to fire in training; most of the magazine
emptied into him and the front of the sampan. The gook's
body jerked around with pieces of cloth and flesh flying
through the air. Dropping his carbine on the deck of the
sampan, he did a bloody dance off the bow and fell into
the canal. He sank quickly, leaving a bloody slick on the

muddy water surface. I glanced behind me and saw that everyone else had hit the deck. As I made my way toward the sampan, I quickly changed to a fresh box of ammo. There were only twenty rounds left from the original 110. I ran up the plank onto the sampan, then pulled back the burlap door, Stoner trained inside. Bruce was lying on the deck looking up at me with a big grin on his face. Next to him was another dead gook, AK-47 laying across his body. Bruce didn't have a scratch on him. The zipperhead Bruce shot got one shot off at him as he entered the cabin and missed. When Bruce opened up, the other gook ran out the forward entrance and, knowing what was going to happen, Bruce hit the deck. He was surprised after I told him I was the only one that fired my weapon outside.

After listening to Quan doing the interrogation and the mamasan's whining, they probably laid low, trying to stay undetected. Everyone in our squad was really pissed off at the gooks in the hootch for lying to us. Quan was really working the lice-infested little bastard over again as I worked my way to the bow of the sampan to recover the Vietcong weapon that had fallen on the deck. The M-1 carbine and the bow were covered with blood. I looked at the carbine; a cartridge was turned sideways, jammed in the action. I realized how lucky I was. That bullet was meant for me. During UDT/SEAL training, an instructor ran over to me and knocked my ass flat to the ground for having my body too high during a simulated combat patrol. After this operation, I would never have to be told to stay low again. I looked over at Quan. The half-naked VC had been blindfolded and handcuffed and was down on both knees.

Quan was one tough little son of a bitch for his size. He hated the Vietcong, and they liked him about as much. As Quan started to put the rag over the dink's face again, enemy rounds started coming into our perimeter from a distant treeline. It was far, ineffective fire, so nobody fired back yet. Here we go, I thought. Mr. Q and Grimes had searched the hootch and found some Vietcong documents. Air support from Binh Thuy was scrambled by Doc, and the medium was notified we had made contact and to stand by. Grimes found a can of gasoline used for the motor on the sampan. He soaked down the inside of the hootch. Mamasan was hysterical. Quan told her to gather her kids and *di di mau* (get lost quick). With a small baby in her arms and two small kids following her, she waddled off down a dike toward an open rice paddy, moaning all the way.

Mr. Q pulled the pin on an incendiary grenade and tossed it into the hootch. "Load up that sampan, now!" he shouted. "We'll take Charlie back to camp for further interrogation."

As the hootch was engulfed in flames, the rest of first squad boarded the Vietnamese sampan. As it popped and crackled, I could feel the heat from the burning hootch clear back where I was. Our original plan was to patrol out through a different canal, but that canal was in the direction of the incoming enemy fire. To avoid ambush we always tried to extract on a different route. We did not make a habit of going out the same way we had patrolled in on. After all were aboard the sampan, we started out the same canal we had patrolled in on. Enemy rounds increased as we left the area, but I think Charlie was just firing in the direction of the burning hootch.

Going out that canal was much easier using the sampan. Maybe Charlie wouldn't know which way we left the area. The dead gook's body was dragged from the cabin and laid beside me as we made our way out the canal. We decided not to use the sampan's engine, as that would give our position away. Instead, we used two long poles to push the sampan out the canal. One of the SEALs was checking the dead gook's body for documents as I crouched on the bow, holding my Stoner in one hand and pushing limbs and vines out of our way with the other. I watched both flanks carefully, trying to detect ambushes.

I looked up through the triple canopy. Two OV-10 Broncos were circling overhead. The OV-10 Bronco was a small two-man fixed-wing aircraft used for close air support. Also called "black pony," the Bronco had a payload of 2000 pounds. Twin Rolls-Royce engines powered that fine plane. It had two rocket pods of eight rockets each and three mini-guns, and it could parachute five real close friends from the aft fuselage. Doc established radio communications with them and directed them toward the burning hootch and the far treeline from which we took the incoming rounds. That would keep the Vietcong occupied while we cleared the area. In seconds the miniguns were firing and rockets were exploding in the distance. Soon we were at the point of our insertion. We waited there until we could hear the medium getting close, then pushed the sampan through the thick undergrowth into Ti Ti Canal. As the medium moved alongside us, the MST crew was astonished at our method of extraction. After all seven of us and our captured tax collector had boarded the medium, I threw a frag into the sampan as we sped away. The sampan, engine, and dead VC went to the bottom of Ti Ti Canal.

Slumping down against the starboard bulkhead of the medium, I thought about the mission: one captured VC tax collector, two VC KIA, one M-1 carbine, and one AK-47 weapon, and a VC motorized sampan sunk. I was still shaking from reaction to the Vietcong I had wasted. It had been either him or me. My training saved my life; he was at the bottom of the canal. Our prisoner lay on the deck, handcuffed and blindfolded. He was kept uncomfortable, giving him little time to get his thoughts together until we arrived at camp.

As the medium cruised at top speed out of Ti Ti Canal and into the Bassac River, MST personnel and SEALs gathered up in front of the medium. Some of them were laughing at me. I didn't see what was so funny, so I went forward to find out. As I got close, Mr. Q held up his hand. "Stop, Young. No offense, but you smell like shit! The back of the boat is all yours. Just stay downwind of us until we get back to camp." I looked down at my muddy, filthy clothes and had to laugh too. I *did* smell like shit!

CHAPTER FOUR

It didn't take us long to get back to camp with first squad's first prisoner. The Seabees were already up, busily running around building up the camp, preparing for the day it would be converted to South Vietnamese control. I was really annoyed at times, looking at all the American taxpayers' dollars being spent in Vietnam. Just about everything the South Vietnamese military used—guns, ammo, boats, planes, helos, buildings, and even food—was paid for with American bucks. That didn't even take into account the most important asset, American lives. It wouldn't have been so bad if they had appreciated it, but most of the South Vietnamese I knew and saw didn't. It made me wonder why I was there.

After the debriefing, some of us cleaned our weapons and gear while Quan drilled questions into Charlie. Quan wouldn't stop until he received the information he wanted, what we called fresh intel. I can't stress too much the importance of good intelligence to military operations. Good intelligence, the element of surprise, and fire superiority would result in a successful operation, the kind that kept us alive, brought back prisoners, and raised our body count. Other intelligence sources for successful SEAL operations came from Provincial Recon Units (PRUs), Navy Intel Liaison Officers (NILOs), District Intelligence Officers (DIOs), the CIA, Army Intelligence (S-2) advisors, or the South Vietnamese people themselves. The South Vietnamese people knew what was happening in their area. Getting them to talk was another thing. They were afraid of what the Vietcong would do to them and their families if they opened their mouths. Sometimes it was necessary to bring civilians in for interrogation purposes, just to find out what type of enemy control might be exercised in their area. We dealt with civilians in a different way than the Vietcong did: we offered them food, clothes, medical supplies, and even South Vietnamese money for their knowledge.

Working over a Vietcong for intel, sometimes we would play "good cop, bad cop," that is, change our tactics and start being nice to him, and sometimes one would lean our way, giving us the information we requested. Sometimes we would use captured money to pay these informants for their information. Sometimes they would even lead us into enemy-held territory, through the safest, least booby-trapped way, to capture their comrades. Every gook was different. Sometimes they earned their freedom for leading us to someone far more important. By capturing the Vietcong's top figures, we hoped we would break down the VC infrastructure and disorganize their forces.

Every two weeks was payday. To receive our pay, we had to go to Binh Thuy, to the Naval Support Facility. Usually we took the medium and cruised up the Bassac to Binh Thuy, where a compound housed the SEAL Team headquarters for the Delta region. Inside the compound was the SEAL Quonset hut, a fiberglass repair facility for river patrol boats (PBRs), an explosive-ordnance disposal team compound, and a disbursing building where we received our pay. Also, there were several large barracks for the men who worked there.

The Binh Thuy facility represented civilization to us, and the personnel stationed there had all the comforts of home. As it was forty miles upriver from our camp, we usually stayed there overnight. That gave us plenty of time to get paid, pick up fresh supplies, and raid the chow hall. At our camp SEALs had chow-hall rights. If we came in late or went out early on an operation, we could help ourselves to the walk-in reefers, crank up the grill, and make our own meals. We didn't even have to do the dishes. Nevertheless, it felt good to get to Binh Thuy, even if it was only for one night every two weeks.

The military personnel stationed in Binh Thuy had nice barracks, vehicles to drive around in, and a super chow hall. Even ice cream. The only problem was the Vietnamese people there. The Vietnamese from Long Phu, the village outside our camp, and from the surrounding area, were what I thought of as the ''real'' Vietnamese people. The Vietnamese from Binh Thuy and Can Tho were like the gooks from Saigon, out to stab you in the back. The same old shit all the time, ''Give me money,'' ''Buy me drink,'' ''Buy me air-conditioned helicopter,'' ''Hey buddy, want number-one drugs?'' As soon as you walked out the gate, they were there, taking advantage of the big-bucks Americans.

I hung around Bruce while in Binh Thuy. He was in-country for his second tour, and so could help me stay out of trouble. But then again, he helped to get me into some trouble too. He was like a big brother to me. Weber, who went through UDT/SEAL training with me, preferred to stay back at our camp. He liked the peace and quiet out in the middle of nowhere, so I usually took a list of things he needed from the PX.

SEALs were as rare to see in town as a Stoner. As we walked down the streets of Can Tho, we always drew a lot of hard stares and suspicious looks from military personnel and Vietnamese alike. Our hair was longer than military specs, some of us had beards, which were not then authorized, and we wore a mix of civilian and military clothing. Levi's jeans, cammo top, protective coral booties or tennis shoes. And occasionally we packed Stoners. Even most military personnel didn't recognize the Stoner. At that time the only people to have Stoners were the Underwater Demolition Teams, the SEAL teams, and the Chicago Police Department (they had six). After taking a look at us, normal GIs would say, ''Who or what the fuck are you?'' Few people in Nam ever got to lay eyes on a Navy SEAL.

We always checked the PX for film; if you wanted film in Nam, you had to be at the right place at the right time. I had a 35mm underwater Nikonos and an 8mm Bolex triple-lens movie camera, both of which came over with me from the States. The 35mm film was hard to find, and the 8mm was damn near impossible. My dad sent me 8mm film from the States. After collecting everything we needed, we returned to the SEAL Quonset hut at the Naval Support Facility, stashed our gear, and headed over to the Navy EOD bar. The Explosive-Ordnance Disposal people had a super bar which they had built out over the Bassac River. SEALs and EOD personnel had a lot in common as far as diving and explosives went, so we got along pretty well. We would sit in their bar, swap stories, and drink whiskey together. On the wall behind the bar was a picture of Ann-Margret. The picture had been doctored to look like you could see through what little clothes she had on, and we drank whiskey chased by beer while we checked out her picture for hours. By the time we left the EOD bar the next morning, we were usually well under way. Then, after gathering our gear and getting a head count, we returned to the medium for the trip back down the Bassac to our camp.

I enjoyed the trip up or down the Bassac River between Binh Thuy and camp. We all took turns driving, and if it wasn't raining, we would lay on the canvas top of the medium and enjoy the sun. Sometimes, taking turns, we would ski the whole forty miles. I could hear the muffled sound of the twin 427 Chevy engines and watch the rooster tail kick out behind us as we cruised on step. I laid on the canvas top, thinking about my last operation. I had almost been shot in the head twice. If that gook's rifle hadn't jammed, he might have hit me. I decided to do whatever was necessary to get back home alive. My job was gathering intelligence by capturing Vietcong or North Vietnamese Army cadre. If they or the regular VC got in my way, I would pull the trigger. If it had to be them or me, I was going to make damn sure it was them. My job was being a SEAL team member. I was going to do it to the best of my ability.

CHAPTER FIVE

It was now well into July, and I don't think any of us had had a haircut since we left the States. That didn't bother me at all. After all, who was going to see us on Dung Island anyway? Besides, we were all ugly sons of bitches when we were cammoed up. Anyone who made it through UDT/ SEAL training had to be crazy: if you weren't when you started, you were when you finished. The final product was a bunch of crazy men who could get the job done. It didn't really matter what we looked like.

I was reassembling my Stoner as Mr. Q approached me at the outdoor weapons-cleaning table. "Young, do you want to go on an ambush tonight?" he asked.

The casualness and informality between officers and enlisted men was one of the great things about being in the teams. An officer could go right up to you and speak directly to you about military matters. There wasn't a lot of time spent on chain of command, since our operating groups were so small. "What are we going to do?" I asked.

"Things have been a little slow lately. We need some fresh intel. Tonight we are going to take the medium back into Dung Island and ambush some boat traffic. Maybe we can grab some prisoners."

Great, I thought, maybe that meant I didn't have to get muddy or wet. I grinned and said, "Yeah, I'll go."

"Okay, Young, meet at the medium at 2200."

At 2200, after I cammoed my face, I found two MST crew members waiting in the medium when three other SEALs and I got aboard.

We cast off and headed on step up the Bassac River. This

was my eighth operation, and I was beginning to get the hang of things. The main thing was to keep your ass down and be quiet! After a few minutes of traveling upstream, we turned off the Bassac to the north on a canal that led into the western end of Dung Island. Melfa guided the boat to a spot about 1500 meters into the island and cut the throttles back to just above idle. Four canals intersected there from all directions, forming an open area free of over-hanging jungle. One of the four canals was the western end of Ti Ti Canal. We picked a spot that had a good field of fire across the intersection, slid the medium under the ov-erhanging jungle canopy to its starboard side and cut the engines. We were in a free-fire zone, so there were no other friendly forces operating on Dung Island. We had the island to ourselves all the time. Anything or anybody moving on the waterways after 1000 hours was an unfriendly suspect.

Our position against the shoreline had excellent cover and concealment for the medium. Using a starlight scope, we took turns scanning the intersection and surrounding area. We weren't there very long when we heard some movement to starboard, the side closest to the jungle. Quietly, some of us covered the area with the starboard .50-caliber, M-60, and a Stoner. We checked out the area with the starlight scope but couldn't see anyone. I thought we might find one of the gooks who fired warning shots; it was a good place for one to be positioned. Listening and watching while maintaining strict noise discipline, we covered the starboard bank and the intersection.

It was a clear night, and the starlight scope, working off the available ambient light, worked well. The night was so quiet I could hear a faint buzz when the scope was turned on.

Shortly after midnight I was watching the intersection with the scope as a sampan eased out of one of the canals and slowly paddled into the intersection. In the green light of the scope I could make out two Vietcong coming straight toward us. I alerted the others by hand signal as I handed the starlight scope to Strausbaugh. I then grabbed a pop flare. We needed to catch them alive, if possible, so we

were going to give them a chance to surrender. When they
reached the middle of the intersection, our kill zone, they
were a long way from shore in all directions. I let the pop
flare rip. We gave the two gooks a chance to surrender by
letting them see the flare go up and ignite. The whole area
lit up like a ballpark at night. Then they made their second
mistake—the first one was exposing themselves—they instantly paddled like hell, trying to reach shore. In an ambush, you usually have about two seconds in a kill zone
before you are killed or wounded; it's doubtful you have
that long if you are ambushed by SEALs using Stoners.
Two Stoners, two M-60s, one .50-caliber, a minigun, and
an M-79 grenade launcher opened up at once. Caught in
the middle of the intersection, they didn't have a chance;
the two occupants of the sampan literally came apart.

As we opened up on the sampan, rounds cracked through
the medium from the starboard side. Strausbaugh and I
switched targets and opened up on the jungle to the starboard
side. Red tracers from every fifth round streaked into the
jungle night from our weapons. One of the MST crew members brought the starboard .50-caliber to bear. The incoming
rounds abruptly stopped. "No time to look for that body,"
Mr Q hollered. "Let's get to the sampan and see what's
left." The medium pulled out into the intersection to find
a body or some documents for intelligence.

As we approached what was left of the sampan, I grabbed
another pop flare and sent it up with the one that was drifting
off and burning out. We found nothing but pieces of sampan
floating on the muddy surface. Three concussion grenades
were chucked out into the water in different directions
around the intersection, in case Charlie was still alive and
had a good set of lungs. You would be surprised how long
a gook can stay underwater when someone is trying to kill
him. But nothing floated to the surface, and the second pop
flare had burned out, so we called it a night.

After reaching our camp, we raided the chow hall, our
faces still cammoed and our bodies still dressed to kill. It
was sure nice coming back dry from an operation. A successful ambush could make a person work up an appetite.

CHAPTER SIX

The Vietcong called SEALs the "men with green faces." They believed we had spiritual powers. They knew we came from the swamp, captured one of their people, and returned to the swamp, and that they never saw their stolen comrade again. And they never knew where or when the men with green faces would show up.

There weren't any operations over the next few days. We spent our time cleaning weapons, firing our weapons, and cleaning them some more. Our nights were filled with guitar playing, whiskey drinking, and writing letters home. Also, smoking a little pot now and then boosted my morale and that of some of my teammates. It was an alternative to drinking heavily, and it made me feel much better without leaving me hung over, but none of us ever—and I mean *never*—smoked before or during an operation. The type of missions SEALs went on required a clear head.

One day, while Weber and I were cleaning up the ammo bunker, Ensign Walsh approached us and said, "I hope you guys enjoyed your time off. First squad has an ambush tonight. The briefing will be at 2100."

We finished cleaning out the ammo bunker and secured the lock on the door. As we walked toward our hootch, I could hear a helo off in the distance. The sound grew louder as the helo neared our camp. Then LePage was walking toward the helo pad with a smoke grenade as an Army slick circled camp. Throwing the yellow smoke on the downwind side of the pad, he walked out of the way as the pilot flew into the wind and descended onto the pad. As soon as the chopper settled, two high-ranking American officers jumped

out and followed LePage to the briefing hootch. One of
them was a SEAL. I didn't know the other one, but he was
also Navy. I thought he might be a Naval Intelligence Liaison Officer. Something big had to be in the works for two
officers to hand carry the intel directly to Mr. Q.

The chopper's blade was still rotating, after the engine
was shut down, when Panella, Weber, Reeves, and I walked
over to the helo pad. The pilot was sitting in the shade
beneath the thirty-foot machine-gun tower, smoking a cigarette. Since he was waiting for the two officers, Reeves
and I tried to talk him into a ride. After crushing out his
cigarette, he said, "Let's go," and walked to the helo and
cranked it up with the four of us inside. After the chopper
was airborne, I slid out of my seat and sat in the starboard
doorway with Reeves, our feet hanging outside. We circled
the camp a couple of times then headed up the Bassac River.
I don't know how fast we were going, but we were really
hauling ass. The chopper was tilted forward and the front
tips of the skids were only a few feet above the water.

We flew up the river like that for quite a ways. Sampans
on the river hurried out of our path as we approached. All
of a sudden, without any warning, the helo made a rapid
ascent from just above the river to about a thousand feet.
Next came a sharp rolling turn to the right. The torque from
the banking turn forced me and my stomach back into the
chopper and against the floor, but it seemed as if the pilot
was trying to throw us out of the door. We clenched the D-
ring tie-downs on the floor till our fingers were white. The
chopper was damn near sideways. I could look straight out
the door and straight into the Bassac. Why did I do this? I
thought. It was too late, the pilot straightened out the chopper and we descended rapidly, heading downstream this
time.

After the pilot figured we had had enough, he headed
back to our camp. By the time we landed, I was glad to
get my feet back on the ground. As we staggered from the
helo, my fingers still white from hanging on, I looked back
at the Army warrant officer who piloted the helo. He didn't
look any older than me, but the grin on his face scared the

hell out of me. It would be a long time before I asked for another ride. As it turned out, while I was almost puking my guts out, our officers were planning our biggest, most important operation to date.

After they finished briefing Mr. Q, the two "upper echelons" climbed aboard the helo and took off across the rice paddies in the direction of Binh Thuy. Not long after, Mr. Q and Walsh made the rounds, informing us the ambush was off and that all fourteen of us and Quan had a briefing at 2100. Mr. Q wouldn't answer any questions. I figured if all fourteen of us were needed for the op, then we would probably be getting ourselves shot at just after first light tomorrow morning. This was to be Juliett Platoon's thirty-third mission in-country. This was also Juliett Platoon's first time to operate as an entire platoon in a combat situation. The importance of the operation required all of us.

After I returned to normal from the helo flight, I headed back to the hootch to check over my gear. After evening chow we watched the movie version of *The Man from U.N.C.L.E.* in the chow hall. After the movie was over, the fourteen of us and Quan assembled in the briefing hootch for our "surprise operation" briefing.

Mr. Q began, "Okay guys, listen up. This mission is called 'Operation Bright Light.' We are to try to liberate two American POWs from a VC prisoner-of-war camp. At 0200 hours we will leave camp and proceed down the Bassac into the South China Sea. Once there, we will turn south and proceed to our insertion point here." With his pointer he tapped our planned insertion point on the picto map.

"After we are inserted, we will patrol two hundred meters inland and set up a perimeter until it begins to get light. We will then patrol farther inland another 150 meters to our objective. Just prior to hitting our target, or upon contact with Charlie, we will scramble our supporting aircraft. They will be on standby on an aircraft carrier off the coast. Navy Seawolf helicopter gunships will be our supporting unit after insertion."

In all the operations we had conducted until then, we had

never been given air support from a carrier. The op had to
be important.

"A Chieu Hoi [a Vietcong who had come over to our
side] will be with us on this op to guide us into the VC
camp the safest way. The Chieu Hoi has worked with the
Vietcong at this camp in the past. He will not be carrying
a weapon. Our objective—to hit the VC camp and free the
two Americans. Intelligence has also informed us there are
as many as thirty Arvins currently being held prisoner at
this camp."

This last piece of information started everyone talking at
once. American POWs. We knew how the Vietcong treated
their prisoners. Mr. Q quieted us down and finished the
briefing. All the operating equipment we were to carry was
assigned, and our extraction and alternate extraction sites
were laid out. We were to extract by helo on this op. Also,
extra helos would be on standby to extract any liberated
prisoners. After leaving the briefing hootch, I went to collect
the special gear I was to use. We were to be armed to the
nuts on this operation.

At 0200 we gathered our gear and met at the dock for
final inspection. Mr. Walsh, LePage, Reeves, and I carried
Stoners and our standard ammo load. Mr. Walsh's Stoner
was modified with a shorter barrel and fed from a 150-round
aluminum drum magazine. Because it was lighter, the
shorter barrel compensated for the extra fifty rounds. Mr.
Walsh's extra belts of ammo were wrapped around his chest.
Weber and Baylett packed chopped-down M-60s with their
standard loads. Bruce and Sitter each carried the M-16/XM-
148 combo, and Grimes carried the CAR-15 for walking
point. Because of its short length, the CAR-15 was highly
maneuverable in tight quarters. The rest of the team had M-
16s. All of us carried gas masks for this op. As well, we
took two PRC-77s; the primary radio was packed by Doc,
along with his medical gear, and the secondary radio was
packed by Shannon. We all carried extra grenades. Mr. Q,
Grimes, Bruce, and Sitter carried extra tear gas. We took
four claymore mines, and Reeves and I carried a LAW
(Light Assault Antitank Weapon) rocket each. The LAW

added 4.68 pounds to my already too-heavy gear. The round, fin-stabilized projectile had a muzzle velocity of about 450 to 500 feet per second. It is percussion fired, and capable of penetrating eleven inches of armor steel, thirty-six inches of concrete, and seventy-eight inches of log-and-earth bunkers. The projectile armed itself after flying about twenty-eight to forty-five feet, and had a back blast area sixty meters wide by sixty meters long. The LAW's killing radius was fifteen meters, and it had a 325-meter range. We used them mostly for attacking bunkers and to slow the Vietcong down when we were being chased out of Charlie's backyard. They were great when they worked. Unfortunately, about half the time Vietnam's humidity and rain made the LAW inoperable; I considered it a one-shot 60mm, disposable piece of shit and hated packing it on my back.

During inspection that morning the team seemed unusually determined. We didn't know if the American POWs were Army, Navy, Marine Corps, or Air Force; it didn't matter. We were going to do what we had to do to free them. The fifteen of us had enough firepower to carry on our own war. After inspection we followed Quan as he escorted the Chieu Hoi onto the medium. The MST crew cast us off, and we were under way down the Bassac toward the South China Sea. Upon entering the sea, we experienced some turbulence. The coxswain continued east for another 400 meters and then turned south. We constantly checked the radar for obstacles and sandbars as the swells from the South China Sea bobbed us around.

After moving south awhile, staying offshore about 400 meters, we located our insertion point on the radar. We turned west toward shore and everybody made their weapons ready. Then the bow of the medium made contact with the bottom in surf only eight to ten inches high.

Splitting into squads, we deployed over both sides of the bow. One man off the port side, one off the starboard, until fourteen SEALs, Quan, and the Chieu Hoi disappeared into the dark. The small waves slapping against shore made just enough noise to hide ours. Reeves and I were the last to enter the ankle-deep water. The saltwater filled my jungle boots. I was surprised to be walking on a solid sandy bottom. We moved quietly up past the high-water mark and set up security. The medium backed out, turned around, and headed out to sea. It was to stay safe, well offshore, in case we needed it for emergency extraction. By keeping a close eye on the radar, the crew could maintain their position offshore and not drift with the current. An easy operation for the MST personnel. If everything went according to plan, we would meet them back at camp after the operation.

Doc and Shannon made their radio checks as we lay there quietly. The jungle canopy was silhouetted against the clear night sky some distance to the west. I could feel the cool damp of the sand penetrating my jeans. We lay there for twenty or thirty minutes, looking and listening for enemy movement.

After a while, one by one, we got up in patrol order and started moving inland. Mangrove roots and large sandy spaces made up the hinterland beyond the surf zone. Triple-canopy jungle lay just beyond. The sand soon disappeared behind us, and good old Mekong Delta mud took its place. More and more mangrove roots popped up out of the mud like human skeletons, but they made for good concealment when we stopped to listen. I patrolled just in front of Reeves, both of us being the rear-security element.

After we penetrated inland for about 200 meters, stopping to listen several times on the way, the signal was passed back to set up a perimeter. The POW camp was not more than 150 meters from our position by then. Watching behind us, I made myself comfortable hiding in the mangrove roots. We were to stay there until it was light enough to patrol toward the camp. Fireflies and mosquitoes buzzed around hungrily as I lay there, thinking of the two Americans. Reeves and I continued to watch the area behind our platoon. We stayed low to the ground, looking up behind us to silhouette anyone who might come into our field of fire, but avoided looking directly at something we wanted to see in the dark. Because of the way the eye is constructed, it's better to look to one side or the other of an object you're trying to see. You can pick up the slightest movement that way.

Ten minutes later we were patrolling again. One hundred fifty meters to go. It was just light enough to see the ground at our feet, and the vegetation was thickening as we entered the triple-canopy jungle. Quan was walking point with the Chieu Hoi, Grimes just behind them. For a moment we stopped again. A small trail was found leading in the direction of the camp. We moved on slowly. We stopped again; this time a trip wire had slowed us down. Slowly, we crossed over the wire one at a time. Six inches off the ground, the trip wire led to a Vietcong claymore mine tied to the bushes along the trail. Each man who stepped over the wire made damn sure the man behind him knew exactly where it was. First one leg, then the other. There ain't nothing like a trip wire to make a man feel like he is the clumsiest man alive.

After successfully crossing the obstacle, I crouched to cover Reeves and pointed with my finger to show him the entire length of the wire and the claymore it was attached to. Before Reeves was able to cross the wire, word was passed back that another trip wire had been found ahead of the patrol. Another sign that we were getting close to our objective. Another sign that we were in Charlie's backyard.

This time, up front, a pineapple grenade with a wire six inches off the ground ran across the trail. I stayed down on one knee to cover Reeves as he crossed the claymore's wire. Reeves put one leg over the wire. As he straddled it, the claymore stared him dead in the face. Just at that time, the grenade up front exploded, a loud crack echoing through the jungle. Reeves's cammo bush hat fell off his head and bounced off the trip wire he was straddling, landing in the mud beside him. Still straddling the wire, he looked at me and I looked at him, our eyes and mouths wide open. Luckily for us, like most Vietcong booby traps, this one was insensitive. Nevertheless, our position had been compromised. Reeves stepped over the wire and reached back to recover his hat. The word was passed back that we had wounded up front and to set up a perimeter around them. We knew Charlie would send someone out to see why the booby trap was detonated, so we set up a hasty ambush.

After moving into my new position up by LePage, next to a small canal that led toward the camp, I was told what had happened. After reaching the second trip wire, the Chieu Hoi turned to Quan and asked for his K-bar knife. Quan gave it to him, and the stupid gook turned and started to *cut* the trip wire to disarm it. Luckily the grenade malfunctioned, blowing ''low order.'' The Chieu Hoi, Quan, and Strausbaugh were the only ones to receive any shrapnel. The Chieu Hoi received only small pieces of shrapnel all over his body. Quan had a nice piece in his leg, and Strausbaugh took a nice piece of shrapnel in one of the M-60 ammo belts on his chest, so he was not wounded. While Doc tended to the wounded, everyone watched his designated field of fire. Sure enough, we heard some noise coming down the canal. Soon, two Vietcong came into view, coming in LePage's and my direction. As soon as they were in our kill zone, we could see the gook in the front of the sampan held a muddy M-1 carbine, and the one in back pushed the sampan with a long pole and had an AK-47 slung over his shoulder.

As they pushed the sampan closer toward us, LePage yelled in Vietnamese, ''Stop, drop your weapons.'' The zipperhead in front raised the M-1 carbine and pointed it in our direction. That was his first and last mistake. LePage, Strausbaugh, and I opened up with our weapons. We damn near cut the gook in half, and he fell facedown into the canal. The other VC jumped onto the canal bank and fell face first into the mud. Seriously wounded, he tried to crawl off into the brush, but we finished him off too. While tending to the wounded behind us, Doc was scrambling air support. LePage and I collected the weapons of the gooks we had wasted. The M-1 carbine had a round jammed in its chamber and was full of holes from our bullets.

Mr. Q gave the signal to move up, so with Grimes in the lead, we started patrolling up the trail toward the camp. But after moving just a short distance, we found the trail to be too heavily booby-trapped, so we dropped down into the canal and continued to patrol forward. Enemy rounds started cracking through the jungle over our heads, but we stayed low in the canal and moved in. About that time, bamboo spikes hidden beneath the muddy water pierced Doc's left jungle boot and stuck in his foot. Grimes and Mr. Q had stepped over them, not realizing they were there. Doc just pulled his left foot off the spikes without making a sound. He was in great pain, but kept it to himself. As we neared the camp, gooks started running everywhere. We hosed down the jungle on both sides of us and moved forward a little more.

Mr. Q decided to shoot some tear gas into the Cong's camp, so we pulled out our gas masks. As our air support arrived overhead, Bruce fired one tear-gas round from the XM-148, but the round hit some overhanging limbs and bounced back toward our position. The wind blew the gas back in our direction, and some of us didn't yet have our gas masks on all the way, so we received the worst of the gas intended for the Vietcong. Another tear-gas grenade was fired into the camp, and we followed it in, being very careful and watching for more booby traps. Meanwhile, Seawolf helicopters were hosing down the jungle all around us and gooks were dropping like flies. We had to alert the choppers to make sure of their targets, because some of the gooks were South Vietnamese prisoners trying to escape.

Once in the camp, we set up a perimeter. Doc was having trouble walking, but stayed in his position within the platoon. The air support continued strafing the surrounding area, and as our security element watched the perimeter, Mr. Q, Mr. Walsh, Grimes, and Quan searched the POW camp for evidence of the Americans, weapons, and documents. A small campfire was still burning with fish and rice ready to eat in large bowls. The spot where the two Americans had been restrained was quickly located: bamboo racks up off the ground had larger ropes for the Americans' hands and feet. In a different part of the camp several smaller cages were located where the South Vietnamese had been kept. As the search went on, enemy rounds continued to crack overhead. In an attempt to suppress the enemy fire, we fired out into our perimeter, even though we were still not seeing the little fuckers. After the camp had been

searched thoroughly, we formed up and searched the surrounding area, still looking for the Americans. The weapons, ammo, and documents we found were carried with us.
But the Vietcong had had good security and good escape
routes in all directions out of the POW camp.

We informed the Seawolf helicopters that no Americans
had been found and asked them to help scout the surrounding
area. They couldn't be far way, I thought as we continued the
search. Until they reached North Vietnam, Charlie rarely kept
American prisoners in any one place more than twenty-four
hours. Absolutely no one had been in the camp when we
rushed it, but there was evidence that lots of people had been
there just minutes before. Sounds of people running through
the jungle around us could still be heard, although not as many
as when we first entered the camp; a few Vietcong must have
stayed behind to harass us while their main force escaped. Enemy rounds still cracked overhead. Since we couldn't see the
little fuckers, we saved our ammo, firing back only when the
enemy's volume of fire increased.

After having searched the entire area, we patrolled back
into the camp. All cages and material usable to the Vietcong
were destroyed. We then collected our wounded, weapons,
and anything useful to Intel and patrolled to the extraction
site, where we set up a perimeter and called in the helos.
A yellow smoke was thrown out to mark our position. After
verifying the color of the smoke, the first chopper descended
into the LZ, which was only big enough for one chopper
at a time. To keep Charlie down as we loaded the wounded
and half the platoon on board, those of us on the ground
fired our weapons into the jungle. Meanwhile, Seawolf helos
strafed the flanks of our position, covering the extraction
helos. As the second chopper touched down, I maneuvered
toward it, firing my Stoner while walking backward. With
all on board, we lifted off. Both door gunners blazed away
as we cleared the jungle canopy. Until we reached a safe
altitude, Seawolfs on our flanks escorted us back toward
camp, then they flew for their carrier.

As I looked down at the green canopy, a sick ache in my
gut came over me thinking about the two Americans left

behind. With all the escape routes Charlie had, it would be next to impossible to find them. Who knows, maybe Charlie had moved them miles away the night before. Maybe they were still in the area, hidden under heavy guard. I will never know. Air strikes were called in to destroy the rest of the POW camp. The medium met us back at camp.

Later that day the area was mopped up by the South Vietnamese, who found nearly fifty of their men who had been held captive, far more than our intel had indicated. Some of them had been prisoners for more than four years. But no traces of the Americans were found.

CHAPTER SEVEN

As the choppers touched down at our camp, everyone departed but Doc and Quan, who were to fly to the hospital in Binh Thuy for treatment. The element of surprise had been compromised by the detonation of the booby trap, and then by the greasing of the two Vietcong in the sampan who had been sent out to check the perimeter of the camp. The operation had been unsuccessful in freeing the two Americans but successful in liberating the South Vietnamese. Seeing the place where the two Americans had been tied up sent a chill down my spine. Not me, I thought, one way or the other. I would not let those gook bastards capture me. Everyone at our camp would miss Doc, including the Seabees. Our bar wouldn't be the same without him. In addition, the corpsman is one of the most important and respected members of a SEAL platoon. Not only did Doc pack the radio and stop the blood from flowing, he also cured the clap when too much time was spent with the bar girls in town. No one ever, and I mean *ever*, wanted to piss off the corpsman.

We didn't operate for the next few days, so I tried to find things to do around camp to keep me busy. Swallows had moved in around camp and were flying in and out around the perimeter. They were thick. For something to do, I grabbed an Ithaca Featherweight Model 37 shotgun and a couple of ammo cans of double-0 buckshot. The Model 37 was an excellent weapon for walking point, especially if the barrel and stock are sawed off to make it shorter.

I took the buckshot out of the cartridges and cut it into tiny pieces with my K-bar knife. I then replaced it in the cartridges and recrimped them. After a good supply of my custom birdshot had been made, I went out into the tall, thick grass around our helo pad. Our Model 37 Ithaca Featherweight was equipped with a "duck bill" shot diverter attached to the muzzle to throw the buckshot in a horizontal pattern. I loaded the seven rounds in the tube magazine and readied my weapon. I had to be just killing something, I guess. Poor little things never hurt anything or anybody. Nevertheless, I crouched down in the tall grass and opened up on them in a safe direction away from camp. The more I shot, the more fun I had. The more fun I had, the more I shot, but I didn't seem to be putting a dent in the swallow population. As they flew overhead darting about, I gave them a little lead and squeezed the trigger. The cut-up buckshot whistled as it spread out in all directions, not giving the poor little blue swallows a chance to fly out of the way. By the time evening chow rolled around, I had one hell of a pile of dead swallows on the helo pad. It helped keep my shooting reflexes in tune, and that alone justified my killing off the swallows. But we had lots of other things to do to keep busy. After dark, when the Seabees were sleeping, we would sneak up to their hootches with long small-diameter wire. Sliding it through the screen windows, we knocked the books, coffee cans of cookies from home, and anything else we could reach off their shelves onto their heads while they slept. Then we ran to avoid getting caught. Seabees seemed to sleep with their heads toward the bulkheads and since they were good carpenters, all had nice shelves over their heads. Usually, three or four SEALs would line up against the Seabees' screen windows at once, each man choosing his target and slowly inserting the wires through the screen at the same time. Then, *wham!* "What the fuck was that?" and mass chaos inside the hootch. With throbbing heads, they would run outside looking for whoever had done it. Of course, by then we would be in the chow hall, innocently eating mid-rats as if nothing had happened.

Another fun thing to do was to grab cans of WD–40, of which we had a lot, and a Zippo lighter, then walk around camp, looking for spiders hanging in their webs. We'd spray the WD across the lighter flame and play the resulting torch over our victims. I hated spiders and enjoyed the crackling, popping sound of their bodies burning and all those legs curling up. Exercising the power of life and death over insects gave me a sense of accomplishment.

Something else done to pass the time was to sit around the hootch cutting notches in every round of Stoner ammo except the tracers. In my opinion, the only good VC was a dead VC. A .223 round left one hell of a nasty wound anyway, but notching the bullets gave them the effectiveness of a hollow point. Chances of stopping Charlie increased.

The next day Mr. Q made the rounds and reminded us to check the claymore mines in the camp's perimeter because the grass was getting too tall and needed cutting back. The Vietcong had been known to crawl up to a perimeter and turn the claymores around. So one had to be extremely cautious when going out to check them. Sure enough, after following the claymore wires out into the perimeter, we found some of the mines turned back toward camp. Charlie had been there.

We collected all the mines, trip flares, and wires so the Seabees could cut back the grass. When they finished, we moved the claymores to different positions around the perimeter. The M-18A1 claymore mine was a directional frag-type mine. Eight hundred steel ball bearings enclosed in a plastic concave shell packed in front of 1.25 pounds of

C-4 explosive that threw the steel balls in a sixty-degree arc. The claymore had a maximum range of 250 meters, but at 150 meters the steel balls would spread out to 160 meters wide and seven meters high. The claymores were packaged six to a box and weighed 3.5 pounds each. Each had two scissor legs that could be pulled out and spread apart to use as a stand. The claymore could be detonated in many ways, from trip wires to time fuses to being detonated by hand. Each mine came with an M-57 firing generator which, when squeezed, created enough electricity to set off an electrical blasting cap screwed into the top of the mine. Being anywhere from zero to sixteen meters directly behind the mine was very dangerous. The claymore was an excellent weapon for ambushes, and we set them around an ambush perimeter for our protection from rear attack or for Charlie when he entered our kill zone.

The next day, since my rating was gunner's mate, Mr. Q assigned me to clean out the ammo bunker and throw out all the MK-2 pineapple grenades. The MK-2 pineapple was outdated and had been replaced by the M-26. To dispose of them, Baylett and I were to dump all the MK-2s into the Bassac River. We loaded them onto our skimmer and drove out into the middle of the river. I was into dumping them like Mr. Q said, but Baylett wanted to pull the pins on them all, one at a time, and throw them. What the hell, I thought. We putted around the Bassac all morning throwing grenades into the river. I expected one to have a malfunction and blow instantaneously, blowing us away. By the time we had finished, all that was left in the ammo bunker were the M-26s and M-26A1s.

The explosive in the M–26 was 5.5 ounces of Composition B. The fragmentation part of the M-26 was made of a notched coil spring, and the total weight of the M-26 was sixteen ounces. The MK-2 pineapple weighed twenty-one ounces and had a cast-iron body molded with notches, and the explosive component was two ounces of flaked TNT. The M-26 had a smooth, thin sheet-steel shell which enclosed the notched coil spring. The MK-2 had a twenty-yard casualty radius, while the M-26 had a thirty-yard casualty radius. Both had a four- to five-second delay. You hoped. So that was the difference. Not only did the M-26 weigh less, but you could blow the shit out of things better. Composition B detonates faster than flaked TNT. Personally, I don't think Charlie knew the difference when it exploded. They either received large holes from the MK-2 grenade, or lots of smaller holes from the M-26. Grenades of all types were a very important and popular weapon used by SEALs on almost all operations.

As I was wasting American taxpayers' money throwing the grenades in the river, I got to thinking about all the sophisticated and expensive toys SEALs got to play with. The Stoner 63A cost the American taxpayers over $10,000 each. That's for just one Stoner weapons system. SEALs had an armory full of them. We used the M-18A1 claymore mine, the M-15 "Willy Peter" (white phosphorus) grenade, M-18 smoke grenades for marking positions or telling wind direction for incoming helos, the M-25A2 CS (tear gas) grenade, the ANM-14 grenade to melt weapons or metal, and the MK-3A2 concussion grenade that worked well underwater and in bunkers. The MK-3A2 only had a casualty radius of two meters, but when used inside a closed room, like a bunker, or underwater, it was much greater. We also used the MK-26 Model O HBX haversack, used for blowing bunkers, opening up blocked waterways, destroying rice, and for underwater work. The MK-26 was composed of eight 2.5-pound cast blocks of HBX. We also used the MK-2 Model O haversacks, M1A2 bangalore torpedoes (for cutting a path through concertina wire), MK-4 and MK-34 haversacks and the MK-8 hose, which, using several woven together, was fine for demolition of a large obstacle. The MK-8 looked like a section of fire hose and was excellent for underwater use. It could also be wrapped around any irregular-shaped obstacle or used to dig a ditch. Most all demolitions used by SEALs were hygroscopic, meaning they could be submerged underwater.

I wondered how much the medium cost, not counting the minigun. We also used weapons ranging from .22-caliber rimfires up to the .50-caliber machine guns. At times our platoon used the Model 39 Smith & Wesson 9mm semi-automatic pistol, with a silencer screwed onto its barrel, to knock off Vietcong guards or silence Vietcong guard dogs. When the Model 39 was fired with the silencer connected, not much more could be heard than the action working. We nicknamed this weapon the "hush puppy." But it was no more effective than the SEAL who fired it. More than once we only wounded a dog and sent him yelping down a dike towards its hootch. Sometimes the same would happen to a Vietcong. When that happened, our position was compromised and the mission was usually aborted, causing an early extraction. But the closer you could sneak up to the VC guard, the better were your chances of placing the bullet in a fatal area. Hitting a target over twenty-five meters away with the Model 39 would be considered good luck. Bullet placement was an important factor in silencing a dog or a Vietcong. The silencing of a guard dog or Vietcong guard quietly kept our presence unknown until it was too late for Charlie to react. By then we had departed the area with our prisoners or intelligence. The Model 39's silencer also fit some of the 9mm submachine guns.

We used a different type of silencer for the M-16s, one which was much longer than the 9mm's because of the higher muzzle velocity of the M-16's .223 cartridge. Silencers were only used on special missions where making our presence unknown was very important. The higher the Vietcong cadre, the more guards he seemed to have protecting him. Using silencers was one way of keeping our position unknown to the enemy. The silencer mainly silenced the muzzle blast, and the Vietcong guard wouldn't hear the crack of the bullet if your shot placement was accurate, turning out his lights.

CHAPTER EIGHT

Our next operation was to ambush a Vietcong tax collector and his guards. Our intel stated they traveled by sampan along a canal on Dung Island often enough for first squad to give this operation a shot.

There are several types of ambushes. A "planned ambush," or "point ambush," was conducted when good intel was available—that is, when we knew when and where to expect Charlie and the intel was fresh and reliable. A good harvest of VC was usually the result.

An "area ambush" was set up someplace you thought was used by VC quite often, but you were not sure when, why, or how many enemy could be expected.

The "opportunity ambush" was set up on fresh intel while an operation was under way, a "get them when you see them" situation. The ambush might not have been planned at the briefing, but we might take advantage of the situation or let the enemy pass by. It all depended on the importance and type of mission.

The "hasty ambush" almost gives itself away: seeing the enemy before he sees you and the entire squad or platoon quickly setting up a position to grease their little asses. Like a well-oiled piece of machinery, we all quickly and quietly moved into our positions. Standard operating procedure. This kind of ambush could be alerted by anyone in the squad or platoon, preferably by hand and arm signals. It was a great ambush to set up while being chased by the Vietcong in a running retreat. If we were far enough in front of the enemy, we could quickly set up and let him come running right into our kill zone.

The "long-term ambush." The "we know Charlie is coming but don't know when" game. For example, finding an enemy trail and waiting and hoping he would come along. Sometimes, an area ambush could turn into a long-term ambush.

The important factors in a well-conducted ambush are: a good plan and patrol order, using the element of surprise, good discipline on the part of all involved (no coughing, spitting, farting, etc.), and concentration and proper control of fire (hitting what you shoot at). Last but not least, make the whole plan as simple as possible. If you had good cover (protection from enemy fire) and concealment, a good field of fire, good visibility of the kill zone, your weapon was cocked and the safety off, and you didn't have to move, you were on a well-run ambush.

Signaling each other while on the actual ambush could be a problem unless all involved knew the platoon's standard signals. Usually, when it was very dark, a light string could be tied to each man. A small jerk on the string and your partner could be alerted to the enemy's presence (or just be kept awake). Sitting in an uncomfortable position without moving was a good way to stay awake and alert. One undisciplined man on an ambush could get everyone blown away.

An ambush included the assault element, killing group, search group, and destroy group (optional). You could have a cutoff team or blocking force to stop the enemy's retreat. If you had enough men, a security element protected flanks and rear from attack on the ambush position. There was also an element assigned to kill or capture enemy leaders, such as the tax collector. One man on the ambush could have several of these jobs, especially if we were operating with less than a squad. Months of training together as a platoon before deploying to Vietnam had made us familiar with the various ambush assignments and kept us in fine tune.

I saved the "counterambush" for last. It's the one you have nightmares about. When *you* are ambushed, you have about two seconds to be killed or wounded in the kill zone.

That's two seconds to react, to save your life and the lives of the members of your element. It all depends on the enemy's firepower and training. Fortunately, the Vietcong weren't trained as well as North Vietnamese regulars, and their weapons weren't as good or maintained as well. That was to our advantage.

Because of fire superiority and training, three or four SEALs could inflict heavy casualties when outnumbered by an enemy force. On most of our operations we used the medium to take us to and extract us from areas of operation. I preferred operating with the medium over the Light SEAL Support Craft because of the awesome firepower of the minigun on the medium. Miniguns were hard to get your hands on in Nam, they were thought of as luxury items. But when 6000 rounds per minute screamed at him, Charlie held his head down long enough for us to extract.

The light SEAL Support Craft was developed and made ready in 1968 strictly for SEAL team use. Specializing in counterguerrilla warfare and intelligence gathering, SEALs required a variety of well-designed craft to support their operations. The LSSC was developed by the Grafton Boat Company, of Grafton, Illinois. The boat was a twenty-five-foot welded aluminum hull with a nine-foot beam. Twin Ford 427 CID Cobra high-performance gasoline engines powered two twelve-inch Jacuzzi water-jet pumps which gave the boat a top speed of 55 to 60 mph, with two MST crew members and seven SEALs and their operating gear on board. The Jacuzzi jet pumps were also in service on the thirty-one-foot PBRs (patrol boat, river) and had already proved themselves in the muddy Mekong. The "light" was designed to have a low silhouette, multiple gun positions, a Raytheon 1900 series two-position seven-kilowatt radar with a maximum range of thirty-two miles. It also had a ceramic armor-plated crew cockpit and engine area, which gave it protection from .30-caliber armor-piercing and .50-caliber bullets.

The Department of the Navy initially rejected the Grafton LSSC design because it had no faith in high-performance gasoline engines and feared the dangers of gasoline fumes and tanks. But when field commanders in Nam became aware of the boat's performance and features, their only concern was how fast they could be delivered. A contract was immediately awarded to Grafton without competitive bidding or publicity. Sixteen hulls were manufactured right away, and the Navy dispatched SEALs to test and train on the factory prototype boat.

The first group of boats was airlifted from Scott Air Force Base directly to Vietnam. This craft was then designated the Light SEAL Support Craft (or light). The light staged from shore bases such as our camp, ships anchored in rivers, or barges. We operated the light on hit-and-run operations with a squad of SEALs under cover of darkness to and from patrol area, canal sweeps, geographic and hydrographic data collection, and, of course, on occasional water-skiing trips. MST (mobile support teams) operated and maintained the craft in support of a variety of SEAL missions. The light was an excellent boat for extracting SEALs and their prisoners from near-impossible extraction sites, usually under heavy enemy fire. Other features included a ceramic armor-plated hull, 12,000-pound displacement at max, aircraft foam-filled explosion-proof rubber fuel cells with a 210-gallon capacity, foam-filled hull which made the craft unsinkable, dual VHF-FM radios (PRC-77 and VRC-46), a custom "silent" exhaust muffler system, with engine exhaust directed through three special chambers then exhausted underwater, and a minimum water depth of nine inches while traveling on step with a full load. The engine covers were designed, while shut, to transit the minimum amount of noise. Painted black or dark green, this baby could turn around in its own length.

The light's standard weapons were three M-60 machine guns, one M2HB .50-caliber machine gun, and one MK-19 40mm automatic grenade launcher. Armament could be arranged to suit the personal desires of the MST crew. As optional equipment, the craft could be fitted with the minigun and a 60mm mortar. Contractual requirements required the boat to survive a drop from fifteen feet into the water loaded with maximum gross weight.

The light could be inserted by helicopter into remote areas not otherwise navigable, making it the first American boat to patrol many of the waterways in the Mekong Delta. This was conducted only on rare occasions, on "unusual operations."

Despite all that, I still preferred operating from the medium. It had more room than the light, and the medium had more cover down inside, where men could stretch out. And it could carry more men and equipment.

So, to ambush the VC tax collector we inserted on Dung Island's north shore. This time, taking advantage of the high tide, the medium nudged up to the bank and we stepped off the bow onto dry land instead of into the usual muddy canal. With the medium downriver and the jungle sounds returned to normal, we began our patrol at 0200 hours. Soon we came across endless punji pits and trip wires leading to various types of homemade Vietcong booby traps. Pointing out to each other all the obstacles Charlie had left for us, we maneuvered past all the crap. Patrolling farther into enemy-infested territory, we stopped about 200 meters south of our insertion point and positioned our squad in the shape of a C along a small canal the tax collector was known to use. We had reached the position long before Charlie was supposed to float into our kill zone, and with weapons off safe, we waited very still and quiet. The center of the squad was hidden in the vegetation alongside the canal while the men on either end covered the flanks and rear. Mr. Q was in the center.

Patrolling or sitting on an ambush with your weapon on safe could result in an unsafe situation. If an enemy ambush was initiated, you might not have time to change your weapon from safe to firing mode. That small detail could mean the difference between life and death. Patrolling with every other man's weapon trained in a different direction and at the ready was the standard operating procedure for our platoon.

After a couple of hours of sitting in the mud, not moving, I had to piss pretty bad. I had no control over having to piss, but could exercise enough self-discipline not to move and blow our position. Without moving a muscle, I soaked my jeans. The insects and small reptiles that crawled all over me didn't seem to mind. In fact, they seemed to be attracted by it.

While sitting on an ambush in a hostile environment in a foreign country, you just can't be moving around. But at the same time, it's hard not to look at some of the strange creatures crawling all over you.

I was positioned behind some mangrove roots in the mud and had a perfect field of fire into the canal in front of me. As the sun started coming up, the jungle came alive with the normal daytime sounds. The mud skippers crawling up my legs would stop and stare at me with their bulging eyes as if they wanted to alert Charlie to my position. The mosquitoes had to be on Charlies's side too. They were natural booby traps in themselves; taking advantage of our not being able to slap at them, they crawled into our nose and ears, leaving big welts everywhere. Small crabs crawled in and out holes in the mud and up our legs, not knowing what they were crawling on. It was a good thing I had the bottom of my jeans closed off with ordnance tape.

Hurry up and wait. After putting up with mother nature that way for so long, blowing away the tax collector would be a welcome change. Not knowing when he might show up, or if he even would, was frustrating. So we sat quietly, waiting for signs of noise or a visual contact.

After several hours when only a couple of snakes floated down the canal, Mr. Q signaled Grimes to patrol out to the extraction site. Moving north, we stayed along the bank of the same canal. As we approached the main river, two more booby traps were found. There were no straight lines in the jungle, and Grimes, knowing this, located the trip wires before he made contact with them. Broken vegetation was further evidence someone had been in the area. After our squad stepped over the two wires, we set up security for Mr. Q and Grimes. They removed two M-26 frag grenades and unscrewed the fuse from each. In its place, a 308-G ADD (antidisturbance device) was installed. After setting the two modified M-26 frags into position near each of Charlie's explosives, the ADDs were armed, giving us eighty to ninety seconds to get the hell away from them. As advertised, once armed, the slightest trembling—like a gook walking by—would trigger the ADDs, detonating our grenades and Charlie's. The ADD was one way of retaliating for all the shit Charlie left behind for us. Underwater, these devices were good to sixty feet and could be used for just about any application. As it had no trip wires, the entire unit could be buried out of sight. Inserted into a claymore, the ADD would have devastating results. But you never really knew what might trigger it: Vietcong, a pig, a crab, or even a Vietnamese child. So we never left them near villages or areas that weren't heavily occupied by Vietnamese. Nobody I knew ever wanted to try to disarm an ADD, or even get close to it after it was armed.

Stepping around several more punji pits along shore, we set up security for the medium to extract us. After extraction, on our way back to camp, we stopped to search a couple of large sampans just for the hell of it. Their owners' papers seemed to be in order, and after searching them, no contraband was found so we let them go on their way. Post-op SOPs were the same: debrief, clean weapons, and raid the chow hall.

CHAPTER NINE

It had been two weeks since our last paycheck, so up the Bassac River we went, on step in the medium. I felt that I had earned every penny of this paycheck. If not for the operating, then for having to deal with the flies, mosquitoes, sticky envelopes from the humidity, and all the warm beer

I had to drink. This was one trip upriver I was looking forward to.

We arrived in Binh Thuy just in time for evening chow. Having a full stomach and keeping my head down seemed to be keeping me alive. We visited the hospital, where we found that Doc was tired of lying around and wanted to start operating again, but his leg was still giving him problems. No way was he getting out of the hospital yet. Quan's injuries would keep him in the hospital a little longer also. It was hard to believe he was a civilian after some of the missions he went on with us. But then again, if he hadn't been working with us SEALs he would surely have ended up a South Vietnamese ARVN.

As we started to leave the hospital, LePage convinced us to do a little partying in Can Tho, so we hitchhiked from outside the gate of the Naval Support Facility. The highway to Can Tho was always crowded with American trucks, bicycles, South Vietnamese vehicles, and pedestrian traffic. Catching a ride was no problem at all.

After climbing in back of an Army six-by, we soon found ourselves in downtown Can Tho. We arrived at our favorite bar, the Dragon Club, and after maneuvering through the crowd of GIs and bar girls, got ourselves a drink. The afternoon slid by with one drink after another. The bar girls were being bar girls, and we SEALs were being obnoxious. As the sun went down, so did the whiskey and beer. Eventually LePage disappeared. Now, LePage had been around awhile and seemed to have his shit together. Our platoon, especially us new guys, looked up to LePage and respected him as our leading petty officer. He was like the papa of our platoon, and even the officers respected his advice. He had been shot in the ass twice and had his head creased by an AK-47 on a previous tour with SEALs. What he didn't know was, he was about to get wounded again. The rest of us waited for him to return downstairs in the bar.

It was getting close to curfew and we would soon have to be off the streets in town or back at the Naval Support Facility in Binh Thuy. A loud *crack!* We looked up. The ceiling had given way. Down came LePage, bare-ass naked. He hit the bar floor with a thud and broke one of his legs. It didn't do much good to the rest of his naked body either. Damn, it was funny. Everyone in the bar was hysterical, even LePage was laughing. We laid him up on the bar and kept him pacified with whiskey, while we waited for an ambulance.

After LePage was hauled away, the rest of us staggered back to Binh Thuy for the night. Then, two in the morning, Doc was sleeping at the hospital. Awakened when the wardroom lights were turned on, he rolled over to see what was going on. There came LePage, lying on his back on a gurney, his leg in a cast. Doc couldn't believe his eyes. After being put in the bed directly across from Doc, LePage lifted up on both elbows. Looking across at Doc, LePage said, "Don't you say a fuckin' word or I'll climb out of this rack and kick your ass." Well, our platoon was another man short, but now we had an extra Stoner.

We spent the night at the support facility after finding some empty racks. I don't know whose barracks we were in and didn't care. The racks were empty, and we were tired and would feel no pain until the next morning, when I felt like I had been through hell week in training all over again. As I sat on the edge of the rack, head in hands, I noticed something different about the place. Shit man, those guys had everything in their barracks. After waking up Reeves, Panella, and Weber, I pointed out all the luxurious items that we didn't have at our camp. "Look at these fuckin' mattresses we slept on last night," I said. "Look at those big fuckin' fans." While the rest of the barracks slept, we quietly carried out several mattresses and two large fans. Packing them down to the dock, we stowed them on the medium.

After regrouping at the SEAL Quonset hut, we took a head count to make sure everyone but LePage was there, then went back down to the Bassac. Inside the medium there was hardly enough room for our platoon, but nobody wanted to give up a mattress, and leaving the fans behind was out of the question. Looking around the dock, Baylett saw an olive-drab skimmer on the bank near the fiberglass-repair building. Just like the boat we used for water skiing at the camp. A large hole in the bow had just been repaired. One of us dragged it off the bank, floated it over behind the medium and secured it to the stern. Then we silently pushed the whole works out into the Bassac. Because it was early morning, avoiding attention from the naval support facility wasn't difficult.

After we drifted downstream until the support facility was far in the distance, the mattresses were passed back and stacked in the skimmer. Then we started the engines and turned the bow downstream. We opened a bottle of Seagram's V.O. and a can of Planter's peanuts as the medium cruised at half speed toward Dung Island with what was left of our paychecks, six mattresses, two fans, and the skimmer. It was 0930 hours, Sunday, 19 July 1970.

CHAPTER TEN

A day later I found myself up to the waist in mud and just about as far into enemy-controlled territory on Dung Island as we could get. Under cover of early morning darkness, first squad, minus Doc and LePage, patrolled up a canal, crawled over several dikes, and made it over Victor Charlie's booby traps undetected. We finally arrived at our objective, a small hootch located by a canal.

At first light Mr. Q gave the signal and everyone on the security element moved into position. Since Doc was in the hospital, Shannon was used as radio man on this op. Back to the door, he squatted down, covering his field of fire like almost always. I was positioned out a ways from the left-front corner of the hootch, while Panella was covering the far-right corner. Bruce was covering our rear. The hootch was completely surrounded. We covered our fields of fire while Mr. Q and Grimes busted in the door. I heard shots being fired inside the hootch, then a real scared Vietcong wearing black pajamas busted through the hootch's nipa-palm wall. He ran straight toward me while looking back over his shoulder at the hootch. I turned my Stoner in his direction just in time for the unarmed bastard to run straight into my flash suppresser. He doubled over the barrel of my Stoner and I didn't give him time to shit his pants—a quick kick to the nuts with my size-ten jungle boots sent him buckling to the muddy earth. He immediately rolled over into the "kneeling Buddha" position, hands pressed together, praying for his life. As he bobbed up and down, I rolled him over facedown in the mud with one knee embedded into his shoulder blades. I bent both his arms behind his back, pulled a plastic handcuff from my cammo top pocket, and bound his hands.

Grimes and Mr. Q had two other VC suspects under their control inside the hootch. While pulling Charlie's head by his hair and covering my field of fire at the same time, I took enough ordnance tape off the butt of my Stoner to gag a horse. The VC's last view of me was as I wrapped tape around his eyes and mouth, leaving only his nostrils exposed.

The other two were brought out and laid facedown with my prisoner, and a search began of the hootch and surrounding area. We didn't have time to do a field interrogation on the suspects as to how many Vietcong and weapons were in the area, we were finding out ourselves— enemy rounds started to saturate our perimeter. Shannon radioed the medium to inform the MST that we had made contact and to order it to stand by.

Under heavy enemy automatic-weapons fire, the six of us and the three prisoners slid into the canal beside the hootch. The canal flowed south back into the canal where the medium was waiting. The tide was out and the mud was deep. The canal was approximately twelve feet wide and four or five feet higher than our heads on both sides. The prisoners were immediately moved to the front of the squad as we patrolled rapidly toward our extraction site, with Charlie close on our ass. Luckily, the canal had not been booby-trapped. That made our quick getaway faster, but we could still only run so fast in the thick, deep mud. Within seconds the Vietcong moved into position on both banks to our rear and began to throw a volley of fire our way. The mud on either side of me splattered from the impact of rounds, throwing crap all over me. Bullets cracked by my head as I forced my way through the mud. Pissed off and scared, I turned and fired my Stoner from the waist, just about emptying the weapon of ammo. I concentrated my fire on both banks behind us to keep the little fuckers down long enough for the front of our element to get farther out the canal with the prisoners. I emptied my Stoner, then turned and ran through the deep mud as fast as I could go to catch up with the others. The mud had been churned up by the eight people in front of me, which made pulling my legs out for each next step seem impossible.

As I ran I extracted the empty plastic Stoner box and dropped it in the mud. I hated leaving anything behind for the VC to find, but did not have time to stow it as their rounds began to splash and crack around me again. I knew Charlie could use anything we left behind for his advantage. I pulled a fresh Stoner box out of my vest, opened the feed cover, and slammed the box home. Laying the end of the linked .223 ammo over the receiver, I slapped down the feed cover and cocked the Stoner, running all the time. Two hundred meters to go, I thought as I turned to face the enemy. Bruce was just ahead of me in the canal, shooting 40mm HE (high explosive) over my head toward the enemy. But the little yellow fuckers kept coming, lots of them. We each threw an M-26 frag grenade up on each bank behind us and turned and ran some more. Pieces of debris from the explosions rained down around us. Rounds cracked past me, hitting the mud with such force they left craters. The Vietcong came closer and closer. As I pulled my legs from the mud, they felt like lead, and I was sinking back down to my waist with each step.

I turned, fired, turned back, and ran some more. Charlie

kept coming, gaining on both banks. There was no time to set up a claymore. It wouldn't have done any good down in the muddy canal anyway. As I turned around again, I noticed movement in the nipa palm on the bank to my left. I hosed down that area and emptied a second box of 110 rounds as the squad moved even farther away from me. Again I turned to run, changing to my third box of ammo. This was it! I knew it. I wouldn't let them fuckers get me without taking as many of them with me as I could! I was getting tired and moving slower. With firmer terrain to run on, the Vietcong were gaining. Mr. Q, who was supposed to be in the patrol's second position, had dropped back to just ahead of me. He was huffin' and a-puffin', gasping for air, pulling himself through the mud, trying to catch up with the others.

Bruce had moved up with the others in an attempt to secure our extraction site. As I caught up with Mr. Q, we both turned and fired at each bank, keeping the little fuckers down a few seconds more. Our prisoners must have been pretty valuable to the Vietcong, who clearly wanted them back, and us too. Again we turned and ran. Mr. Q was slowing down; just he and I were at the rear of the patrol. Bruce was far out ahead, but his 40mm HE rounds were still buzzing overhead and exploding behind us.

I said, "Come on, Mr. Q, come on," as I turned and fired my weapon some more. By now the two .50-calibers on the boat were hosing down the jungle to our flanks and shooting overhead. We were getting close! I yelled, "Come on, Mr. Q, we can make it." I was rear security and wasn't going to let Mr. Q drop behind me. If he wasn't going to make it, neither was I. The front of our element had reached the medium and had set up a perimeter, covering our asses as we got closer. My ears were ringing from the explosions behind me. Fuck, I was gasping for air as I pulled myself farther out of the canal, watching enemy rounds hitting the mud beside us. I knew one of those rounds was going to be mine in a second.

My legs were numb from running through the mud; I couldn't go much farther, but Mr. Q was far worse. Bruce and one of the MST crew were still shooting HE over our heads, but the gooks were still coming. I emptied my weapon of ammo behind us, letting Mr. Q get ahead of me. I turned and ran again, changing to my fourth box of ammo. I could see the medium now, and its weapons were smoking. The prisoner handlers literally threw the three prisoners over the side and into the medium. All of the SEALs except Bruce had boarded the medium and were covering us with automatic fire, but because the minigun was mounted on the stern of the medium, it could not be brought to bear. Mr. Q caught up with Bruce, and I fired at the banks while they climbed over the bow with help from the SEALs already aboard. Still firing my weapon behind me, I moved to the front of the boat and hung one arm through the nylon net hanging off the bow.

The medium began to back out into the canal, dragging me with it. I threw my Stoner up on the bow and was pulled up by my teammates. Enemy rounds kicked up in the water around the medium. I flipped my body down into the hull of our boat, my Stoner in hand. Beside our prisoners, Mr. Q and I lay on the deck, gasping for air. The medium turned and opened up its throttles to get us the fuck out of there.

As the stern turned about, the minigun opened up. The most beautiful sound I had heard all day, music to my ringing ears. I couldn't miss its workout, no matter how exhausted I was. Still gasping for air, I jumped to my feet and stuck my Stoner over the gunwale. With the minigun blazing away beside me, I emptied my fourth box of Stoner ammo. As we sped off down the canal, the jungle disintegrated behind us from all the firing. All traces of enemy movement stopped. The 7.62mm god had spoken.

There hadn't been time to do a field interrogation because our position had been compromised. Since Quan was still in the hospital with Doc, the interrogation would have to be conducted back at camp by ourselves. After what I'd gone through on this op, I sure hoped the prisoners had a lot of intel. The sooner we could interrogate them, the better. During our retreat from the hootch, the prisoners wouldn't cooperate with the prisoner handlers and had to be dragged to the medium most of the way. That slowed us down and damn near cost us our lives. If we hadn't needed intel so badly, two of the prisoners would have been left behind, making our retreat much easier. We kept them uncomfortable till we got back to camp.

After we returned to camp, the prisoners were put into the prisoner holding boxes, all but one. We had to keep them separated. The oldest of the three was escorted, still handcuffed, gagged, and blindfolded, to our briefing hootch. Normally, the debriefing was the first and most important business conducted after returning to camp. Since a field interrogation had not been executed, this was first. Our debriefings were never formal. Although very important, they were conducted as a group, not on an individual basis.

After the first interrogation had been completed, all three one at a time, we had three different stories. So, keeping Charlie blindfolded, we continued the process, and would continue until some straight questions were answered. I left the briefing hootch and walked down to the dock. My face was still cammied and my clothes full of Mekong mud. I looked across the river to Dung Island. What was I really in Nam for? I thought. Who was I really fighting for and why? Something was missing: I couldn't put my mind on it. In the background I could hear the questions being put to one of the gooks again. The small waves from a breeze slapped up against the metal drums of the dock. The sun was just coming up and the sky was bright orange to the east. A beautiful morning in a hellhole.

CHAPTER ELEVEN

My mother wanted me to go to Canada. She didn't want me in Nam. She had been born in Belfast, Northern Ireland, and was raised in London during World War II; she had seen enough war for the both of us. I had sent home some 8mm movies I took of our camp and some of the prisoners in their holding boxes. She wrote back saying she felt sorry for the prisoners in the boxes. She was a good lady, not just because she was my mother, but because she had never hurt anything or anybody in her life. An Irish woman, she would tell you what was on her mind. I wrote a letter back to her chewing her out about feeling sorry for Charlie. What about the Americans the Vietcong or NVA had their hands on? Our prisoners had a different lifestyle than Charlie's prisoners. The rumors I had heard from friends were that the Vietcong cut up bodies of Americans and displayed what was left of them on the river banks. What about the two Americans we tried to liberate from the prisoner-of-war camp? They were never kept in one place for more than twenty-four hours. What kind of condition did she think they were in? Yes, Charlie had it all right while being in our hands. Hell, they got better food than mamasan fed them back on Dung Island, medical attention too. One thing for sure, the Vietcong would never take me alive.

I loved my mom. Sometimes I wished I had taken her advice about Canada. But my granddad and my dad had been in the Navy, and I felt I had to fulfill my military obligation to my country. I thought, Maybe if I join the Navy I could stay out of Vietnam. But at the same time I wanted to see what war was all about. I joined the Navy so the Army draft wouldn't get their hands on me. Loving the ocean and being a strong swimmer steered me toward Underwater Demolition Training.

SEAL units in Vietnam were small and very flexible. We didn't always go by the book as other, larger units did. This contributed to the low casualties and the high success rate of SEAL missions in Vietnam. SEALs were trained and cross-trained to be able to handle any position on the patrol: officer-in-charge, point, or rear security—corpsman included. If the front element of a patrol got into a "world of shit," word was passed back and rear security became point and led the patrol in the opposite direction. We could drive the support boats, fix them if they broke down, repair and fire all the weapons on the boats, minigun included. That flexibility saved our lives and the lives of many others.

SEALs are good at sports. There wasn't a Seabee or Vietnamese at our camp that could knock Grimes off his feet in boxing. Only a few would even attempt to step onto the helo pad with him. All the support from the Seabees' buddies cheering them on wouldn't help either. During our time off we played volleyball, in the mud, baseball, in the mud, football, in the mud, and even threw frisbees. Yes, in the mud.

Another fun thing we did during slack time was swim across the Long Phu River at low tide and make mud slides down the steep bank on the opposite side. A few South Vietnamese from our camp would swim over, wanting to join in on the fun, but it always ended up in a nasty, anything goes, mud fight with us instead.

Early in July Mr. Q began to call me "Chuy," which means "banana" in Vietnamese. If we had no contact and were extracting through a banana grove on the island, I would cut off a bundle of bananas with my K-bar and extract with them. More than once I had to drop the bananas as we ran for our lives, Charlie close behind. It reminded me of when I was a kid back home getting chased out of an apple orchard by an old man with rock salt in his 12-gauge. There was no lack of bananas hanging in our hootch.

Nearing the end of July, some of us still hadn't had a

haircut since we left the States. We sure didn't look military.
It didn't bother anyone but the officer-in-charge of the Seabees. One day he complained about our shaggy appearance
to Mr. Walsh, who replied, "If you want to start operating
with us on Dung Island, we'll get our haircuts. Besides, it
helps camouflage us in the jungle." I don't think the Seabee
officer took too kindly to Mr. Walsh's answer, but we never
heard any more about the matter. The smell of shaving
cream alone could give our position away to the enemy, so
we rarely shaved.

Two SEALs named Passyka and Berta showed up at our
camp one day. They were to replace Doc and LePage until
Doc got out of the hospital. Passyka was from a platoon
stationed at a camp named Sea Float on the Ca Mau Peninsula. They were welcome, and shared the whiskey, beer,
water skiing, and operating with our platoon.

I had moved out of the rafters into LePage's rack, and
the first night down there I noticed a big difference in the
heat. The temperature was more comfortable, but I still had
problems sleeping at night, and not only from the heat. I
seemed to dwell on the next morning's op until my guts
ached, causing me to spend much of my nights in the chow
hall. August also brought the beginning of the monsoon
season, and at times the rain made so much noise on the
metal roof of the hootch that we had to yell just to communicate. But taking advantage of the downpours, we would
grab soap and run outside, bare-ass naked, for a shower.
Showers were usually limited at our camp because of a
shortage of fresh water.

Doc had been released from the Third Field Hospital in
Binh Thuy and arrived by six-by at our camp. Passyka had
returned to Sea Float, but Berta stayed with us a little longer
to operate. Doc's primary objective was to hit the bar, and
that he did. He still had a light limp but was ready to return
to operating.

Early one morning, second squad brought back some
prisoners from Dung Island, so we took turns taking pictures
of each other holding our K-bars to their throats. The gooks

shivered with fright as we had our fun. But it was just part of making them uncomfortable before interrogation. They had given second squad a bad time while trying to extract. Sitter said, "If it had been up to me, I would have left them at the bottom of the Bassac with their comrades."

Weber and I played cards a lot between ops. But no matter what game we played, Weber usually won. He was a farm boy from Nebraska who had never seen an ocean before he started UDT/SEAL training. I remember him standing on the Silver Strand looking out over the Pacific Ocean, staring out into the blue water. "Golly, look at all that water," he would say. Weber was a quiet guy and it took a lot to piss him off, but once he said "Dad-gum it," he was angry and you had better get out of his way. Even though he'd never seen an ocean before he joined the Navy, Weber became a fine SEAL operator, earning the nickname "Gedunk," Navy slang for junk food. Seems nobody ever saw him without a piece of candy or something else in his hand to munch on.

The Seabees had poured a new concrete slab and built a shower stall around it. The water supply came from an old tanker trailer parked behind the shower and was pumped to the shower heads by a gasoline engine. Showers were few and far between, but due to our gross condition after operations, we cranked up the engine whenever we needed it and walked into the shower clothes and all, washing off the Mekong mud.

Even after our clothes had been washed by us or by the Vietnamese women who worked at our camp, they still had that moldy, mildew smell to them. Our jungle boots were washed out in the shower or the Bassac, and when dried, were stiff as a board. I had two pairs and would let weird things grow in one pair while I wore the others, and vice versa. I went barefoot as much as possible and my feet were pretty tough.

The lack of fresh intelligence found us sitting in the briefing room. Under cover of darkness after South Vietnamese curfew, we were going to take the medium through the west end of Ti Ti Canal all the way through to the South China Sea. I didn't mind operating on the medium this way; except for our cammoed faces, staying in the boat kept us dry and clean. I hated putting that stuff on my face, but without it we might just as well have stayed at camp.

The Seabees thought camouflage paint was really neat, and while gearing up for an op we sometimes had quite an audience. Seabees would stand around and watch us gearing up, giving them something to write home about. Joking with each other while getting ready would boost our morale and get our minds off the mission. When we test-fired our weapons before going on an op, I sometimes let Seabees shoot my Stoner.

At 1100 hours four SEALs and two MST crew members boarded the medium and headed up the Bassac. Soon we were entering the west end of Ti Ti Canal. The boat slowed to just above idle. The tide was high and the night was warm and clear as the triple-canopy jungle closed in on us. The farther down Ti Ti Canal we went, the narrower the canal got. It was one excellent spot for Charlie to set up an ambush.

The jungle grew into the canal there, and rubbed up against both sides of the medium as we continued toward the South China Sea. Mr. Walsh climbed out onto the bow and studied the canal ahead and the banks on either side with a starlight scope. You wouldn't catch *me* out there on the bow standing straight up looking through the scope. Not in Ti Ti Canal. But Mr. Walsh loved to operate. The jungle closed in even more, and soon Mr. Walsh had to move limbs and vines out of his field of view. While he stood on the bow, I crouched down in the hull expecting a B-40 rocket or an ambush to initiate any second. As we slowly moved through the tightest spot of the canal, I could hear the muffled big-block Chevy engines laboring under their soundproof covers and our wake lapping on each bank. Mr. Walsh turned around, crouched down on the bow and said in a low voice, "I smell pot." He returned to his standing position and looked around some more with the starlight scope. He soon turned and crouched down again, this time

saying, "Do you think the Vietcong are smokin' pot?"
The medium moved slowly through the narrowest part of
the canal, and then it began to widen out again. I sighed
with relief as the canal grew larger, but at the same time
we were deep into enemy territory without support from
friendly forces. Our boat was okay in that part of the canal
as long as the tide was high. With the narrow channel behind
us and the sandbar down by the sea in front of us, we could
be stranded at low tide if we ran into trouble.

We were damn near due north of our camp at that point,
but back into Dung Island quite a ways. That place had
always been a hot spot, even for the platoon we had relieved.
One of the members of that platoon had earned the Navy
Cross for gallantry there. Whenever we inserted into that
area we almost always made contact with Charlie and ended
up in a fierce firefight which caused us to extract.

Mr. Walsh climbed back into the hull with the rest of us.
Looking up, I saw the silhouette of the triple-canopy jungle
against the clear night sky. The jungle on either side of us
was pitch-black, showing absolutely no detail whatsoever.
As I mentioned earlier, depending on the enemy's firepower,
we had about two seconds to react to an enemy ambush,
but we might also receive "far, ineffective fire," like the
shots the Vietcong used to warn their comrades of danger.
It might be aimed at us or in the air over the zipperheads
being warned. Anyway, if they even hit the boat, we would
be surprised.

It might be "far, effective fire," from a long ways away.
Charlie might hit the boat or, worse yet, wound or kill
someone. It could be "near, ineffective fire," meaning
Charlie was close to us but was a poor shot. No accurate
shooting. Last and worst, "near, effective fire," in the kill
zone of an ambush—Charlie shooting accurate. Anyway, I
always hit the deck when I heard any shooting.

The Vietcong didn't have the gear to clean their weapons
that we did, so they had a lot of malfunctions, and that
usually cost them their lives. In case of a near, effective
fire ambush, the SOP is to start an immediate assault on the
enemy. This is why we kept our weapons off safe while

patrolling. If we took near effective fire while in the boats, we would automatically open up with all our fire power in the direction of the ambush, trying to suppress the enemy's fire by putting out more rounds than we were receiving.

While patrolling, SEALs used the clock system, the leap-frog method, and fire and movement. Using the clock system, upon command from our patrol leader, we would move in the direction of his command. Five o'clock, eight o'clock, or whatever, moving from the direction we were already patrolling, which would be twelve o'clock. The leap-frog method had part of the platoon or squad moving up or back while the others covered it, and vice versa. Fire and movement was firing weapons while taking cover or getting the hell out of there.

SEALs went on patrols so heavily armed that it was usually not difficult to suppress the enemy's fire. The situation depended on the training and the weapons of the enemy. NVA soldiers were well-trained and well-armed compared to the average Vietcong. We could usually tell the difference between them in a firefight. The Vietcong was a part-time fighter, part-time family man. Usually, the rank and file VC were made to fight by high-ranking Vietcong, who made a full-time job out of being a VC.

Among the VC, the hamlet chief was usually in charge of his small area, being under the district chief. Mr. Hamlet was in charge of the local Vietcong guerrillas. His staff was broken down into a hamlet secretary, deputy secretary, and various staff sections, all of whom were Vietcong, the Vietcong we tried to capture for their intel. The Vietcong under the hamlet chief would farm his rice by day and try to blow your ass away at night. It might not be what he wanted to do, but what would you do if your mother was held at gunpoint, part of the harassment the Vietcong pulled on the South Vietnamese in the rural areas. Sometimes we pulled operations to bring in specific Vietnamese civilians in VC-controlled territory and interrogate them about enemy supplies and movement.

The sex or age didn't matter much, but kids seemed to open their mouths a little more. Dung Island was a sort of

R&R (rest and relaxation) locale for Vietcong and NVA moving south. They could stop for a while, rest, and eat while having tight security and plenty of warning of danger. VC security was one reason we operated at night, taking advantage of the dark and bad weather like rain and wind— being someplace where we weren't expected under adverse conditions. Sneaking in during a wind or rainstorm would hide any noise we made, catching Charlie off guard.

Conduct on patrol was a mix of discipline, flexibility, adjusting (to the conditions present at the time), and acting (knowing immediately what to do in case something came up)—and doing it. That's where SEAL SOPs (Standard operating procedures) came in. By radioing back to camp at certain intervals, giving our coordinates and letting our standby element know we were okay, or in a "world of shit"—that is, a situation we couldn't handle ourselves— our teammates could be coming to our assistance in minutes. That is where having two operating boats come in handy.

Well, cruising down Ti Ti Canal at just above idle was asking for it. Sure enough, we started receiving incoming rounds from the starboard shore. Lucky for us it was near, ineffective fire. Enemy rounds cracked overhead and in the water around us. I hit the deck immediately as the rounds cracked through the medium, then lifted my Stoner over the gunwale as we returned fire. Like hail from a lightning storm, empty .308 shells bounced off the deck and engine cover from the minigun. M-79 40mm HE exploded in the nipa palm on shore. Our fire superiority suppressed the enemy's fire within seconds. We estimated four or five VC had been trying to set up on us. They fired a few rounds our way, and we returned at least 1500 rounds into their position, not counting the 40mm HE rounds. We had to be careful not to slip on the empty brass on the deck.

We hung around the area, giving Charlie a second chance, while everyone reloaded and made the weapons ready. I don't think we were wasting ammo, because the harassment kept Charlie uncomfortable and all our firepower had to have a psychological effect on him. Besides, I hated the warning shots the little fuckers fired off.

After a few minutes we proceeded on down the canal on step. The tide was going out and we wanted to make sure we cleared the sandbar at the east end of the canal. Maybe we would run into a sampan trying to cross the canal on our way out. Soon, not too far from the last place we took fire, we heard a shot, so the minigun and a couple of 40mm HE rounds were fired in response, but the medium kept going. If for nothing else, just to let Charlie know we could shoot too. Going to shore to chase the zipperheads could only have gotten us into trouble: a larger force of VC could have been waiting for us. On the other hand, we knew where to expect the warning shots in the future, and that meant some higher-up dink in the area was being warned.

Canal sweeps were common, conducted to keep the Vietcong uncomfortable. We finally reached the end of Ti Ti Canal, and just in time. The medium scraped bottom a couple of times as we entered the Bassac. We turned west and headed back to camp. We were still dry and without mud on our jungle boots.

CHAPTER TWELVE

We didn't clean our weapons till the next morning. The MST crew cleaned their weapons on the boat while we cleaned ours up by our hootch. The smell of WD-40 permeated the air around camp. Pieces of weapons covered the top of the four-by-eight piece of plywood used for a table.

I was glad I had been raised in the country; I never did like the big cities, and felt at home in the woods, the farther out the better. I could relate to a lot of what I was doing in the Navy. The training my dad had given me on rifles and handguns since I was a young boy fit right in with my job in Nam. Hunting Vietcong was a lot like hunting deer and elk, only they didn't shoot back or set booby traps.

Get up early, sneak in, shoot the game, extract with meat (intel), and have a beer, etc. Obviously, training from my dad was helping me stay alive in Vietnam. My dad's plan for a hunting trip was similar to some of our operations briefings, only not as complicated. He would point out on the map where the deer and elk might be, insertion points, how fast or slow to walk, concealment in the brush, trees, shadows, and where and when to extract. Even before I could handle a weapon, I followed him through the woods quietly while he hunted.

My dad was drafted out of the Navy and into the Army Air Force during WWII. Because he was color-blind, he could pick out ground targets from the air better than the average man. He ended up on a three-man crew on board an A-20 Havoc, a twin-engine, fixed-wing, low-altitude strafing bomber. His plane was shot down over France four days after D-Day. For several days the three men of the crew evaded capture by the Germans. The engineer gunner was killed by the Germans a few days before they were liberated. My dad woke up one morning while hiding in the hedgerows to find the engineer gunner nowhere around. He then woke up the pilot, who was hiding close by, and informed him of their missing comrade. The pilot decided he and my dad should stay put under cover and wait. Since they had been cold at night, the pilot thought the engineer gunner had tried to sneak back to their plane wreckage to recover a parachute to keep them warm. Machine-gun fire was heard in the direction of the downed plane a short time later. He had been shot in the back seven times by machine-gun fire. My dad's stories about evading the enemy stuck in my mind, and I thought about them a lot on ambushes and other ops. I knew one thing, I wasn't going to let those fuckin' gooks get me, at least not alive.

I finished cleaning and reassembling my Stoner and grabbed an M-79 grenade launcher to clean next. The M-79 weighed 6.16 pounds empty and was capable of firing several different types of cartridge. It had a smooth aluminum bore of 40mm, and a steel receiver. It fired an antipersonnel high-explosive fragmentation round that would arm itself in fifteen meters by set back and centrifugal force. Composition B with an RDX booster was the explosive used in the HE round, but the M-79 could also use canisters of buckshot with 1/4-inch ball bearings. Also, white, green, and red paraflares, and CS and CN tear-gas cartridges, were available. The barrel was fifteen inches long and the muzzle velocity was 250 feet per second. The front sight was fixed, and the rear sight was folded down for targets a hundred yards away or less and was marked with twenty-five-yard increments. Maximum range was 450 meters, but 300 meters was the maximum effective range. The XM-148 and the XM-203 grenade launchers attached to the barrel of an M-16. Also, it attached to the Stoner, giving you the world's most advanced weapons technology. Both grenade launchers squeezed out ten more feet per second than the M-79 and had a maximum effective range of 400 meters. We preferred the XM-148 because it was more dependable. While some SEALs carried the M-79, most liked the XM-148/M-16 combo because of the extra firepower. Attach one of these units to the Stoner, and ''Whoa, watch out Charlie!'' Only the Stoner 63-A weapons system fills all small-arms requirements.

Mr. Q walked into our hootch one morning and advised us we wouldn't be operating for a few days. Having some time off, I decided to visit some friends at Sea Float, a group of barges 360 feet long by ninety feet wide, anchored in the middle of the Cua Lon River, on the Ca Mau Peninsula. I caught a ride from our camp to Binh Thuy with some Seabees in their six-by. From there, after waiting several hours, I rode an Army slick on down to Sea Float.

On board the helo, besides the pilot and copilot, were three high-ranking officers. A door gunner and I were the only enlisted men. I sat next to a Navy captain. I was wearing Levi's jeans, a standard moldy cammo top, and coral booties, which were normally used by Underwater Demolition Teams while performing hydrographic beach recons in coral-infested waters. Made of hard rubber bottoms with a gray canvas top and laced up like a tennis shoe, coral booties were issued to every member of the UDT and SEAL teams. They could be used with or without swim fins. My hair and grubby beard didn't seem to bother the captain; he was more interested in my Stoner, not ever having seen one. While he stared, I looked down out the port helo door and watched miles of defoliated jungle.

As our helo circled Sea Float, I saw Seabees cutting back the jungle on both shores so Charlie couldn't sneak up on their camp. Members of SEAL Team One, Underwater Demolition Team 13, swift boats, Seawolf helicopters, a Psychological Warfare group, Seabees, and some South Vietnamese Montagnard troops were all stationed at Sea Float. The Seabees were building plywood hootches on the west bank and had just completed a new helo pad there also.

Up until a few days earlier everyone ate, slept, lived, and operated off the barge. I met Blocker, another member of Training Class 53, and Passyka there. Blocker had gone through UDT/SEAL training with my class and had been assigned to UDT Team 13. He told me how you could sneak through a hole in the perimeter fence and go to a nearby village. Just being in the village, which was off-limits, was like an operation in itself.

For me, sleeping on the barge at night was next to impossible. At different intervals twenty-four hours a day, concussion grenades were thrown into the Cua Lon River around the perimeter of the barge to protect the barge from enemy sappers swimming downstream. As the grenades detonated, the entire barge vibrated and the explosion echoed through the hollow steel barges. During the day, between concussion grenades, we would swim to shore or back out to the barge. We made damn sure the sentries on duty knew we were going into the water first.

The jungle surrounding Sea Float had been sprayed heavily with Agent Orange. Elmo Zumwalt III was stationed there with the Swift Boats, and his father, Admiral Elmo Zumwalt Jr., was a strong advocate of the use of Agent

Orange to reduce casualties among American troops by killing everything that grew around the base camps, rivers, and
canals in certain areas. By depriving Charlie of cover and
concealment, it was harder for him to set up ambushes.

During my stay at Sea Float we took a skimmer upstream,
where the Vietcong had put signs in different areas saying,
YOU DIE. Sometimes the VC also put the name SEALs on
these signs. That had a psychological effect on some SEALs
but just angered others. The area around Sea Float was
mostly under enemy control. As we traveled up the river,
I couldn't believe how much Agent Orange had been sprayed
around there. Miles of defoliated jungle, nothing but snags
and mud, looking much like a forest fire had gone through
the area. Zumwalt's son didn't even have to be in the area,
but since he was, his dad, in an attempt to help protect his
son, sprayed the stuff everywhere.

In one of the hootches on shore at Sea Float a ham-radio
operator managed to contact a town close to my hometown
back in the States. A collect phone call from that point was
transferred to my parents. For the first time since I left the
States, I talked to my parents. Because we were talking on
the radio and two people couldn't talk at once, each party
had to say "over" at the end of his transmission. I assured
my mom I was okay, had plenty to eat, and was keeping
my head down. She said, "That sounds like you. Over."

After a week at Sea Float it was time to return to camp
on the Bassac. Saying good-bye to my friends, I climbed
on board a chopper bound for Binh Thuy and started my
journey back. I hadn't paid too much attention to the defoliated areas on the flight down to Sea Float, but I studied
them carefully on the way back. Forest fires didn't burn in
wide, long strips. Looking at the skeleton jungle below made
me wish that Dung Island looked like that. Especially the
Ti Ti Canal area. I didn't then know the health hazards of
Agent Orange, so its use didn't bother me. Any time Charlie
had no concealment was all right with me.

After a while we landed in Binh Thuy. Since it was
already getting dark, I spent the night in the SEAL Quonset
hut. Man, was it cold. The SEAL hut had an air conditioner

that kept the place cool. By then I was used to the temperatures prevailing in Vietnam, and I damn near froze my nuts off that night. Visiting the hut every two weeks wasn't bad, but the night there was too cold for me. The cool air felt good as I fell asleep, but when I woke up I was freezing. That was the first and last time I ever slept on a cot there.

The next morning I grabbed all the mail I could find for our platoon, found a chopper going my way, and was Long Phu bound. After a brief stop to let off an Army lieutenant and a couple of gooks at a Vietnamese outpost, the slick continued on in the direction of my camp. With only the noise of the chopper and the view of the top of the green jungle canopy below, I was hypnotized in my own thoughts. Flashing back to my first morning in Nam, I thought about the five SEALs who had crashed and burned from a thousand feet. I wondered how many Vietcong or NVA were down below looking up at me. That scared me. My mother always used to say, "It all comes back." I wondered what wrong I had done in my life, and hoped it wouldn't "come back" on me while I was in Nam.

The change in pitch of the rotor blades ripped me away from my thoughts as the chopper banked into a starboard turn circling camp. Believe it or not, the dirty rat-infested camp looked great to me. I had some good friends down there, and even being away only one week, I missed them. As I looked down at the Bassac, I saw Baylett, Bruce, and Panella water skiing. The Seabees looked like ants from up above, running around the camp, building the place up so the zipperheads could take over one day. One of the SEALs threw out a yellow smoke so the chopper pilot could judge the wind direction. As we descended past the tower, I made eye contact with Weber, who was standing on top. He gave a big wave and smile and I returned with the same.

I was already standing on the starboard skid as the helo touched down, and ducking my head—mailbag in one hand, Stoner in the other—I ran from the helo over to the bottom of the tower. Weber climbed down, and grabbing the mail bag in one hand, shook my hand with his other. We headed over to our hootch as the chopper left. Weber passed out the mail to everyone present and they all went off to their private places to read the news from home. I left the hootch after hanging my Stoner and vest by my rack and walked down to the water's edge behind the chow hall, where Baylett was just pulling the skimmer up on the muddy bank. The tide was out, and Baylett, Panella, and Bruce had to wade through knee-deep mud to get up to the camp. The light and medium were stranded high on the mud bank next to our dock. I told them about my experiences at Sea Float and about all the Agent Orange sprayed down their way.

After the skimmer had been secured to shore by a long rope, we went directly to the bar, where Doc, Sitter, and Mr. Q were shooting craps. As I pulled up a chair beside them, Mr. Q said, "Hi, Young, how was your trip?"

"It's good to be back."

Mr. Q smiled. "We have an operation tonight. We're low on bananas." Everyone in the bar laughed. I was invited to join the game, but not knowing how to shoot craps, I declined. I was never really good at gambling and couldn't even win at penny ante poker. I grabbed a cold beer and walked out of the bar. As I looked over at the cage we kept our pet snake in, I saw Mr. Walsh and Grimes. As I approached the cage, Melfa, our medium coxswain, met me there. Grimes opened the cage door and crawled in with our eight-foot, three-inch python. Grimes seemed to communicate with the thing better than with some humans. He let the snake wrap itself around his body while holding its head in one hand. No thanks, not me. Snakes didn't bother me as much as spiders, but that didn't mean I had to play with them. I didn't mind trapping live rats and throwing them into the cage for snake food, but Grimes could play with the damn thing all he wanted.

After Bruce had washed the mud off his legs, he asked me if I wanted to walk to the village of Long Phu, two and a half miles away up the Rach Tra Bu canal (we called the canal the Long Phu River). A small rough road, more like a large path, started at the gate at the southeast corner of our camp. The small village outside the gate was just several nipa-palm hootches on either side of the path. The village was only 200 meters long. Then a small wooden bridge that the Seabees had constructed crossed over a canal. From there the road turned to the left at a small Buddhist temple. It continued south for about two miles through rice paddies on both sides and dikes leading out at ninety-degree angles from the road which connected with smaller dikes farther out. As it was often mined by the VC, the road was checked by ARVNs each morning. Just a large dike itself, the road was barely wide enough for the Seabees' six-by.

After Long Phu the road improved the farther you went toward Soc Trang. Bruce and I no sooner got out the gate when all these kids gathered around us from out of nowhere. "Give me candy, GI. Give me food," they said. Same old shit, not like the big cities, though. After all, the first American to walk through the village had probably passed out candy and started a situation that snowballed. I really couldn't blame the Vietnamese kids.

The farther we walked into the village, the more kids followed us. Even some of the older people came along. I felt like a celebrity even though they didn't ask for my autograph, just the basics. As we reached the far end of the village I swear every kid in town had congregated around us. I reached into my pocket, pulled out a piece of Dentyne gum, and threw it as far back as I could. The kids ran after it, giving Bruce and me a chance to run down the road to evade them. But after the hasty dog pile for the gum was over, they came again. And I was almost out of gum. The farther away from the village we walked, the fewer kids followed us. First the littlest ones turned around, then some of the older kids started returning to the village.

Down to just a few kids now, we continued on toward Long Phu. Not wanting to walk the distance to Long Phu unarmed, Bruce had packed his Model 39 Smith & Wesson 9mm auto loader while I carried my Smith & Wesson Model 15 .38-caliber revolver. We had extra cartridges in our pockets, but hoped we wouldn't need them.

As we walked I would turn to the little pests and say, "Di di mau," pointing in the direction of their village. All but one obnoxious little guy got the hint and started back the other way. About halfway to Long Phu Bruce and I decided to walk out into the rice paddies on one of the dikes, hoping the little gook would leave us alone. But as we walked out onto the dike, the little fucker just stood in the road and watched us.

Everywhere I looked there was rice, dikes, and water. A few jungle treelines could be seen off in the distance to the south and back across the Long Phu River to the northeast. About a hundred meters out on the dike we stopped and sat down to smoke a joint. Blue skies with an occasional cumulus cloud and flat rice paddies made me feel small.

After a few hits off the doobie, the little gook back on the road starting yelling "VC, VC," as he pointed all around us. I looked at Bruce and he looked back at me, still hitting off the joint. We scanned the surrounding area and saw nothing. Looking back at the gook, Bruce yelled, *"Di di mau,"* but the kid just stood there. As the doobie got small enough to burn our fingers, I suggested we continue on our way. The kid was making me paranoid, the more he stood there yelling "VC." I thought of our chances of holding off with our handguns three or four Vietcong carrying AK-47s. Hide behind the dike, I thought. Run for camp. Throwing the roach into the rice, we walked toward the road. Maybe the kid was trying to tell us something. Maybe being stoned got me thinking too much.

After reaching the road we continued on toward Long Phu, but the kid walked behind us saying "VC, VC," as he continued pointing out into the rice paddies. Down the road we walked, looking at each other, then all around us. I turned and told the kid to go away several times, but he still continued to harass us. Finally, right in the middle of one of his "VCs," I turned and yelled *"Di di mau!"* as loud as I could. The kid froze in his tracks and stared at me, then ran away. I felt bad for a moment, but I was glad he was gone.

Still checking the surrounding area, we reached the end of the two-mile straightaway. The road turned right there and tall palm trees and nipa palm lined both sides. The Long Phu River was to our left, and Long Phu was just ahead. I felt more secure the closer to Long Phu we got. Long rows of banana plants with a triple-canopy jungle in the background were to the right as the village appeared before us. Going to and coming from Long Phu's marketplace, sampans of all sizes weaved in and out on the river. Long Phu village was much larger than the village outside our camp, and was the largest village in Long Phu district. It had a couple of concrete stores, a large marketplace that sold rice, fish, bananas, and fruit, the usual nipa-palm hootches, and some fancier ones made of cement.

Every small village in the country seemed to have its Buddhist temples also. There were no bar girls or the likes of that in this village; it was a true South Vietnamese village, not Americanized in any way. Situated in the middle of nowhere, if some of the villagers were Vietcong, you would never know it.

Upon entering the center of town, we decided to check out a small store. Once inside, we each bought a warm beer and looked around at the merchandise—everything from beer to fish nets. The owner or manager, I don't know which, seemed happy to see Americans in his store. A couple of older men with goatees stood in the entrance of the store watching us as betel nut dripped from their toothless mouths. Then, sitting on a shelf, a wire-cage trap about eight-by-eight-by-twelve inches caught my eye. Rat trap, I thought. Bruce laughed as I paid for it and two more warm beers.

We continued to look around, drinking warm beer as our audience still hung around the entrances smiling. It must have been the sale of the day or something; we couldn't have been the first white men they had ever seen; it was 1970. What was so interesting about us, I didn't know. A few kids were congregating at the door, but the owner wouldn't let them enter. He was giving Bruce and me the run of the store. I have to admit, it was hard to call this guy a gook because he was so friendly.

Putting down the empty beer bottles and picking up my cage, Bruce and I started toward the door; then I heard the owner mumble something. I turned around once more, looking at him. He was pointing to the ceiling and then to my trap. I looked up and there it was, just what I always wanted, a foot-long lizard. Damnedest thing I ever saw. Much prettier than Grimes's snake. Large feet with long toes and a long green tail, I had to have it. The gook—I mean very friendly Vietnamese—grabbed a long pole and began to herd it toward the nearest wall. The locals standing at the entrance came in and began to help the owner, all of them commenting in Vietnamese. Probably the most exciting thing they had done all day. As the lizard climbed down, its big toes clinging to the wall, one of the Vietnamese men grabbed "the thing." I put it in the cage and offered to pay for it, but the man didn't want any money. He shook my hand instead. I felt I had just made a friend. Saying our good-byes, Bruce and I left the store and wandered back through the village to start our two and a half mile walk back to camp. We didn't stop for anything on the way. All I wanted to do was get back to camp, so I was checking out the area while I also checked the road for mines. There were places in the road where it was obvious some had been dug up before. But we got to camp without any problems.

I walked into the hootch carrying the lizard in the cage. Melfa, who had been drinking, took one look at the lizard and fell in love with it too. Slurring his words, he named the lizard Reptilicus. The guys in the hootch stood around us as I opened the trap door and let Reptilicus free. He ran up the wall and into the rafters, where he stayed. I then went to the chow hall to get some scraps for my new trap. Setting the trap, I put it inside one of the sandbag bunkers around the perimeter, hoping to catch a rat for Grimes's pet snake. I shouldn't have worried: as the days went by, I averaged six rats a night—our snake was never without food.

CHAPTER THIRTEEN

At 2200 hours the door of the briefing hootch was secured with the members of first squad inside. The briefing began with Mr. Q telling us about our early morning mission. "Our objective is located on Dung Island," he said. "Intelligence from the CIA in Soc Trang states there are three hootches located along this small canal"—pointing to the hootches on the picto map—"one of which contain a large Vietcong rice cache. Charlie has been taking rice from the farmers on the island and storing it in one of these hootches to feed the VC and NVA soldiers in the area. Our job is to destroy the rice with explosive.

"The patrolling order will be as follows: Grimes will be point, myself, Doc with the radio, Panella, Bruce, and Young as rear security. All involved will carry their standard weapons and ammo. Panella and Bruce will each carry a MK-133 Model 2 demolition haversacks, and they will be responsible for setting them up prior to departure of the mission. You two guys can get together on that after the briefing. Use the M-2 fuse as the igniter."

One of these setups would have been enough to do the job, but we always took along two of the more critical items to ensure the success of the mission. "When we reach our objective, Grimes and I will place the charges on the rice cache and I will pull the fuse," Mr. Q said. After the call signs, time of departure, air support, insertion area, and extract sites were discussed, Mr. Q asked if there were any questions. No questions were asked; everyone knew his job, so we all left the briefing hootch to get our shit together.

I got the key to the ammo bunker and passed out the

ammo and explosives we needed for the mission. The MK-133 Model 2 demolition charge assembly consisted of an MK-2 Model Ø haversack with an explosive component of an MK-26 Model Ø, which was an explosive charge of eight 2.5-pound cast HBX blocks, two-by-two-by-eleven inches long wrapped in olive-drab cardboard. The explosive HBX is cast onto twenty-five feet of detonation cord with thirteen inches of detcord between each block. A 50/50 phenolite booster is cast in the center of each block on the detcord every twenty-four inches to ensure detonation.

The MK-133 Model 2 demolition haversack is a general purpose demolition and could be used on underwater operations in which the charge assembly had to be submerged. The eight blocks could be cut apart and used separately if needed. HBX has a rate of detonation of 24,300 feet per second, and the haversack has a flotation pouch so it can be floated to its objective if required. The total weight was twenty pounds. Five feet of detcord on each end of the sack could be pulled out to secure it to other haversacks, or one end could be pulled out, securing it to a blasting cap. The blasting caps were a nonelectric spherical type with a priming charge of fulminate mercury and a base charge of 13.5 grains of PETN, making it the equivalent of a civilian Number 8 nonelectric blasting cap. This cap was connected to enough time fuse to burn one minute. The time fuse was connected to the MK-2 ignition fuse, which was also waterproof. After pulling the cotter in from the MK-2 fuse, we had approximately one minute to evacuate the area. Sometimes, when large amounts of explosives were carried by Underwater Demolition personnel, lots of South Vietnamese ARVNs would accompany them as a security element.

On this operation just us six SEALs would do the job. After checking over my gear, I returned to the briefing hootch to study the picto map of Dung Island. I always wanted to know exactly where our objective was in relation to the camp, in case I had to make it back on my own. By studying the maps available to us, by aerial reconnaissance, and by crawling in Dung Island's mud itself, I was getting to know the island and its canals pretty well.

Dung Island was actually several islands separated only by natural and man-made canals. Each island had its own name, with Dung Island being the largest. Cu Lao Tron and Cu Lao Con Coc were next in size, with Nai and Cha islands joining together to make one at low tide. The islands were all together in the middle of the Bassac River at its mouth, where it entered the South China Sea. No roads existed on them, only trails and large and small canals. South Vietnamese traveled the waterways by day, Vietcong and NVA by night.

We test-fired our weapons after evening chow and were ready for our early morning operation. Not wanting to smoke a joint, I tossed and turned all night thinking about the mission. Maybe I should have smoked—it would have relaxed me—but I just couldn't do it, before or during an operation. Just thinking about where the rice was on Dung Island scared the shit out of me. We always made contact with Charlie in that area.

After I was cammoed up and on the island, actually doing my job, the danger never bothered me—I almost enjoyed it at times. But thinking about the operations I was to participate in really got to me sometimes. Sometimes I wished someone would drop one big bomb on that fuckin' island.

Just after 0200 the next morning the medium entered the east end of Ti Ti Canal, the longest, widest canal, and one of the narrowest navigable canals on the island. Past the danger of the sandbar, we proceeded quietly into Charlie's territory. Solid triple-canopy jungle lined both banks. You couldn't see twelve feet through that jungle in the daytime. Soon our MST crew and Mr. Q had located the insertion point, a small canal on the starboard side.

After the boat pulled up into the small canal that meandered north from Ti Ti Canal, all six of us slid over the bow silently, to set up a perimeter as the medium maneuvered away. As usual, the boat would make a few fake insertions away from our position to throw Charlie off.

The muddy water instantly filled my jungle boots and soaked my jeans. In chest-deep water we waited quietly along the canal bank for the normal jungle sounds to emerge and any signs of enemy movement. The canal we had inserted on was one of three canals 300 meters apart that intersected about 500 meters inland on the island. We were to patrol to our objective on the middle canal and patrol out on one of the others, either of which could be used for extraction in case of an emergency.

Waiting for the normal jungle sounds to return was very important. In most cases, even the little noise our boats made would silence the creatures near the insertion. Even very late at night some kind of animal was always making noises in the jungle; if the sounds didn't return after a while, it could mean Charlie was close to our position. It was the same while patrolling—not only were we listening for the enemy, but for the normal jungle sounds too.

Mr. Q signaled Grimes to move ahead. We followed one at a time up the canal, stopping and listening at times, until we had patrolled about 200 meters. At this point the canal made a sharp turn to the right. I knew exactly our position on the island because I'd studied the picto maps so closely earlier. At that point our squad climbed up onto the right bank of the canal and set up an LP (listening post). Because we were deep into enemy-occupied territory, we had to move very slowly and concentrate on hearing any noise the enemy might make. He might walk right by us as we lay there in the mud, and we would let him go so that we could carry out the mission as planned.

We lay there for a long time, not in the most comfortable positions, not moving. If Vietcong had been active in the area, we would have heard them. The picto map kept flashing through my mind as if it were embedded in the back of my brain. Everything sounded normal. Carefully checking for booby traps, Grimes silently stood up and began to patrol slowly down a trail on a dike to the east, inching forward toward our objective.

The rest of us followed, one at a time, weapons off safety ready to fire at any instant, until there were only about 100 meters to go. My mind was engulfed with tension as the squad patrolled. Suddenly, the normal jungle odors were altered by the smell I had become accustomed to on previous operations, mosquito coils burning. Gook hootches were nearby.

Unexpectedly, an abnormal sound was heard to our left flank. The squad dropped down and became motionless, expecting an ambush. Again we waited and listened, all eyes and ears trained in that direction. Finally, after listening for a while with no result, we moved on again. Sooner than I had expected, we reached the first hootch of the three. The security element covered the hootches and behind us, as Grimes scouted the trail beyond. The other five of us followed Grimes after he motioned us ahead, me covering our rear at all times without making a sound. According to our intel, the third hootch was to have the rice cache in it. Not wanting to make contact with Charlie, we silently passed the second hootch. Just a short way to go now.

No Vietcong guard dogs this time. That was strange. Maybe Charlie had eaten them with some rice to supplement his diet. Security was set up around the third hootch, and Mr. Q and Grimes were handed the explosives to cook the rice. Doc stayed close to Mr. Q in case the radio was needed. I covered the area behind us, toward the two other hootches. Within seconds Grimes rounded everyone up and we moved a short distance down the trail toward the eastern canal and set up security again while waiting for our boss. Mr. Q pulled the M-2 fuses on about two tons of rice and quickly— he only had one minute—came to meet us. The rest of us right on his ass, Grimes started to patrol toward the extraction canal.

Thirty seconds and fifty meters down the trail, we heard several VC talking loud and moving toward our position. With the forty pounds of HBX about to blow, we couldn't return toward the hootches, but we didn't want to walk into an enemy's kill zone either, so the signal was given to slide off the trail and lay low on the opposite side of the dike. The closest man to the hootch, I lay as flat as I could and covered my head to avoid the blast.

Suddenly the sky lit up with a white flash, and limbs and debris flew through the jungle over the top of our position, damn near burying us alive. My ears were ringing as rice came falling to earth like a monsoon rainstorm. The zipperheads down the trail must have been surprised as the white flash and concussion came their way. Not long after the falling shit had settled, enemy tracers started filling the night sky. As their bullets ricocheted off the surrounding limbs and vines, word was passed back for me to take point and lead us to our alternate extraction site. I was blinded from the flash and I couldn't see shit in front of me, so I stayed as low as I could and made my way back toward the hootches to the west. All that was left of the rice cache was a crater in the mud. The two hootches down the trail in front of me were leveled also.

Enemy rounds were still coming in our direction as we ran down the trail we had come in on, and I could hear our rear element firing back down the trail behind us as we tried to evade. The Vietcong were hot on our ass, and while still running down the dike, Mr. Q passed the word to set up a hasty ambush. No sooner had we gotten into our positions than three Vietcong came running down the dike into our kill zone, firing weapons down the trail in front of them. But their bullets cracked over our heads, because we were hidden in the nipa palm below the dike. They didn't see us as we opened up: three gooks fell facedown on the muddy dike, their bodies smokin', but we could hear more Vietcong running toward us. With no time to check the bodies for documents or to recover the VCs' weapons, we started down the dike in the same direction, Grimes in front this time. We could have been running into one of Charlie's ambushes by then, but that was a chance we had to take. We knew the dike hadn't been booby-trapped, at least not back as far as the canal we had come in on.

Finding the three dead gooks on the dike must have slowed the others down, which gave us time to reach the canal we had patrolled in on. Mr. Q hesitated for a moment, trying to figure out our next move. That took about two seconds. The squad crossed the canal while Mr. Q and Grimes covered us, then we covered them as they crossed.

We set up another hasty ambush on the opposite bank. More Vietcong came running into our kill zone, more cautiously this time. Didn't do them any good, they went down too. One of them fell into the canal directly across from me and started floating out with the tide, his intestines floating behind him. The gook's AK-47 lay in the mud on the opposite bank. With no time to recover those weapons either, we continued on to the next canal.

With the tide changing, we had little time to waste. Our alternate extraction canal was approximately seventy meters ahead of us. We patrolled toward it, Grimes moving out swiftly but being very careful of booby traps and punji pits. I watched our rear, my Stoner pointed in that direction. The medium had been alerted to our situation and was on standby, engines running. The Vietcong behind us must have thought we went out that first canal, since they didn't seem to be after us anymore. I hoped we wouldn't run into any more in the direction we were headed.

The dike trail had stopped at the canal behind us, and we now patrolled through thick nipa palm. We took advantage of the concealment, and with no visible trail to follow we slowed the pace, making our movement much quieter. As we reached our alternate extraction canal, I could hear Vietcong searching in the distance behind us. The picto map of the area was embedded in my mind, so I knew we still had another 200 meters to patrol in that canal before reaching the extraction site.

As we slipped down into the muddy water and patrolled south, stopping only to listen for short periods, it was getting light to the east. We continued on, hoping the VC wouldn't cross the canal and come our way. I watched both canal banks behind us carefully.

Finally, the extraction sight was reached. A perimeter was immediately set up on both banks at the mouth of the canal. We concealed ourselves in the mud, water, and vegetation as Doc radioed the medium. This was the part of a mission I liked best—extracting after a successful operation without any casualties of our own. But it wasn't over yet; not until we were all on board our boat, out of Ti Ti Canal, and into the Bassac River could we relax.

Charlie was beating the brush far behind us, but we could

hear him getting closer all the time. My ears still had that HBX ring to them as I heard the muffled sound of the medium coming up Ti Ti Canal. After he had a visual on it, Doc used his radio to maneuver it into our position.

All the MST personnel were wearing flak jackets and helmets, standard equipment for them. They were manning the weapons, and all that was visible of them was part of their heads peering over the gunwales. They were a welcome sight, but Charlie had to have heard the medium's bow nudge up on the muddy bank. One at a time we left our hideaways and, Mr. Q and I being last, climbed over the bow and down inside, taking cover. Melfa put the craft in reverse and we backed off the muddy crab-infested canal bank and out into the canal, weapons still trained at the shoreline.

Melfa pulled back the throttles. The bow raised out of the water as the stern dropped down, and we got the hell out of there. Scraping the sandbar with the hull of the medium a couple of times got us out of Ti Ti Canal and into the main river channel just in time.

Back at camp, the sleeping second squad got a rude awakening as first squad entered the hootch yoo-hahing and throwing our gear around. The debriefing was mercifully short, and I still had rice in my hair and was wearing my muddy clothes and cammoed face when Bruce and I returned to the dock alone to have a smoke and unwind.

CHAPTER FOURTEEN

By now us "new guys" had been combat-proven. Although I always understood why the training we had gone through had been so rigorous and demanding, I appreciated it even more now. The weak and incompetent personnel had to be weeded out of our training class, leaving behind stable men who could depend on each other under any circumstance. From a bar fight to a combat situation, it didn't matter.

I flashed back to my UDT/SEAL training as I stood in the shower washing off the mud and face paint. Some of the trainees attending BUDS (Basic Underwater Demolition/ SEAL Training) had been injured during training evolutions and, not wanting to quit or drop out, were reenrolled in the next class. Usually this resulted in waiting for the next class to catch up to where the injured person had left off. Just finishing UDT/SEAL training with your original class was quite an accomplishment. People who were dropped back had to start where they left off, even if that meant going through hell week again.

It took determination to make it through BUDS. To become a team member you had to earn your way. While in training one day, my class was running the obstacle course on the Silver Strand. I was halfway through obstacle number thirteen, the "slide-for-life." Three long telephone poles buried in the sand about twelve feet apart came together above the ground forty feet up. Metal spikes driven into each side of the poles served as the steps of a ladder, and if two trainees met at the obstacle, one man climbed one pole and the second man climbed the other. At the top a large platform and two thick ropes led down and out in two different directions to two smaller telephone poles, twelve feet high. The objective was to climb to the platform, slide down one of the seventy-foot ropes, and kick the bottom pole first before dropping to the ground and running to the next obstacle. By the time a new trainee finally got to the slide-for-life after going over, through, and under twelve other obstacles, UDT and SEAL instructors on his ass all the way, the trainee was gasping for air and his arms and legs felt like lead.

As I was hanging upside down, inching my way toward one of the bottom poles, I looked back up at the man coming down behind me. He had just left the platform, and the strain of pulling himself over the twelve earlier obstacles had caught up with him. He lost his grip and started to fall. He tried to hang on by his legs, but the weight of his body sent him flipping end over end until he bounced four feet off the ground. That encouraged me to get a tighter grip on the shaking rope. I inched my way along the rope as the instructors used an IBS paddle to throw sand on the man who had fallen, yelling at him to climb the slide-for-life again. He complained about arm pain as he started up the obstacle a second time.

I was not far from the bottom pole by then, still looking up the rope behind me, still hanging upside down. Again he wrapped his legs around the rope and, sliding off the platform feet first, started to pull himself down the rope with his hands. No sooner had he left the platform than his strength gave way again. This time he flipped over in mid-air like a cat, then his face and the side of his body bounced off the sand below. I kicked the bottom pole, dropped to the ground, and ran to obstacle fourteen, looking back at the man as he lay there groaning.

Again the instructors gathered around him, yelling at him to get the fuck back up that pole. He grimaced with pain as he held one arm with the other, staggering toward the pole. Using his elbow and one hand, he climbed to the top again. Yelling at him to slide off the platform, the instructors were gathered at the bottom of the anticipated drop zone. I was nearly done with my next obstacle when the poor fucker fell a third time. I didn't know a man could flip over in midair like a cat, but he did it again, just in time to bounce off the sand from forty feet up once more. The instructors seemed to be really pissed off at him as they threw more sand on him, this time yelling at him to go on to the next obstacle. Finally, he finished the whole obstacle course, with the exception of the cargo net, his teeth gritted with pain, his face covered with sand and sweat.

After the last man finished the obstacle course, we formed up and ran back to the amphibious base for chow. Our sweaty clothes and faces were plastered with sand from the Silver Strand. The injured man went to the dispensary instead of going to chow. The next time I saw him, both arms were in casts. He didn't want to give up UDT/SEAL training, so he was dropped back to Class 54. He graduated with that class and was assigned to one of the Underwater Demolition Teams. *That's* determination.

Nobody makes it through BUDS easy. The whole time I spent in the teams, not once did I see an officer who wouldn't clean off his diving tanks and gear with freshwater and stow them away after a dive. Even the commanding officers of SEAL Team One and the three UDT teams on the west coast carried their own diving bottles, cleaned them and their gear, and stowed them away in the dive locker after a dive. After all, working together makes a team. That's what I liked about the officers on the teams: they would jump into the ditch with a shovel and help out, earning respect from their troops.

We had several operations in August, some of which were real dick-draggers, and I wondered how long we could continue to operate without further casualties: so far we'd had only minor shrapnel wounds. I attributed most of it to the training we had gone through. On most of our operations, dodging enemy bullets and exploding booby traps was routine. How long till our luck runs out? I thought. Who will be the first to get it? Will it be me? I tried not to think about it.

LePage had broken his leg falling through the ceiling and had finally been sent back to the States. His injury didn't

count. Doc and some of the other members had stepped in
punji pits and collected a little shrapnel, but that didn't slow
them down long.

Fighting side by side with some of the South Vietnamese
people was as close to suicide as I wanted to get. Some of
them had the "Let the Americans do it" syndrome. In a firefight with Charlie, they sometimes dropped their American-
made weapons, turned, and ran, leaving us to fight their
war. That really pissed me off. At times I felt like I was
shooting the wrong gooks. But not all South Vietnamese
were like that. The few who worked with us were usually
strong fighters dedicated to their country and their job.

At 0200 hours one morning first squad loaded up on board
the medium and was bound for Dung Island again as second
squad settled back down to sleep in the hootch. It was raining
so hard, our boat had to stop several times to wait for a
break in the storm. I thought the canvas top on the medium
was going to collapse.

We maneuvered the shallow-draft boat back into the part
of Dung Island that made me toss and turn the most at night.
But after listening to Mr. Q's briefing earlier, the operation
seemed safe enough. Maybe I was just getting used to the
routine. Hell, we had the bad weather on our side—it would
conceal noise we might make as we inserted and patrolled
toward our objective. Sneak in, be where we weren't expected, apprehend the gook asshole, then get the fuck out
of there without being detected, and extract with the little
slant-eye. Not much different from most of our operations.

Upon inserting this time, we didn't get muddy. We were
already soaked from the monsoon rain. The bow of the
medium nudged right up to the bank of the canal, level with
the bow. One step off the bow and we were hidden in thick
nipa-palm jungle. With the rain still coming down like a
minigun pounding the earth, we could barely hear the medium maneuver away from our insertion point. At least the
handkerchief wrapped around my head helped to keep some
of the water out of my eyes. We immediately set up a secure
perimeter to listen for enemy movement, but all I could
hear was the rain battering the nipa palm leaves as I covered

my field of fire. I didn't mind the rain at all; it felt good, keeping the sweat to a minimum, and the noise from the rain made patrolling to our objective easier. And there were no mosquitoes to bug us.

Finally, Mr. Q signaled Grimes to scout the area ahead in the direction of the objective. As Grimes left our perimeter, I wondered whether he would come back or if it would be several gooks with machine guns.

It wasn't long before he returned and signaled us to follow. The other five of us rose slowly from our hiding places, one at a time, and silently followed him deeper into the jungle. As I patrolled, I strained to hear movement to the flanks or behind me over the pounding of the rain. Metallic sounds are never natural in a jungle. Since there were no friendly forces on Dung Island, if one heard unnatural noise, it was a good sign of the Vietcong being in the area. But a sound would have to be *loud* to be heard over the downpour.

Nothing on our bodies rattled or made noise, not even if we ran. Taping the pins on our grenades and other gear stopped their rattling and snagging on limbs and vines, so we slipped through the thick vegetation easily.

The rain came down. Traces of cammo paint ran down my face and into my mouth. My back was drenched but warm. The rain was still better than those fuckin' mosquitoes. SEALs are used to disregarding their personal comfort for the success of their mission. That starts on the first day of BUDS training, long before we arrived at Nam. If you couldn't hack it then, you surely couldn't hack it in Nam.

We stopped to listen again. Never lay down your weapon, keep it at ready, I thought, still flashing back to my training days. We never stopped training, not even in Nam. Every operation was a training evolution. At least I didn't have that goddamn LAW rocket hanging off my back on this op. I hated it.

After patrolling farther, we were approaching our objective. Although we could take fire commands from Mr. Q, each man in the squad knew exactly what to do in case of an emergency: commencing fire, shifting fire, target responsibility, rate of fire, etc. Knowing what to do and when to take action. Automatically performing your duties without command. We patrolled on. Grimes passed word back that we were in a danger area, meaning we were at our objective or anywhere our security element might have to be used. Fuck, the minute we left camp we were in a danger area.

The rain continued but had let up considerably. A banana grove stretched for several hundred meters beyond the tree line of nipa palm. The lack of thick jungle out in front of us made seeing much easier. A short distance down the rows of bananas I could make out one nipa-palm hootch. Grimes had identified our target and was sent out to look for Vietcong guards and dogs. As he scouted the perimeter of the hootch, I scanned the area in the direction we had come from. The others covered Grimes from along our position in the tree line. The sky to the east was beginning to lighten; we had reached our target on schedule.

Grimes returned, crawling back most of the way. He informed Mr. Q that two Vietcong guards were roaming the area around the hootch, a good indication the man we wanted was inside. Mr. Q signaled us to move closer and set up positions around the hootch, but the two gooks would have to be taken care of before we could rush it. Grimes crawled in as close to the hootch as he could and hid behind a banana tree. As one of the guards approached his position, Grimes—9mm hush puppy at the ready—fired his silenced round, hitting the zipperhead. The gook dropped his weapon and fell to the ground, moaning and flipping around loud enough for the second guard to hear him. The second guard came toward Grimes with his weapon ready. Still lying down at the bottom of the banana tree, Grimes fired another shot, hitting him in the chest. As that gook fell to the ground, his rifle fired a single shot, alerting the whole island. Two more dead gooks to add to our body count. Automatically, we rushed into our positions.

One of the members of our squad checked the two bodies for signs of life, collecting their documents and weapons. The rest of us covered our fields of fire from our positions as Grimes and Mr. Q went swiftly to work. They had two prisoners inside the hootch blindfolded and handcuffed before the VC knew what the hell had happened.

The rain had stopped by then, but water was still dripping off the jungle canopy and from the banana trees. Since we would soon be extracting, I looked around my perimeter for signs of enemy movement and some ripe bananas. At first I couldn't believe my ears. Concentrating, it became clear to me. The sounds of approaching Vietcong, lots of them, were outside my perimeter. As I saw the first signs of movement down the rows of bananas, I opened up with a burst of automatic fire and yelled to warn the others. Doc got our boat on the radio and told them we had made contact. Meanwhile, Panella noted movement on his side of the hootch.

Steam rose from the damp ground as the Vietcong quickly surrounded our position. Charlie's bullets started cracking over our heads and into our perimeter as he opened up. Twigs, leaves, and tree limbs were falling to the ground around me as I crawled across the muddy earth to a more secure area with better concealment. In an attempt to suppress the enemy's fire, everyone in our element opened up with a volley of fire that would have knocked down the Victoria Hotel. I didn't know how many of the fuckers had surrounded us, but their firepower seemed to overwhelm ours as we exchanged tracers. As heavy enemy automatic fire kept coming into our position, kicking up the mud around me, I lay as flat to the ground as I could and changed to a fresh box of ammo. There wasn't much cover in the banana grove. Outside our perimeter there were explosions from Bruce's XM-148. On a signal from Mr. Q, we tried to leapfrog in the direction of the medium, taking along our prisoners. We threw grenades and fired our weapons as we maneuvered, but heavy automatic-weapons fire pinned us down again not far from the hootch. Doc was scrambling air support from Binh Thuy as I squirmed deeper into the mud, trying to make my body disappear. A .30-caliber tracer, ricocheting off the limbs above me, landed in the mud an arm's reach from my head, still burning with a red

flame. That really pissed me off. As the steam rose from
the earth, I flipped over on my back holding the Stoner
above me and blindly fired into the jungle beyond. With all
the incoming enemy rounds, I didn't dare poke my head
up.

After emptying the second box of ammo, I flipped back
over on my stomach and changed to a full box again. We
didn't seem to be gaining fire superiority. Once more our
element put out its maximum rate of fire, but we still
couldn't suppress Charlie's incoming rounds. We tried and
tried again. Finally we had to start saving ammo until our
air support arrived from Binh Thuy. Until that morning we
had never engaged in a firefight with so many Vietcong.
Our asses were flat pinned down as VC rounds continued
to pound our position. Bruce's 40mm HE rounds still exploded in the background. Whoever we had captured must
have been real important to Charlie.

The prisoners lay bound and gagged inside our perimeter,
ready to be dragged out to the medium. I squirmed deeper
into the mud, leaving my sweat and some of the cammo
paint from my face embedded in my bodyprint in the mud.
The squad's position was an oval, each man covering his
field of fire. Staying several meters apart from each other
prevented everyone's getting hit from any one incoming
grenade. As I lay there in the mud I thought, No gook will
take me alive, not without one hell of a fight. As many of
them as I could get would go down with me, if necessary.

As the steam rose from the ground and water dripped
from the jungle canopy, we lay in the mud waiting for our
air support, occasionally finishing off a brave gook who
tried to assault our perimeter. Our ammo was slowly disappearing and things began to look pretty grim. Then, after
thirty minutes of heavy fighting on both sides, two OV-10
Broncos began to circle overhead. What a welcome sight.
Doc established radio communication with one of the pilots,
who told him to mark our position. Doc threw a red smoke
grenade in the direction of the medium. Making radio contact with the pilots again, Doc asked them to identify the
color of the smoke in case Charlie threw one out also to

confuse the pilots. After they identified the smoke and its position, Doc asked them to make their air strikes 180 degrees and forty meters south of the smoke. "Roger that," they replied as the first OV-10 started its first run.

As the first rockets pounded Charlie's position, Charlie made a desperate attempt to take our position. Bullets ricocheted in all directions and grenades exploded everywhere, theirs and ours. The OV-10 Broncos—"Black Ponies," as they were sometimes called—carried two rocket pods of eight rockets each, three miniguns, and two M-60 machine guns—quite a lot of firepower. I looked up behind me from my position in the mud as the second Black Pony started its run. Enemy tracers streaked out of the jungle canopy toward the twin-engine fixed-wing aircraft as it fired two more of its rockets. The rockets looked as if they were headed right toward me. I yelled "Oh shit" and turned my face down, covering my head with my hands and trying to make my body sink deeper into the mud at the same time. The concussion from the impacting rockets picked me up out of my bodyprint and slammed me back to the muddy ground. Pieces of debris from the jungle flew in all directions. "Fuck!" I yelled. "Whose side are those planes on anyway?" Charlie's rounds continued to pound our position, and the planes maintained their strikes uninterrupted by Charlie's small-arms fire. Again and again I was picked up out of the mud then slammed down as the rockets fell on the enemy's position.

By then the rockets had cut quite a hole through the jungle in front of us. My ears were ringing as the steam from the ground mixed with the smoke from exploding rockets and grenades. Mr. Q crawled over to Doc, took the mike, and informed the pilots we were starting out through the hole they had made in the enemy's position. After reloading our weapons, we started to fire and maneuver toward the smoking hole in the jungle. Laying down a maximum rate of fire toward both flanks, we took our prisoners with us. First, half the squad moved up firing its weapons while we covered them, then it was our turn, dragging the prisoners with us. Flopping back down in the mud, I covered the area behind us as our first element moved ahead again. Charlie tried to cut us off, but the pilots hosed down our flanks and behind us with their miniguns, giving us a chance to run for it.

My turn again. My body felt like lead—from physical exhaustion, and from psychological—as I picked myself up, running forward while firing behind me. Finally reaching the point of rocket impact, I threw myself down again, changing to my last box of ammo. Beside me in the mud was a gook's leg that had been blown off at the hip. The body was nowhere in sight. From behind, enemy rounds cracked overhead and into the nipa palm beside us as we started to run again, hoping that whatever booby traps may have been in this area had been detonated by rockets and falling trees and limbs. Then rockets were pounding to earth behind us, the concussion bending the nipa palm leaves in the direction of the medium as if to point the way to our extraction site. I tripped over debris, got back to my feet, and ran some more. We made for the boat, dragging our prisoners with us and firing to our flanks. I jumped over and ran around several dead gooks in my path, some with bullet holes in them, some just pieces hanging in the bushes and trees.

The Bronco pilots had a good view of the area and continued to unload their armament behind us as we ran for our lives through the nipa palm. If it hadn't been for the air support, we would have been in deeper shit than we were already. I turned around, flopped down in the mud and fired part of my last box of ammo into the jungle behind me, hoping to hit some more of the invisible little bastards. The mud seemed to glue me to the ground as I tried to get to my feet again, but I made it, turned to catch up to the others and ran like hell. Although not as thick as before, tracers still streaked through the nipa palm and around us as we neared the canal. If I made it out of this one alive, I would owe the lieutenant commander flying one of those Broncos a bottle of whiskey.

The medium had been monitoring our conversations with the Black Ponies, so the bow rammed the canal bank as our squad approached. Nobody needed to be told to get on board. I turned around and emptied the last of my Stoner ammo into the jungle behind us. With one quick leap I was on the bow and then under cover of the ceramic-tile armor plates on the bulkheads. Even though we weren't, I felt secure for a few seconds. On most ops the Stoner usually made me feel that way, but not on this one. We were unsuccessful in gaining fire superiority, but without the weapons we did have, it would have been disastrous. Still catching my breath, I dropped my Stoner and grabbed an M-79 grenade launcher lying nearby. With the two OV-10 Broncos, our minigun, and everyone on board firing into the jungle, we turned the medium around and got the hell away from the canal bank. I fired 40mm HE rounds from the M-79 back at the jungle until we were out of the launcher's effective range.

The Black Ponies made their last run, expending the last of their ordnance. Steam still rose from the ground, water still dripped from the jungle, but first squad had its prisoners. The medium headed back to camp at full speed. The Broncos were last seen heading northwest up the river toward their base when Mr. Q came aft in the medium and said, "Hey, Young, why didn't you get any of those bananas?"

"I couldn't find any ripe ones," I answered. Maybe I should have been a Seabee.

CHAPTER FIFTEEN

Interrogating the prisoners as soon as possible was an important factor in getting reliable intelligence. Important information on Vietcong movement, weapons, food, supplies, reinforcements, and higher ranking cadre could usually be obtained from a successful interrogation. Maybe a whole new operation could be constructed from the information collected from our most recent prisoners. We hadn't come up against such an organized resistance of Vietcong like this on Dung Island before. My ears were still ringing as I thought about the firefight and the pieces of Vietcong hanging in the trees.

After the interrogation and debriefing, I went to morning chow. Fuck cleaning my weapons and gear till after I ate. The Vietcong's leg, blown off at the hip, didn't seem to bother me as I mugged down my breakfast. After chow, face still cammoed, I changed into my UDT trunks, field stripped the Stoner, and cleaned it thoroughly. Not once, on or off a mission, had my weapons failed me while in Nam. I was going to keep it that way. American technology and our intensive training was the reason I was still alive. Everyone in the element had kept his head under fire while heavily outnumbered by an enemy force. My nylon vest was very light without any ammo or grenades in it. The only thing left in it was one muddy smoke grenade and four empty Stoner boxes. After filling the ammo boxes, I put them in my vest with a couple of extra frags. I didn't mind the extra weight, because it might save my life or the lives of my comrades some day. As rear-security man, it was difficult at times to know what was going on up at the front of the patrol element, especially in the thick dark jungle at night. That's where SEAL standard operating procedures came in: it was very rare that a word or some sort of signal wasn't passed back to inform us of what actions were being taken up front. Knowing what actions to take, and when, came from training in SOPs.

As I entered the hootch to stow away my Stoner and gear, Reeves and Weber were sitting on their racks laughing. When I asked them what was so funny, they said, "Jump school." A smile flashed on my face as I sat down nearby. I had gone through airborne training with them. Five of us SEALs and one UDT guy, five of us being from the same BUDS class, attended a jump school at Fort Benning, Georgia, together. What a joke. Basically, jump school was three weeks of running, PT, parachute-landing falls (PLFs), and learning about how to steer a parachute. The average person, at least in the Navy, could learn how to do a PLF correctly in the morning and be jumping that afternoon. I guess the Army airborne course was strenuous—by Army standards.

It was hard to stay out of trouble at Benning, and at times we had to restrain ourselves to avoid being kicked out of the training. I called our natural high spirits "boosting morale," but the Army had a different name for it. Six of us Navy types and hundreds of Army guys.

Just out of BUDS training a few weeks earlier, the six of us were in the best possible physical condition. The push-ups we had to do at jump school didn't even come close to the demands of UDT/SEAL training. In fact, I had done more push-ups in my six months at BUDS training than most people do in a lifetime, and most of those were done while soaked to the bone with saltwater in the surf zone of the Pacific Ocean.

SEALS and UDT personnel were sent to Fort Benning just after they completed BUDS training, although I do know some SEALS who went to Okinawa and other places around the world for their airborne training. As much training as SEALS do anyway, I always wished they had their own airborne training in Coronado. The airborne instructors at Benning were called Black Hats because they wore black baseball caps. They were everpresent to harass the troops. Our Black Hat seemed to take a likin' to us Navy types and gave us special favors, such as allowing us to run in circles around the Army formations while they ran, doing extra push-ups, and running extra laps. But the one I liked best was making the SEALS run at the back of the formation to keep the Army guys from dropping back behind the group.

Though we were not authorized liberty, or to leave Benning, our Black Hat would sneak us off base after each workday, taking us to his house to meet the wife and kids for dinner, taking us to the country with lots of beer, taking us to downtown Columbus to the best topless bars. Joe Instructor during the day, Joe Guide after hours. He even bought the beer.

Just before we graduated from jump school, another group

of UDT/SEALs arrived at Benning for jump training. After dark one night, wearing nothing but field jackets, all six of us walked across the base to their barracks. Since it was January, it was pretty cold outside. Upon entering their barracks, we unzipped the jackets and walked through the crowd of Army guys, looking for our friends. Most of these Army types thought we were abnormal, and you know, they were right, we were unique in our own Navy way.

Come jump time, we really pissed off some of the Black Hats. The jump zone was located across the state border, in Alabama. A field a mile long by a half mile wide was used by the Army there. Buses parked on one side of the field toward the center, out of the way of the jumpers. Directly across from the buses, on the opposite side of the jump zone, was a large pond, the edge of which extended a few meters into the jump zone. Since we were Navy, after we exited the aircraft and checked our canopies, we steered toward the pond, hoping to get wet. The instructors looked up and, using megaphones, yelled, "Steer toward the buses, steer toward the buses." So after hitting the pond, we were assigned more push-ups. Each time we jumped into this jump zone, we steered toward the pond. I enjoyed looking down at the Black Hats on the heads of the instructors running toward the pond yelling up at us, "Steer toward the buses."

As we sat in our hootch reminiscing, it began to rain again, rattling off the tin roof so hard it sounded like a snare drum. In seconds, puddles outside our hootch became lakes. Grabbing soap, we ran outside naked and stood under the eaves, letting the water run onto our heads. It was difficult to hear anyone talking over the pounding of the rain. Our freshwater collector, an extra radar shield from the light, was turned upside down and left under the eaves also. It was full and running over. I washed the cammo off my face, and as quick as the monsoon cloudburst started, it stopped.

Later that day, as I lay in my rack, I thought about our last operation. At times it was hard to believe it was me actually doing these things, like maybe the time I spent operating I was somebody else—a mysterious person out-side my own body. Thinking of my other self, I dozed off.

I dreamed about being back in the States, deer hunting with my dad and my younger brother. We were walking through the woods very quietly, using hand and arm signals, spread out a hundred yards apart in a skirmish line down a mountainside. As we moved slowly along the slope, we worked as a team looking for deer. I heard sounds behind me and dropped to the ground in a flash. My dream turned into a nightmare. I got up and started running through the woods in the opposite direction from the sounds I heard. Tripping and falling down, I got up and ran some more, firing my weapon behind me all the way. They were catching up, couldn't let them get me, at least not alive. There's one, then another. As I ran, the tall pine trees became nipa palms and jungle, right before my eyes! Oh God, I thought as I stumbled through the thick shit with "them" right on my ass. Got to get to the boat, I thought as I jumped into a muddy canal. But the mud stuck to my legs like some fantastic new adhesive on the market. The Vietcong seemed to run through the jungle faster than I, without snagging on anything. They jumped onto the mud and ran on top of it as if it were hard-packed dirt, their wide toes working like snowshoes. How could they do that?

I desperately tried to free myself from the unforgiving canal, but the gooks quickly surrounded me. I turned my Stoner on them, it had never failed me. I pulled the trigger, but I was out of ammo. One of the fuckers reached out and grabbed me on the shoulder.

"Oh, no!" I yelled as Weber shook me. "Time for chow," he said. My heart was pounding, my body and rack were soaked with sweat. I went to chow. The Seabee cook had whipped up some kind of Vietnamese chow. It was hard enough living and fighting for them, I didn't have to eat their food. Instead I chugged down a couple of glasses of fake milk and returned to the hootch. Weber finished his Vietnamese chow and returned too. Didn't matter to him what he ate; Weber would eat anything flopped down in

front of him. I swear, at times I wondered if he even had
any taste buds.

With enough daylight left, Weber and I got our Model
15 Smith & Wessons and walked out to the ammo bunker.
The day had been hot and humid. After I unlocked the metal
door, the hot air inside rushed out, bringing with it the smell
of crated ammo and explosives. Weber dug around and
found a case of .38-caliber ball ammo. We opened the
wooden crate with our K-bars and he pulled out an olive-
drab metal ammo can. We took it, secured the ammo bunker
door, and headed toward the machine-gun tower.

The ammo bunker was a metal container, eight feet square
and eight feet tall, surrounded by and covered over with
sandbags, which were supposed to protect it from a mortar
attack. After climbing to the tower, we started shooting in
the direction of an old Vietnamese cemetery, our camp's
designated fire zone. Our .38s were SEAL-issue handguns,
used as backups while operating. I always cleaned mine and
kept it in tune, but I never had to pull it on anybody during
an operation.

Soon, Grimes and Shannon joined us in the tower, Shannon
with his M-16 and Grimes with a CAR-15. Bruce, looking out our hootch door, couldn't stand not getting in on the
action, so he grabbed his M-16/XM-148 combo and ammo vest and joined us. Weber and I climbed down and all of
us lined up on the helo pad, pointing our weapons at the arch
by the cemetery. Tracers started ricocheting off the arch and
concrete crumbled everywhere from Bruce's 40mm.

After the dust cleared, the arch still stood. By this time
the bar had emptied and was watching, and some of the
other SEALs joined us on the firing line. We opened up
until our weapons were empty. Grimes borrowed Bruce's
grenade launcher for one more round of HE. It seemed like
everyone in camp watched as the round of HE armed itself
on the way to its target. With a loud explosion echoing back
to camp, the arch crumbled to the ground. The tops of the
tallest palm trees beyond the cemetery made good targets
also. Concentrating our fire on them, with an M-79 HE
round or walking tracers from an M-60 into the tops at full

auto, would send the limbs falling to the ground. Several palm trees already looked like tall telephone poles with splintered tops.

I loved my weapons and enjoyed working with them and shooting them. All that firepower. I loved the section in UDT training when our class was out at San Clemente Island. The UDT trainees had their own camp on the north end of the island. The camp and surrounding area were off limits to civilian and all military personnel except UDT trainees and the instructors. A big black civilian, the only one I ever saw there, cooked for our camp, and that guy could put out a meal. The instructors always made sure the training class had plenty of explosives and ammo to work with, so we could blow things up and shoot the shit out of things—from old dump trucks to refrigerators, anything we could think of to place a charge on, we turned into smaller pieces of scrap.

As the days went by out on San Clemente Island, the twenty-eight remaining students of the original seventy-eight did everything from setting demolitions on underwater obstacles to six-mile swims. One day, while working with some C-4 plastic explosive, our class walked around the demo area looking for something to demolish. I found an old projectile from a ship's gun lying in the cactus. Filling in the hollow projectile with C-4, I placed it next to the frame under the bed of an old dump truck. I then tied det cord onto a trunk line that was also det cord. All the trainees tied into the same trunk line after their explosives had been set in place.

One guy filled the refrigerator with TNT and tied into the trunk line with his det cord. After all twenty-eight trainees had tied their det cord to the trunk line, we moved into a log bunker, where the explosives were electrically detonated from one "hell box." Rocks, dirt, and metal flew everywhere when the handle was turned. It seemed like minutes had passed before the instructors would let us out of the bunker. We couldn't believe our eyes after the dust cleared. The refrigerator was gone, evaporated. Not a trace of it could be found. The dump-truck bed was pushed up over five feet and one side of it was missing. A huge piece of the frame was gone too.

As I looked over the damage I had done to the dump truck, I found a piece of leaf spring about ten inches long by three inches wide by one-quarter inch thick. I then cut out a piece of explosive called data sheet to cover the piece of leaf spring. Data sheet was a plastic explosive that looked much like an olive-drab mud flap off a truck. It could be cut to any shape or size and was very flexible. Next, I looked around for one of the many lizards that inhabited the island. I found one, thumped the little critter good with my finger, so he wouldn't move, and put him on the leaf spring. Next I took the piece of data sheet, same size as the leaf spring, and carved my middle name backward right in the explosive itself. That would have the effect of making my middle name a shaped charge, leaving it (I hoped) and the lizard embedded on the metal spring. I then wrapped det cord around the leaf spring and data sheet to hold them together. Before securing the det cord to the trunk line, I buried the whole works under several large rocks so I could recover it later. Then I walked around the demo area watching other members of my class experimenting with other explosives. Finally, the trunk line was rolled out and we all secured our det cords to it. We regrouped inside the bunker, and like before, pieces of rock, metal, wood, and whatever filled the air as the twenty-eight different explosive experiments were detonated at the same time.

After everything settled, we walked back up to the shards and craters. Sure enough, my middle name and the lizard were pushed into the steel and left there forever, right down to the claws and tail.

Day after day, underwater and on the surface, we blew the shit out of the north end of the island with all types of explosives, until the instructors figured we were explosive-wise. Once in a while a Navy LST would maneuver offshore and lower concrete obstacles with pieces of steel sticking out of them into the water. The next morning we would conduct a recon of the beach, locate the new underwater obstacles, and make a map of their positions. Next we would figure out how much "demo" we needed. After the map was made and the demo calculated, we would destroy the obstacles during a simulated combat-swimmer operation. Needless to say, we UDT/SEAL trainees knew what we were doing with explosives by the time we left that island; the instructors made sure of that.

CHAPTER SIXTEEN

The Seabees were going to Binh Thuy. It was now the middle of August, 1970. Since the platoon had no ops planned, some of us were going to ride along with them. After morning chow, Bruce, Panella, Doc, Reeves, Grimes, Strausbaugh, and I climbed into the back of the Seabees' six-by. With one Seabee driving and another riding on the passenger's side, the gate to our camp was opened and we drove out.

Grimes and Strausbaugh had their bags packed for R&R to Hawaii. They planned to stay in Binh Thuy until they could catch a flight to Saigon. The journey by six-by usually took half the day if everything went right. It was a rough ride and a boring trip, not like the ride of the medium. As the six-by drove slowly through the village outside our camp, children, chickens, dogs, pigs, and old papasans moved to the side of the road. None of "them" had cars, trucks, TVs, or even bicycles. The only bike I saw around there was owned by the camp's assistant Seabee cook.

The Long Phu River's dirty water was just to our left. Some of the hootches were built right over the water on stilts, and the nipa-palm walls of others almost rubbed the side of the six-by. Easy for them to park their sampans, easy for them to fish, easy for them to shit in the water. Most of the hootches, hamlets, villages, and cities in the

Mekong were located along a canal or river bank, using the water to travel on as we would use roads in the States.

As we continued down the two-mile straightaway, I wondered if the ARVNs had checked the road for mines that morning. Knowing how they operated, I guessed they probably had not. The six-by turned west and slowed down a little as we entered Long Phu.

As we started out at the south end of town, I grabbed my first ball cap. On the right side of the road, in the direction we were going, a thin Vietnamese man with big ears walked unaware of us as we approached. He was wearing a plaid shirt, pressed slacks, and thongs, and the little fucker didn't even step to the side. He was trucking along as our six-by rolled past him. Hanging onto the truck with one arm and one leg, I grabbed the blue cap off his head, breaking his trucking stride. For a moment the Vietnamese man just stood there, surprised, but with a smile on his face. As we rolled along, picking up speed, his facial expressions started to change to that serious look; he knew he wasn't getting his hat back. Everyone on the six-by laughed at the expression on the victim's face as his big ears seemed to stand out more without his hat.

We relieved three more unsuspecting Vietnamese of their hats before we left Long Phu behind. Reeves had the hard side of the truck for grabbing hats. Most of his victims were walking toward him, so he had to grab quickly, before they knew what was happening.

The six-by rolled right along now. The road had improved a little, and it had been a long time since I had ridden that fast on the ground. Not many Vietnamese people were along that stretch of the highway, but there were several small villages.

Though wider, the road was still a dirt surface on a dike. The Kinh Bang Canal was on the left, and miles of rice paddies were off into the horizon to our right. Tall palm trees lined both sides of the road, small nipa-palm hootches appearing here and there. The road was long and straight.

The closer we got to Soc Trang, the more foot traffic and motorcycles congested the road. We soon arrived at Kinh

Saintard Canal and had to stop. The Vietcong had blown up a bridge downstream from there, and the Cau Tan Lick ferry had to take its place. South Vietnamese soldiers stood guard on both banks behind sandbag bunkers. The ferry wasn't very big, but would hold a six-by.

We sat on the east shore watching the ferry cross to our side. It was powered by a man who pulled on a rope that was attached to each bank and ran through two steel rings attached to the boat. It had a single deck, with a ramp on each end that could be raised or lowered, enabling the vehicles to drive on one side and drive off the other without having to turn the ferry around midstream. After a busload of pigs, chickens, and Vietnamese disembarked, the Seabee drove the six-by up onto the ferry and we helped the old codger pull us to the opposite shore. Looking downstream, I saw what remained of the old bridge. The center pier still stood, with pieces of twisted steel hanging off it, and a section on either bank was intact. The Kinh Saintard Canal was a major waterway, and heavy boat traffic traveled it in both directions, dodging the ferry as they passed by.

Soon our six-by had climbed the muddy bank on the opposite shore. The road from Long Phu to Soc Trang was called Highway 118, and we now drove on a two-lane dirt surface. Bicycles, Hondas, and other military rigs used the highway, and the traffic increased the farther toward Soc Trang we went. In places, South Vietnamese rice farmers had piled stacks of rice clear out onto the highway, drying it in the sun.

As we entered the outskirts of Soc Trang, the dirt road became a two-lane paved highway. The Army Corps of Engineers was paving Highway 118 and other roads in the area, more American money being pumped into Nam to make the Vietnamese a little more comfortable. The hustle and bustle of military and civilian traffic increased. Soc Trang was a good-sized village that functioned as the capital of Quan My Xuyen district. Having no reason to stop, we continued on.

Eventually our six-by reached Can Tho, where the traffic was "stop, move up a little, stop again." The traffic kept on that way until we were halfway between Can Tho and Binh Thuy, where we accidentally ran over the Honda-55 step-through of a Vietnamese who apparently took offense at our lifting his hat when we'd passed him earlier. The little fucker hung onto our bumper, like an olive-drab bumper sticker, as the traffic backed up behind us. We couldn't have pried him off with a crowbar.

We sat in the middle of the highway, blocking traffic, until a gook officer drove up in an American jeep. He parked right where the Honda had been parked, in front of our truck. Finally, the guy stuck to the front bumper let go and the two gooks started mumbling and jabbering together in Vietnamese on the side of the road. Very little traffic was getting around us while the officer and Vietnamese soldier discussed the matter. The little turd was pointing to his hat and down at his Honda, still underneath the back duals of our truck. Then as we stood in the back of the six-by, the Seabee popped the clutch, ramming the back of the gook officer's jeep. Everyone hung on as the two gooks dove for the ditch, the jeep rolled into the rice paddies, and the Seabee went through the gears.

The road was clear for a long way ahead by then. Looking back, I watched the two gooks climb out of the ditch before the vehicles and dust blocked them from my view, while the Seabee broke speed records toward Binh Thuy.

We drove the truck onto the Tactical Air Support Base across from the Naval Support Facility in Binh Thuy, then we went our separate ways, to stay low for a while. The truck was well hidden on the small base, back behind the chow hall. Bruce, Reeves, the Seabee driver, and I went to the Explosive Ordnance Disposal bar back across the street—who the hell would look for us there? Too late to start back to Long Phu, and too drunk to drive, the Seabee suggested we start back in the morning. That sounded all right with us; it was better to keep the six-by out of sight anyway.

The next morning on the way to breakfast, I noticed several parked jeeps with the keys in them. I knew how bad our platoon needed one. The target was sure tempting, but

I didn't have the guts to "borrow" it. After chow we all gathered at the six-by for the ride back. Grimes and Strausbaugh had gotten a helo to Saigon the night before, so we wouldn't see them for about ten days.

As we left the air-support base, the highway to Can Tho was already crowded with jeeps, trucks, and buses, and the sides of the road were packed with Vietnamese foot traffic. The truck rolled through Can Tho and out the other side, then began to pick up speed. Reeves and I stood in the front of the truck bed, hanging onto the bang board and watching the people and traffic. As we rolled along, I noticed several Vietnamese kids huddled up along the right side of the road. As the six-by passed them, one of the little fuckers threw something up into the air over the truck. The object landed right in the middle of the truck bed. It was a homemade bomb. This really pissed me off.

I looked back at the kids, but they ran off in different directions. The bomb was a .50-caliber cartridge with the bullet removed and mounted below the primer to work as a firing pin. Two strips of bamboo attached to the sides of the cartridge case had been folded across the bottom, holding the bullet-firing pin in place. The top of the case had been crimped over. The weight of the bullet on the bottom kept the bomb stabilized in the air until it hit a hard surface and the bullet fired the primer, detonating the cartridge's contents. A wound from that type of booby trap probably wouldn't kill you, but it could put you out of service for a while, especially if some kind of high explosive had been put in the cartridge case. Without knowing what components were inside it, we were very careful with the bomb.

I felt like going back and breaking the little fucker's arm, or better yet, his neck. But chances of finding him weren't too good. We waited until the truck crossed over a canal and then threw it into the water. That sort of thing never happened around Long Phu, only in the big cities.

If I ever make it home alive, I'll never come back here to fight for these slant-eyed fuckers again, I thought, staring into a canal as we drove through the countryside. Was this mosquito-infested hellhole and the people in it worth losing my life over? I couldn't answer that question. If we weren't getting pinned down by a South Vietnamese outpost, or friendly fire like second squad ran up against early one morning while returning to our camp, the gooks in the cities were trying to stab us in the back. While in Binh Thuy I had bought a bottle of V.O. I opened it to get my mind off Vietnam. Passing the bottle around kept us occupied and out of trouble, at least for the moment.

Before long we had driven through Soc Trang and were waiting for the ferry again. We couldn't seem to catch the damn thing empty and on our side of the canal. But finally it was our turn. The crossing was fun, and we were greeted warmly by the guy who ran the ferry.

After we reached the other shore, I threw the ferry's skipper what was left of our whiskey. He smiled toothlessly and bowed as we got under way again.

Day by day my dislike for what I was doing for these people, and the people themselves, grew. Something was wrong, but I couldn't place it. After arriving back at our camp, I found I had received several letters and a package from home. A helo had brought our mail down from Binh Thuy the day before. I never saw anyone wrap a package like my old man. An M-26 frag grenade couldn't have blown it open. After damn near breaking the blade on my K-bar opening it, I discovered some 8mm film, 35mm film, a pair of Levi's jeans for operating in, and some chocolate-chip cookies. The cookies and the film didn't last very long.

CHAPTER SEVENTEEN

During UDT/SEAL training you are assigned a swim buddy. He is your partner throughout the duration of training. On timed ocean swims you are to stay within six feet of each other. When my class first started training on 30 June 1969, my swim partner was a first class petty officer. A few days after training started, my swim buddy couldn't hack it and dropped out. That had a bad effect on me. Maybe I should quit too, I thought. But I did not want to be a quitter, and I enjoyed the physical training, so I stuck around and Weber became my new swim buddy.

Weber wasn't as fast a swimmer as I was, and he slowed me down at times, but since we were swim buddies, I stayed by his side. As far as partners went, Reeves and Fisher were the top swimmers in our class, with Weber and me usually finishing second. During our swimming screen test, I came in first out of seventy-eight men with a personal time of 5:45 for the 300-meter swim. That was before we were assigned swim buddies or fins. From the day Class 53 started training, I learned to take pain and punishment. If I wanted to make it through, there was no such word as "can't."

Seventy-eight men started and twenty finished: fifteen of us started with the original class, and five men dropped back from Class 52. The day before hell week started, we lost seven men on our sixteen-mile run from Coronado to Mexico. A four-wheel-drive ambulance followed us on all our training evolutions, picking up the injured and the quitters. I finished our runs in the top ten percent of our class and kept Reeves and Fisher honest at swimming by staying on their ass, making Weber stay up with me. Starched greens, shined boots, polished belt buckles, and short hair were the order of each morning's inspection.

First Class Petty Officer Moy was our class instructor. We nicknamed him Mother Moy, and he hated it. Every morning, first thing, was our class inspection. A smudge on your boot, a belt buckle not polished, or unpressed greens would get you what was known as "hit the bay"—that meant jumping off a causeway in front of the barracks and standing in San Diego Bay until after the inspection was over.

Surviving an inspection by any of the instructors was rare. Some mornings Moy would walk out of the instructors' building for our class inspection. At the same time our class would yell, "Hoo-yah, Mother Moy!" He would stand and glare at us, then finally say, "About face, forward march," and the whole class would march off the causeway into the bay, starting us off wet for the day's evolution. Some mornings during inspection, just our looking at Mother Moy gave him the excuse to point to the bay. By the time hell week was over, only thirty men out of the original seventy-eight were left to continue on with Class 53.

Hell week was also called motivation week, the one week in UDT/SEAL training when most of the weak and incompetent personnel drop from the class. During that week, the instructors rotate their duty among each other to keep the class awake and working twenty-four hours a day, one evolution after another with a meal every six hours. A trainee is wet for most of the week, getting little if any sleep. After hell week, with the class down to a manageable size, things moved along more smoothly. One night during hell week we single-filed into the chow hall at twelve midnight, wet and full of mud, but the last man in line always carried a mop to clean the floor behind us.

Living each evolution from meal to meal seemed to keep me going. I would take a baked potato in tinfoil and hold it between my wet legs to cool it off and warm me up because I knew that in a few more minutes I would be doing more push-ups in the surf zone of the Pacific Ocean. Any relief from the wet and cold was welcome. Being dry for thirty minutes in a row was rare for hell week. One night we all got to put on dry clothes and portaged our rubber boats across the highway from the amphibious base to the ocean side. I can't remember fucking up, but Moy said, "Hit the bay, Young."

Fuck! I thought, as I ran off into the foggy night to throw my body in the ocean. Once out of the instructor's sight, I waited for a wave to rush up on the beach, barely getting my boots wet. Putting my hands in the cold water and dabbing them on the front of my greens made them look wet. Returning to report to Mother Moy before returning to my boat crew, I yelled, "Hoo-yah, Mother Moy," in a hurting sort of voice. In the dark night I must have looked wet, so he replied, "Recover," meaning get back in my boat crew. Putting one over on an instructor and getting caught could earn you enough push-ups in the surf zone to have meat hanging out your ass.

Whether it was a hot meal at the amphibious-base chow hall or a box lunch in the mud flats, we had a meal every six hours. Late one afternoon, after we'd been awake about four days, the instructor told us to run into our barracks, put on dry clothes, and return with a pillow and blanket. He gave us five minutes to do this and be back in formation in front of the causeway. After reassembling outside, the class was marched in formation to a football field close by. Once there, we all laid our blankets and pillows down in boat-crew order on the soft grass in front of us. We were then ordered to lay on our backs and watch a beautiful Pacific sunset without falling asleep. Fuck, it felt good to be dry again. As we lay there, one of the instructors turned on a radio and tuned to some soft music. Anyone falling asleep had to hit the bay and stand in chest-deep water until an instructor told him to recover. I don't remember closing my eyes, but I woke up to find Mother Moy was thumping on my chest, telling me to hit the bay and bring up some bottom samples.

As long as I could keep moving, I was okay, but when we had to stop training, I would want to fall asleep. One of the last nights of hell week, what was left of our class

was supposed to assemble to watch a training film. We had
five minutes to change out of our wet clothes and assemble
in a classroom. Staying awake through the half-hour movie
was one of the hardest things I ever had to do. My comrades
were hitting the bay right and left. Finally, the fuckin' movie
ended. Three or four of us had survived it as the instructors
walked around the room with flashlights, watching for us
to fall asleep. As the lights were turned on, there was Mother
Moy. "Congratulations, men, you stayed awake, hit the
bay!" That son of a bitch! I thought as I hit the bay. I loved
him.

You couldn't get up from push-ups or out of the bay until
an instructor yelled "Recover." Sometimes he would yell
"Seatcover," and everyone would drag their bodies out of
the bay, falling into formation once again. After we were
there he would announce, "I said, 'seatcover,' dummies,
hit the bay." Some mornings Moy would walk up to us for
inspection and he wouldn't even have to point or say a
word, the whole class read his mind and we hit the bay on
our own. We grew accustomed to the "hit the bay glare,"
After hell week our barracks looked empty because so few
men remained.

On 9 July 1969 I swam one mile under the qualifying
time and earned my UDT duck-feet swim fins. All the swimming our class had done until then was done without fins.
The black hard-rubber fins meant a lot to me after what I
had gone through to get them.

In June 1969 the San Diego–Coronado Bridge had just
been completed across the bay. One night after dark Reeves,
myself, and a couple of other guys from our training class
swam from the amphibious base to the west end of the
bridge. We carried a can of yellow spray paint with us.
After reaching shore, we climbed up under the bridge onto
a catwalk that went underneath. We walked on the catwalk
until we came to one of the two tallest center piers that
supported the bridge. We then climbed down onto the pier
and crawled along the top of it until we were on the outside
of the bridge, facing the amphibious base. As we laid on
top of the concrete pier, we could look down on Navy ships

passing down below us. After lying there for a while, we decided it was time to use our paint. Climbing up onto the huge metal I-beam, we painted a big yellow 53 on the freshly painted blue bridge. Hell, we didn't know the phone company was planning to photograph San Diego from the amphibious base, looking through the new bridge at the city, and to use the photograph on the new edition of the San Diego phone book. After spending half the night under the bridge, we returned to the bay and swam back to the base. The next morning our class was standing tall as Mother Moy walked out of the instructors' shack, not looking too happy. The shit was about to hit the fan.

"It doesn't take a brain to figure out how that fifty-three got painted up there last night," he yelled. Then he informed us about the phone company. "I don't know who is responsible for it, but it had better be gone by tomorrow morning." The whole class got to hit the bay and bring up bottom samples in our hats throughout the morning, followed by one of the hardest PTs we had ever seen in training. After dark that night we swam back to the bridge, with blue paint this time. After climbing back out onto the bridge again, we painted over the 53. The blue paint we had didn't quite match the paint of the bridge, but it passed Mother Moy's inspection the following morning.

This bridge had a unique construction. The section in between the center's tallest piers had been built with watertight doors much like those of a ship. In case the bridge ever collapsed, the center section was supposed to float, enabling it to be towed out of the way of naval ship traffic. The inside of that section was well lighted, and the sound of the traffic above echoed throughout the chamber. A steel ladder led to a manhole cover in the center of the bridge. Climbing this ladder, one could lift the cover just enough to see, and peering out, could watch the traffic traveling in both directions. The bridge had five lanes for traffic, two westbound, two eastbound, and the center lane used for service vehicles and emergencies only.

About a week after we were out under the bridge, some trainees from Class 54 decided to go out there. As they

lifted the manhole cover up enough to look out, a bridge
service truck drove over them, straddling the hole with its
tires. Noticing the cover up, the service truck drove directly
to the toll booths on the Coronado side and reported it.
Thinking the bridge was being sabotaged, the Coronado
police and San Diego police were alerted. The San Diego
police started from their side while the Coronado police
started moving from their direction toward the center of the
bridge, on top and underneath on the catwalks. The Class
54 trainees were surrounded and held at gunpoint, then
escorted to the San Diego jail. During the middle of the
night Mother Moy was called to get his tadpoles out of jail.
Needless to say, the whole class paid for it the next day.
The personnel involved damn near were kicked out of training. Reeves and I realized how lucky we had been.

UDT/SEAL training consists of eighteen rigorous weeks.
The training is divided into three phases of six weeks. The
first phase of training is several weeks of very strenuous
physical and psychological conditioning. It takes a very
motivated individual with a positive attitude to complete
even the first phase of UDT/SEAL training, which weeds
out the weak and incompetent men and thins the training
class for the more special training of the next two phases.
Stress is applied throughout the training to measure the
ability of individuals to function under extreme hardship
and under combat conditions. One must demonstrate endurance, alertness, maturity, reliability, and teamwork to
successfully complete all the phases. A progressive buildup
of physical and psychological demands placed on the trainees, like calisthenics, ocean swims, rubber raft paddles, and
runs, all in limited times, test the individual to the limit.

The last week in first phase is called hell week, as I
mentioned above. That is just what it means, staying awake
for six days and nights doing evolutions while the UDT/
SEAL instructors rotate their duties to keep the trainees
moving and awake. This week particularly tests the trainees'
ability to function under extreme physical discomfort and
mental stress.

The second six-week phase of training teaches demolition

of special explosives above and underwater, beach terminology, beach reconnaissance, land warfare, rappeling from cliffs and helos, techniques of unconventional warfare, weapons, patrolling and ambushes with small units, and the fundamentals of UDT work. Although the training seems to be a little easier than the first six weeks, the necessity to function as a team under very stressful conditions is still present. From securing several pounds of explosives on underwater obstacles to swimming into a beach through thick kelp beds and heavy surf in the pitch-dark night for a beach recon, the physical and psychological demands are always present. But after hell week, anything seems easier.

The third six-week phase of training consists mostly of diving: being trained to use open circuit, semiclosed, and closed-circuit scuba gear. Open circuit is compressed air, semiclosed circuit consists of mixed gases (nitrogen and oxygen mixtures), and closed circuit is pure oxygen. As does phase two, this phase requires using the mind: performing day and night underwater compass swims, setting explosive charges on ships, bounce dives with decompressions, and diving physics.

In the final days of training the trainees must successfully complete a series of diving and battle problems utilizing all the skills taught during training, while working together as a team.

To qualify for UDT/SEAL training one must be between eighteen and thirty-one years of age, possess a General Competency Test score of 45 or more, be physically and psychologically qualified in accordance with Bureau of Medicine Manual Articles 15 through 30, possess basic integrity and loyalty, have a minimum of twenty-four months of obligated active service upon completion of UDT/SEAL training, and have performance evaluation marks that are indicative of an individual who works hard and is capable of self-discipline. It definitely takes a highly motivated individual.

By the time Class 53 finally made it to the diving phase of training, only twenty-two men out of the original seventy-eight were left. I had a hell of a time doing the diving

physics part of phase three. We received a dropback from
Class 52 that gave us a total of twenty-three men. In November 1969, on the graduating day of Class 53, there were
twenty men standing tall in their dress blues, fifteen of the
original class and five men from Class 52. Five of us out
of the twenty received orders to SEAL Team One, four men
received orders to Underwater Demolition Team 11, and
eleven men received their orders to Underwater Demolition
Team 13.

I had successfully completed UDT/SEAL training. Now
that I had become a SEAL, my training started all over
again. Jump school, SERE (Survival, Evasion, Resistance,
and Escape) school, JEST (Jungle Escape Survival Training)
school, and training day after day with my newly-formed
platoon. After arriving at the SEAL compound in Coronado
ready for duty, the new SEALs are assigned into newly
formed platoons. From that day on the SEAL training continues. This training together lasts up to nine months before
the platoon is actually deployed to Vietnam. The new members of a SEAL platoon must successfully complete SERE
school, JEST school, parachute training, and cadre training
before being deployed overseas. Many hours are spent patrolling together, sitting on ambushes together, and in various other types of training to get to know each other's
habits and how each man performs as a SEAL platoon
member. The world's toughest military training was behind
me. I was a member of the most elite unit in any military
service in the world.

CHAPTER EIGHTEEN

It was now 17 August 1970. At times I thought I was going to be in Nam forever. I stood in the briefing room, back out of second squad's way as they had their next operations briefing. The weather was hot and humid outside, the only relief a jump into the Bassac River. Mr. Walsh briefed his men on their late evening's ambush on Dung Island. They were to use the light on this op as first squad was using the medium early the next morning. Second squad was to insert on the north side of Dung Island, patrol inland, and set up an ambush on a small canal. They were to return from their mission as my squad was departing on ours. The platoon was short-handed because Grimes and Strausbaugh were in Hawaii and LePage had been sent back to the States. By rotating the men in our platoon, we were able to continue to operate at the same pace. Some of us were operating back to back, going out with first squad, and upon returning to camp, going back out with second squad.

About 2200 hours second squad had geared up and boarded the light. After helping them get ready before they left on their op, I turned out the lights and returned to my rack. I could hear the light fade off in the distance, heading upriver. It was good to have some peace and quiet after all the commotion of second squad gearing up. Grenades dropping to the floor, Baylett's M-60 ammo being dragged around, Baylett tripping over his M-60, Baylett—damn, that guy was noisy. He was the noisiest SEAL I had ever known, at least while he was gearing up for an op.

I was soon fast asleep, best night's sleep I'd had in a long time. A few hours later, still sleeping, I was not aware of the five heavily armed men as they entered our camp from the river. Quickly covering the ground from the river to our hootch, they quietly entered as I slept. Slowly they approached my rack, making sure I didn't hear them. As soon as they grabbed me, my eyes snapped open. I tried to fight them off but they held me tight as they lifted me out of my rack. Fuck, my heart was beating, my capillaries were pumped full. Twisting and squirming, I continued to try to free myself as they carried me out of the hootch and into the dark. At first I thought it was a dream, but as they carried me closer and closer to the river, I knew it wasn't. I twisted and turned, then, without warning, I was airborne. Without time to catch a breath, I was suddenly submerged in the muddy Bassac. As I tried to fight my way to the surface, everything was dark. It was hard to tell which way was up. As I finally surfaced, second squad was standing on the bank laughing and yelling, "Happy Birthday, Young." Fuckin' Weber, I thought. He was the only one that knew my birthday was August eighteenth. The light had developed engine problems before they inserted, and their operation was aborted. It took them half the night just to return to camp, arriving about 0100.

Within two hours first squad was on its way to the western end of Dung Island. Mr. Q, Bruce, Doc, Panella, Reeves, and I were to set up an ambush in a hootch that two high-level Vietcong were supposed to have a political meeting in. Our objective was to capture the two if conditions permitted, otherwise to eliminate them and their bodyguards. From our intelligence we knew exactly the hootch and the approximate time the enemy was supposed to be there. Before first light we were to take control of the hootch and its occupants, long before Charlie was to arrive.

Our medium was on step toward Dung Island's western end, 0300 in the morning. We turned into Dung Island on the canal that led to the intersection of three other canals. As we approached the intersection, the medium slowed to just above idle, then we turned, taking the left canal. We had used this intersection several times before on successful ambushes against Vietcong. Ti Ti Canal was to the right,

UDT/SEAL Training Class 53, Basic Underwater Demolition
School, November 1969. Class 53 began with 78 men. Bottom
row, left: Darryl Young. Top row, third from left: Tim Reeves.
Middle row, seventh from left: Ron Weber.

Second squad, Juliett Platoon, 1970. Top, from left: Lloyd "Doc" Schrier, Tim Reeves, Ron Weber, Nicolas Walsh, Peter Panella. Bottom: Barry Strausbaugh. Walsh is wearing Levi's jeans.

Lloyd Schrier

SEAL camp. Long Phu River at bottom, Bassac River at right, village of Ap Vinh Hung to left of camp. Buildings on left side of camp were under construction by Seabees. Barge in Long Phu River was used by Seabees to haul sand and gravel.

SEAL camp near Long Phu, June 1970. SEAL hootch in middle with door open. South Vietnamese patrol boats at left; Dung Island across the river.

Tim Reeves

Sitter, Walsh, Shannon, and Bruce assembling portable tents for a briefing hootch at the SEAL camp.

Vietnamese sampan, Dung Island, September 1970. Are these people Viet Cong? Nipa palms line the far shore.

Time Reeves

Darryl Young, 1970. Left: Stoner with box magazine and extended cocking handle. Right: modified M-60 with cut-back barrel, bi-pod and sights removed, helo door gunner's buttstock.

Darryl Young

OV-10 Bronco (Black Pony), Juliett Platoon's air support for most operations on Dung Island, at Binh Thuy, 1970.

Darryl Young

Light SEAL support craft. On stern is a .50-caliber machine gun mount, with .50-caliber ammunition to left; engines have soundproof covers. Radar mount and compass bubble can be seen in midsection.

Medium SEAL support craft with catamaran-type hull. On sides are covered .50-caliber machine guns; on bow, a hanging net used for extractions. South Vietnamese patrol boats are anchored in background.   Darryl Young

Darryl Young

6,000-round-per-minute General Electric minigun mounted on the stern of medium SEAL support craft. The minigun has flash suppressors on all muzzles and a flexible ammo guide.

Darryl Young

Seal toys. Top: LAW. Second row: M-79 rounds, incendiary, luminous marking, tcargas, yellow smoke and fragmentation grenades, emergency day and night signal flare. Third row: fluorescent paint spray can, claymore. Bottom: illumination parachute flare.

Darryl Young

Tim Reeves ready for a
night operation, August
1970. Blond hair could
be a problem
sometimes.

Tim Reeves

Nicolas Walsh

Darryl Young (with
bananas) and Bill Bruce
returning to SEAL camp
from an operation on
Dung Island, 1970.

Patrolling toward second POW compound through canal, September 1970.

Tim Reeves

American POW retaining area, September 1970. A nipa palm mat covers the floor; a wooden bowl, canteen, and canteen cup sit next to pole.

SEALs waiting for
extraction helicopters
with wounded South
Vietnamese man
liberated from POW
camp, September 1970.

Tim Reeves

View from chest-deep in a canal into front entrance of Viet Cong
commandant's living quarters, where the short wave
radio was found. September 1970.

Tim Reeves

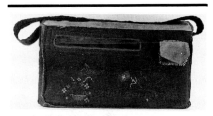

Shortwave radio with
cover, captured on
Dung Island. Cover is
embroidered with
birds, flowers,
Vietnamese writing, a Viet Cong flag, and a hammer and sickle.
Captured in an operation that also netted the SEALs flags,
uniforms, another radio, and sewing machines.

UDT compound, Da Nang, September 1970. From left: Roger
Banfield, Ron Weber, Lucas Palma, Tim Reeves. The next day
Palma was KIA.

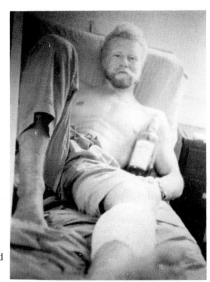

Steve Grimes with shrapnel wound and painkiller at Third Field Hospital, Binh Thuy, October 1970.

Tim Reeves

Walter Baylett in Viet Cong attire with AK-47; Tim Reeves at right. October 1970.

Tim Reeves

Darryl Young

Nicolas Walsh with Viet Cong suspect captured on Dung Island.

Left: Walter Baylett with Stoner and binoculars. Right: LTJG
Joseph Quincannon with M-16, wearing Levi's jeans, belt knife,
and vest for carrying M-16 magazines.

SEAL training camp for South Vietnamese LDDNs, Cam Ranh Bay, 1970. Trainees are grouped below flags; roofs are sandbagged.

Darryl Young surfing in Cam Ranh Bay, December, 1970.   Tim Reeves

Darryl Young

Children from Ap Vinh Hung village, 1970. Some show peace signs; others the Vietnamese equivalent of a raised middle finger. Tu Lin is the small girl at middle bottom of picture.

back behind us as we moved up the canal the first time. We made a couple of fake insertions. The canal narrowed steadily the farther up it we went, until the boat turned to starboard for our final insertion. As soon as the medium came to a stop, everyone involved went over the bow very quietly and set up a perimeter. The boat headed back down the canal to wait for the signal to recover us.

From studying the maps earlier, I knew the nipa-palm jungle was only about fifty meters wide there, with a dike and then a large banana grove beyond. Several hootches were aligned parallel to the dike which kept the high tides from flooding the bananas. By the density of the nipa palm, you would never know it was just a fifty-meter strip along the canal. Knee-deep mud and water were our footing until we reached the dike. We lay low, listening for signs of enemy movement. The jungle sounds reappeared as we lay there. We waited longer. It occurred to me that I could think of ten or twelve other places I would rather be on my birthday.

Time to patrol. We start. I'm tense. My mind is working a mile a minute. At any jungle sound, normal or not, I hold my breath to help me listen better. I crouch low in the mud and nipa palm; I don't move. Again we move, again we stop, it's taking us hours to patrol fifty meters. Maybe it's fifty minutes. I'm holding my breath, taking in a big listen instead. It helps me hear better. My heart is beating. Finally we reach the dike. Hundreds of fuckin' mosquitoes have followed me from our insertion point, some riding on my cammoed face and hands, some hovering close by, waiting for their turn. I strain my eyes to see through the dark behind us. The sound of water filling in our footprints is all I hear, except for the fuckin' mosquitoes and the normal jungle sounds. Reeves is with me. That, along with our Stoners, gives me a secure feeling. They're off safe, ready to kill to avoid being killed. The whole squad is crouched behind the dike on the canal side in the "ready to get the fuck out of here if we have to" position. The hootches are visible to us; we are not to them. The smell of *nuoc mam* filters through the air, reaching my nose. I've smelled better things to eat. Up till now, no pungi pits or booby traps.

We wait, listen, watch the hootches. It looks clear, so the signal is given to move in quietly. Mr. Q and Bruce go first, the rest of us cover them. They enter the hootch we wanted without knocking. All is silent inside. Soon the hootch is secure. The signal from Mr. Q for the rest of us to enter the hootch is given. Papasan and mamasan are on the dirt floor, hands bound, mouths gagged. The same with their two baby sons, except only their mouths are taped. Everyone in our element takes up positions inside the hootch. Mine is to the right of the front door, the only door, with a good field of view through the cracks in it. I can see the dike and jungle beyond, the way we came in. We are ready for Charlie now. Hurry up and wait.

Inside the hootch is a mud and log bunker. The smell of mosquito coil reeks in the air. The residents are placed in their bunker with instructions to be quiet. Reeves is covering the far corner of the hootch, looking through the cracks in the nipa-palm wall. He's alert, he's excited, he's not scared. A dog barks in the distance, a pig snorts beside the hootch, the normal jungle sounds are everpresent. Just being on Dung Island keeps me awake. No one talks, everyone listens, everyone waits. At times I felt like a criminal running around the island with a machine gun. At times I felt guilty for what I was doing. Just a little more than a year ago I was in high school. That was hard to believe.

Mr. Q was on the left side of the door next to me. Everyone had a position inside the hootch so they could look at the perimeter through the cracks in the walls. The Vietnamese squatted in the back of the bunker. Outside, it was getting light; Charlie should be coming soon. Roosters were crowing in the background, and a hundred meters away, from the hootch closest to this one, sounds of people stirring could be heard. The pig behind the hootch was rooting around and rubbing his side against a banana tree.

We could hear voices now, toward the other hootch. They sounded normal, as if they knew nothing of our presence. As I looked through the crack in the door, I saw a young girl walking on the dike trail, coming in our direction. I quickly signaled Mr. Q and the others. She turned toward our hootch from the dike and walked straight toward the nipa-palm door. She was saying something in Vietnamese as she pushed the door open and entered the hootch. Quickly grabbing her, I put my hand over her mouth while Mr. Q handcuffed her. She was placed in the bunker with the other Vietnamese. The mosquito coil continued to burn.

About twenty minutes later a small boy came down the dike from the same direction. I alerted Mr. Q again as he too turned toward our hootch, and upon entering received the same treatment. Tears ran down the kids' faces as they crouched to the back of the bunker. I turned from staring out the cracks for a moment to look back at Reeves. He was looking at the kids and, with both hands, pretending to pull off one of his thumbs while making weird faces. His face already looked weird with the cammo paint on it. The kids seemed occupied with Reeves's clowning around, which stopped them from crying and making noise. I looked back out through the cracks as Reeves continued to entertain the Vietnamese kids. This would have been a good training aid in cadre training back in the States, I thought.

As the kids sat quietly in the bunker, still staring at Reeves's green face and wondering what it was he was doing to his thumb, I spotted an older girl walking down the dike trail in our direction. I signaled Mr. Q again, this time shaking my head in disbelief. She turned toward the hootch. She came right through the door, as the others had. She ended up staring at Reeves's green face also, from the back of the bunker. Mr. Q leaned over to me and whispered, "Hey, Young, they're all coming to your birthday party." Looking back at Mr. Q, I gave him a big grin and whispered, "Maybe Charlie sent these kids here to check out the hootch for them." All we could do was wait and see.

About a half hour went by when I noticed mamasan coming in our direction, probably looking for her kids. She too walked right through the door and was immediately apprehended. We decided to do a field interrogation on her and the other two adults, in case Charlie was setting us up.

As the grown-ups were being interrogated, the kids started to get nervous again. Reeves was constantly trying to entertain the little fuckers to keep them quiet, but he was running out of faces to make. We received no information from the older Vietnamese, so decided to start our extraction, taking papasan with us for further interrogation.

After checking the perimeter outside the hootch carefully, security was set up to cover Reeves and me. We reached the dike with no problems and checked out the area beyond. Reeves and I covered the rest of the squad until we all regrouped in the nipa palm. The medium was notified of our extraction as we patrolled back toward the canal. After reaching the canal, a perimeter was again set up while we waited for the medium to reach our position. Since we had a secure extraction site, the bow of the medium pulled up into the nipa palm. Within seconds we were all on board and headed back to camp. As the medium got on step out of the canal and into the Bassac, I thought about the possibilities of Charlie sending the kids into the hootch first. Charlie wasn't dumb at all. It wouldn't be the first time he used kids to do his dirty work.

When we finally reached camp, the prisoner was escorted directly to our briefing hootch. During the interrogation, the Vietnamese papasan began to open up to us. We told him he would probably never see his family again unless he told us about the Vietcong activities in his area. Begging for his freedom, he told us about the Vietcong having meetings in his hootch in the past and that one of those meetings was to be held the next morning. This Vietnamese man was nothing but a banana grower, but Charlie used his hootch at times, with him having no control over them. He was worried about his wife and kids, and we assured him they would be all right. After the interrogation was completed, a CIA officer in Soc Trang was notified of our prisoner. He drove to our camp to pick him up for further interrogation back in Soc Trang. Mr. Q suggested we hit the same hootch early the next morning by inserting from the air, using an Army slick.

You just couldn't call Joe Blow and ask for a helo. All

tactical helo requests were submitted to the Tactical Helo Support Facility in Binh Thuy. This request had to be submitted by 1200 hours the day prior to the scheduled operation in the following format:

a. Number and type of helicopters required.
b. Person to report to, meaning Mr. Q, include phone number, frequency, and call sign.
c. The time period required.
d. Who will provide gunship cover, Navy Seawolfs or Army gunships?
e. Command control, from the ground, embarked, Seawolf, etc.
f. Control headquarters, normally appropriate NOC.
g. Staged from:
h. Briefing on operation, on arrival.
i. Control frequency and call sign.
j. Size of unit to be lifted.
k. Center of mass of operation, using a six-digit coordinate.
l. Other information, predark reconn, insert after dark, standby on location, extract on call, and rehearsal if required. etc.

Mr. Q's job wasn't easy. The same type of information would be required for Seawolfs or Army gunships flying cover, which happened mostly on the bigger operations.

While Mr. Q worked on the night's briefing, I checked over my gear for the next morning's operation. While I was in our hootch inspecting my gear, Weber informed me that a mike boat, a flat-bottomed landing craft, was coming down the river. This boat was designed to carry troops and supplies. Since most of the ship traffic was on the north side of Dung Island, because the Bassac River was deeper and wider on that side, seeing anything other than our own boats, Vietnamese sampans, or an occasional plane or helo flying over once in a while, was rare. Weber and I walked down to the river as the mike boat maneuvered into shore and dropped its ramp to unload supplies for the Seabees. Grimes and Strausbaugh had caught a ride back to our camp on the boat after their R&R. It was good to see them again.

The boat brought everything from canned food to corrugated metal for the buildings the Seabees were assembling. As they walked toward our hootch, I told Grimes and Strausbaugh they hadn't missed anything since they left. I noticed large South Vietnamese and American flags on board the boat and asked one of the mike-boat sailors if he wanted to trade for them. He asked me what I had to trade, and I offered him a K-bar. Personally, I liked a knife half the size, as they were less weight and the same job could be accomplished with the smaller one. SEALs always had extra K-bars lying around, and everyone else usually wanted one, so they made excellent trading stock. The sailor and I made the deal, and before long the mike boat was unloaded, the ramp was raised, and it backed out into the muddy Bassac. As the mike boat turned upstream, the diesel engines roared and the flat bow slapped against the muddy water. I watched them go upstream and thought about what good duty those guys had. Cruising up and down the major rivers and canals, dropping off and picking up supplies at the different bases and outposts, with a lot of free time on hand.

The mike boats were very slow, taking hours to get to and from their points of service. Armed with little more than M-16 rifles, they stayed out in the middle of the major rivers and canals to avoid an ambush or a B-40 rocket. Mike boats came in different sizes and could haul anything from tanks to troops. With their flat bottoms—they were designed for use in the naval amphibious forces—they could maneuver right up to the beach to unload or load whatever they carried. We used mike boats in UDT/SEAL training for bounce dives in the Pacific Ocean. Those days were called "easy days" in training because of the amount of time it took to travel from the amphibious base, out San Diego Bay to the ocean where it was deep enough for the particular dive, and back to the base again. Travel time took up the major part of the day for a half-hour dive. That didn't bother me at all, but it was a good idea to take along a magazine and a box lunch. It was also a good time to catch some zzz's.

Seals used a modified mike boat called a Heavy Seal Support Craft (HSSC). It was slow, but its armament was impressive. Sections of tubular steel were welded a few inches apart and away from the sides, back, front, and steering cabin to make it invulnerable to rocket attack. A B-40 rocket has a shaped-charge effect on contact, but detonation on the tubular steel—a few inches away from the boat itself—broke up the shaped-charge effect. Equipped with a 57mm recoilless, miniguns, .50-calibers, and M-60, the HSSC could go anywhere there was enough water to float it and turn it around. But because it was diesel powered, it was much noisier than our gasoline lights and mediums.

Grimes and Strausbaugh drove us nuts telling us about all the round-eyed women in Hawaii. As they talked they had the undivided attention of our platoon and half the Seabees. It had been a long time since any of us had seen a round-eye. Weber and I had talked about going to Hawaii when our time came for R&R; we'd had a pretty good time there on our way to Vietnam. But our turn for R&R wouldn't come until about November fifth. The men of our platoon usually took R&R in pairs, although they didn't have to go to the same place; one man could go to Hawaii while the other man went to Australia.

That didn't have anything to do with the helo Mr. Q requested for the next day's operation. After the Vietnamese we brought back that morning had been interrogated in Soc Trang, the CIA officer contacted Mr. Q to confirm the political meeting of the Viet Cong the next morning. The helo had already been requested, and our intelligence had been confirmed and double-checked. Early the next morning we were to drop in and pay Charlie a visit. I didn't care for helo operations in-country. Maybe it had something to do with the five SEALs getting killed the day before I arrived in Nam. With the noise of the helo and early morning daylight combo, everyone on the ground would know we were coming. Another objection I had was the fact that we had been in the hootch and brought back the papasan who lived there. Charlie was sure to know about that and not show up.

A helicopter makes a pretty good target, and even Charlie, as bad a shot as he was, could hit one if he tried. Back in the States I enjoyed parachuting, playing war games in a simulated combat mission, and rapeling from a helo. After all, Charlie wasn't shooting at us in the States. Traveling around Nam in a helo was the best way to travel if you were not operating. And, I have to admit, they were great for getting us the hell out of a sticky situation.

The only LZ (landing zone) close to the hootch was a small rice paddy seventy meters to the north, but the Army slick couldn't land in an LZ that small in a wind ten knots or more. Because of this, an alternate LZ was located 200 meters to the northwest, also in a rice paddy. We would not use that LZ unless we absolutely had to, because by the time we landed and patrolled to the hootch, Charlie would be long gone. It would do for an alternate extraction LZ, though.

After the late-night briefing, Mr. Q, Doc, Grimes, Panella, Bruce, and I returned to our hootch for the night. I didn't get much sleep. Thinking of the early morning's op by helo occupied my mind as I tossed and turned.

At first light the helo circled our camp right on schedule. We were cammoed up and ready to go. A yellow smoke was thrown out downwind from the helo pad and at treetop level over the Vietnamese cemetery; the olive-drab slick descended into our camp. With all involved on board, the big green target headed in the direction of Dung Island as the Phoenix program continued. I would be uneasy until my feet were back on the ground, even if it was on Dung Island.

Nose down, picking up speed, we proceeded up the Bassac River, circled around the west end of Dung Island and hit our enemy from the opposite side. At jungle-canopy level, we all cocked our weapons as the chopper rapidly moved toward the LZ. As we landed, Vietcong were running in all directions, some carrying weapons. The six of us jumped to the ground and immediately set up security. The helo blades changed to a loud pitch as it lifted from our LZ.

Enemy small-arms fire started coming our way. Laying down a maximum rate of fire, we suppressed the enemy's fire and sent Charlie running, gaining fire superiority. Then we assaulted the hootch in an attempt to capture the two political officers before they split out the back way. As we approached the first hootch, three Vietcong, two of them carrying weapons, ran toward a mud and log bunker near the dike that held the Bassac water back. We opened up on them. One of the gooks fell to the ground with his weapon and another was wounded. With a little help from his friend, the wounded Vietcong was dragged into the bunker. Panella and I took cover, watching the bunker and surrounding area as Bruce and Grimes searched the first hootch. Doc and Mr. Q recovered the dead Vietcong's weapon and checked the body for documents while keeping their weapons trained on the bunker. Grimes and Mr. Q then circled around behind the bunker while the rest of us watched our perimeter. Nothing was found in the hootch. Grimes could hear the two gooks inside the bunker but couldn't persuade them to come out. Instead, the little fuckers fired their weapons at the bunker entrance, really pissing Grimes off. Grimes pleaded with them again to surrender, and again they answered him with small-arms fire. With Grimes on one side of the bunker entrance and Mr. Q on the other, Grimes pulled an M-3A2 concussion grenade from his H-harness. Mr. Q made eye contact with Grimes and nodded his head. As Mr. Q took cover, Grimes pulled the pin and tossed the grenade into the bunker, taking cover himself. After a short hesitation there was a muffled explosion and the mud roof of the bunker lifted up and collapsed on the two assholes inside.

Grimes returned to the bunker as smoke and steam drifted from what was left of it. Noticing a hand sticking out of the mud debris, Grimes grabbed it in an attempt to recover one of the Vietcong. He pulled on it, expecting a dead Vietcong to follow, but just an arm detached from the shoulder came out. About the same time, more enemy rounds started coming overhead in our direction. Charlie must have been reinforced after regrouping and was coming back. Doc was told to call the helo in for our extraction as we started to patrol in the direction of the LZ. As we passed the hootch, Mr. Q tossed an incendiary grenade into it. Moving away from the hootch swiftly, we set up a perimeter in the banana trees just outside the LZ. The hootch was already engulfed in flames as the chopper descended toward our position. Doc had thrown out a green smoke marking our position and the chopper pilot had identified it. As we returned Charlie's small-arms fire, suppressing it long enough for the helo to touch down, both door gunners on the helo were blazing away toward the treelines to help keep Charlie's heads down.

As I ran past the front of the chopper, I noticed the nervous look on the pilot's face. His eyes were open wide, staring at the burning hootch. He looked like he wanted to get out of there as bad as I did. With all on board, the helo lifted off and proceeded at treetop level in the direction of our camp. I looked down, firing my Stoner into the jungle canopy, and saw the hootch I had spent my birthday in collapse to the ground as the smoke swirled from the chopper blades behind us. We were back at camp within two minutes.

This operation took less than ten minutes on the ground. Being where and when we weren't expected resulted in eliminating a few more gooks, adding to our body count. We didn't capture any documents or prisoners, just one SKS 7.62mm semiautomatic carbine in poor condition, like most of Charlie's weapons. Leaving what was left of Charlie in the collapsed bunker would give his comrades something to do by digging them out.

After the informal debriefing, we stowed our gear and headed for the chow hall, still cammoed from the operation.

CHAPTER NINETEEN

Down in the Mekong Delta region the Vietcong was hard to reinforce and resupply. Not only was the terrain hostile, but he constantly had to watch out for South Vietnamese and American troops. For this reason, Charlie used just about anything and everything he could get his hands on to help him win the war. Besides pungi pits and setting booby traps of all kinds, the Vietcong carried a variety of weapons. The one he liked the most was the AK-47. The AK-47 (pronounced "Ah-Kah"—for Avtomat Kalashnikov—by the Vietnamese) 7.62 x 39mm submachine gun carried either Russian or Chinese markings, and could be fired full or semiauto. Designed by Kalashnikov in 1947, it fired the Russian M1943 7.62 (.30-caliber) intermediate round. It could fire a PS (ball), T-45 (tracer), BZ (armor-piercing incendiary), and Z (incendiary tracer) ammo. The East-bloc 7.62 cases could not be reloaded due to the poor manufacture of the cartridge case. Tracers were normally painted with a green or red tip, and the armor-piercing had a silver tip. The AK's effective range is 440 meters on semiauto and 300 meters on full auto. It is short and stubby and has a thirty-round banana-style magazine. The weapon carried its cleaning gear in the rear stock and under the barrel in the front. The main spring, bolt assembly, chamber, and bore are completely chromed, which means fewer jams and easier cleaning and also reduces rust and corrosion. With a low jam factor, and being able to take a lot of abuse, it was an ideal weapon for Charlie, given his living conditions. If he could get his hands on one. The three-position safety on the weapon was also a fire selector switch. Up, the weapon was

on safe; halfway down, it was on full auto; down, it fired
semiauto. The safety switch was hard to move and noisy
when it was moved, which was to our advantage. Since
there are no naturally occurring metallic sounds in the jungle, the sound of the safety might alert us to a possible
ambush. The AK-47 was available in four versions: wooden
stock one-piece receiver, metal stock one-piece receiver,
wooden stock two-piece receiver, and metal stock two-piece
receiver. The metal stock is the folding type. The chrome
barrel slows down the bullet, decreasing the bullet's knockdown efficiency; the M-16's steel bore allows the M-16's
bullet greater knockdown power because of the higher velocity of the 5.56 bullet.

At least, that's the theory. But it was hard for me to
believe since the .30-caliber bullet weighs much more than
the .22-caliber bullet. I would rather sit in a warm jail back
in the States than pack the M-16 in combat. Even though
I was issued an M-16, I had never carried it on a combat
mission in Nam and I never planned to. You could make
mine the AK-47. The AK is very accurate for a submachine
gun, and could group six inches at a hundred meters in the
semiauto firing mode. This accuracy was accredited to its
firing from the closed-bolt position. In Nam the AK-47 was
very well distributed around the country and was dreaded
by all the allied forces. It was gas-operated and selective
firing, and weighed 10.58 pounds loaded. It is 34.25 inches
long. Muzzle velocity reached 2329 feet per second, while
the rate of fire was 600 rounds per minute. SEALs used the
AK-47 quite often on clandestine operations. This weapon
was called different names in different countries, AK-47
being Russian, Model 58 being Czech, Type 56 being
Chinese Communist, and A-KA 56 being North Vietnamese.

Back in Coronado there was a foreign weapons board
located in the SEAL armory, and all SEALs were well-
acquainted with the small arms likely to be found in Southeast Asia (and the rest of the world, as far as that goes).
We knew the weapons inside and out and could use them
reliably anywhere, any time, as long as we had the am-

munition for them. Besides the AK-47, the most dreaded weapon we faced in our operating area was the B-40 rocket, because our aluminum-hulled river craft were very vulnerable to them. The Vietcong had been known to run trip wires across a canal to a B-40, using them for a booby trap for our boats to trip. One rocket could put a boat and its crew out of action permanently.

One of my favorite parts of UDT/SEAL training, besides the swimming, was working with the weapons. Even before UDT/SEAL training, while I was in boot camp Company 156, I scored 153 points out of a possible 180 firing the M-1 Garand for my first time. I scored highest in my company and sixth overall in the battalion. That wasn't bad for the first time having an M-1 Garand in my hands, but I'm sure glad I didn't have to pack that heavy piece in-country.

Navy boot camp had very little small-arms training, that's one reason I wanted to join the Underwater Demolition Teams. After I became a SEAL, I worked in our armory. There were all kinds of expensive toys to work with, and I was highly motivated to get to Nam and try them out on real live targets. I had a completely different perspective of this after my first live human target shot twice at me before I laid him to rest. Statistics proved that a Navy man—even a SEAL—had a better chance of surviving a tour to Vietnam. Most SEAL casualties in-country were accidental, and very few SEALs were killed in combat. A group of SEALs had been killed and some of them wounded in their own hootch because one of them had been fucking with a captured Vietcong mortar round, a very unfortunate mistake. And there were the five who crashed and burned on the helo ride on the way to Saigon for a good time.

I decided to forget about that. With four more months to spend in-country, I still felt safer with three other SEALs deep in enemy territory without a steel helmet on my head or a flak jacket strapped to my body. SEALs had their shit together and knew what they were doing and where they were going, not like a lot of the ground-pounders that were in-country waiting for their places on the KIA list.

* * *

The date, 30 August 1970. The Vietnam War continued. Still no haircuts since we left the States. It didn't bother most of our platoon, and it was the last thing I was going to suggest. We had several successful ambushes and body snatches in the last few days. I was getting used to Nam, used to the flies, the mosquitoes, the bug bites, the mud, my hootch, the food, my rack, our shitter, the Bassac, the Seabees, the weather, the changing tides, the rain, the heat, the sweat, my cammoed face, getting shot at, the good pot, the rats. I wasn't getting used to some of the gooks, the officer-in-charge of the Seabees, the wasted taxpayers' dollars, the metal buildings being built for the Vietnamese, the Vietnamese running from the Cong and leaving their weapons for Charlie to use against us, the gook rip-offs, and dealing with death on a daily basis.

Finally, September first, a well-needed break, a payday, a trip to Binh Thuy. I enjoyed a peaceful ride up the Bassac River on the medium. Even Weber went along this time. It was raining like hell as the medium backed away from our dock into the river far enough to avoid Charlie's "near, effective fire" from the shoreline. Northwest of Dung Island the river channel opened up to nearly 3000 meters wide in places. There were endless large and small islands in the river channel on the way to Binh Thuy. Some were just sandbars, others had hootches, rice paddies, and bananas. Some had nothing but triple-canopy jungle. Where the larger islands were, the river channel narrowed. As the islands dropped back behind us, the channel would open up wide again. On the south shore thick, dark green jungle lined the banks in places, while the muddy water gave way to rice and large cumulus clouds in others. Small and large canals entered the Bassac in several places on the south shore, some natural, most man-made. We weaved in and out of Vietnamese fishing nets strung way out into the river on long poles stuck in the muddy bottom. Vietnamese in sampans waited for the low tide so they could reap their day's catch from the nets. Leaving Quan Long Phu District, we entered Quan Ke Sach District; it all looked the same. The channel narrowed again, maybe to 400 meters wide on our side of Cong Dien Island. Finally, the rain stopped, but it wouldn't be long before the next cloud emptied on us again. It was a cool day, by Vietnam standards. Sandbars appeared on the downstream side of most of the islands with a one- to four-fathom-deep channel, it all depended on the South China Seas tides. Large and small nipa-palm hootches lined the south shore, which was more heavily populated where the canals entered the Bassac.

I took my 8mm movie camera and my 35mm camera out of their carrying case and photographed the treeline and hootches along the south shore. Standing on the stern of the medium, I took a picture looking forward over the canvas top of our boat, with Reeves driving and the Bassac River out in front of us. Then it began to rain again, so I put my movie camera away. It was hard to believe I was in a war zone, until I looked into the nipa palm along shore. That reminded me of all the insertions. As we continued north-west on step, our boat weaved in and out among the sampans moving in both directions and across the river. I wondered how many VC were slipping through the South Vietnamese checkpoints at the intersections of major canals by using phony papers identifying them as South Vietnamese. It was mandatory that every person in South Vietnam carry iden-tification and present it upon request to any authorized South Vietnamese or American.

Main channel for a ways, then island, main channel, island, all the way to Binh Thuy. Some of the smaller islands had mud dikes built around their entire length to keep out the high tides and let only irrigation water enter. Some of the islands were nothing but mangrove swamps. All the islands were long and thin, some much larger than others. It was easy to tell the difference between the natural and man-made canals. The natural canals meandered, and the man-made were built straight, like a large ditch, through the countryside. All the man-made canals were made by human labor, some carved out hundreds of years ago. Where in the United States we have county roads, in Vietnam there is a district canal. Down in IV Corps, everything not built up above the tidal high-water line was wet, it was a countryside formed by thousands of years of Mekong River mud and sand deposits. A real paradise, except for the smell of pollution and the fuckin' war. Each changing tide took some of that away. If it weren't for the mosquitoes and the Vietcong, the islands would have been a neat place to visit for a while, perhaps to do a little fishing. Unfortunately, that was not possible without a Stoner and 550 rounds of ammo.

The land was rich with plants and animal life of all kinds. Even though I don't care much for insects, I will have to admit some of them were interesting. The fireflies, the dragonflies, and even some of the enormous beetles didn't bother me, but some of the things that crawled over us on ambushes made me wish I was at the North Pole, a bug-free environment. Vietnam was an interesting place, but at times it was hard to enjoy, particularly when lying in the mud while trying to gain fire superiority. When that happened, I usually wished I was someplace else, not smelling the burned gunpowder, theirs and ours, and the Bassac mud one inch away from my face. In Vietnam, even in the most pacified area, a man wasn't safe. Didn't matter if you were a cook, truck driver, or a SEAL.

Two Seawolf helicopters buzzed over our heads towards Binh Thuy, breaking me away from my thoughts, reminding me I was really in Nam. As they moved upstream away from us, I could see daylight through their empty rocket pods. Maybe they had been used for air support for another SEAL platoon operating south of us. There were never more than 200 SEALS or UDT personnel in-country at any one time. There weren't many more SEALs and UDT personnel than that, period. Seawolfs and Army gunships could place their rockets to within twenty meters of our position while engaged in a dick-dragger with Charlie. It would have had to be a dick-dragger, or they would never have been called upon for help. The fewer people involved in a SEAL operation, the better, in most cases. But when they were needed, getting them involved saved many a SEAL's life.

The two Seawolfs were out of our sight, upriver, in seconds. Rong Island was to our right by then, a 4000-by-300 meter island strung out in the center of the Bassac. This island was mainly planted in rice, with a few jungle areas scattered on it. Then the boat channel closed to 800 meters.

Binh Thuy was located in Tinh Ba Xuyen Province, the same province Long Phu District was located in. The center of the main channel of the Bassac was the stateline between Tinh Vinh Binh Province and Tinh Ba Xuyen Province. The main channel was wider on the sides of the island, that was where the line was, separating the different islands into different states. Most often, the main channel was situated on the north side of the islands, giving Tinh Ba Xuyen Province control over most of them on the river.

The sun finally came out, so I took off my cammo top and my reversible tee-shirt (the outside navy-blue and the inside yellow-gold; it could be used for signaling if necessary). I climbed up onto the canvas top of the boat, between the bows, and used it as a hammock, lying in the warm Vietnamese sun. The light bouncing of the medium, hitting the wakes of Vietnamese sampans, along with the sun and several miles to go, put me to sleep. I was awakened as the throttle was pushed forward and the medium settled down into the water when we turned left into the docks of the Naval Support Facility in Binh Thuy. The river went on.

The smell of fiberglass resin filled the air. A couple of PBRs up on shore, sitting outside the fiberglass repair shop, looked like olive-drab Swiss cheese. Charlie had done a number on the boats, and we wondered what had happened to the crew. With the bow line in his hand, Mr. Walsh jumped from our boat to an empty spot on the dock big enough for the medium. Everyone on board made damn sure anything of any value was taken off the boat and stored at the SEAL hut. If we didn't, it was sure not to be there when we got back.

Bruce and I walked over to the PBRs for a better look. One of them looked beyond repair and had to have been lifted out of the jungle by helo. It had been stripped of all usable gear and weapons by Charlie or the Americans. We walked through the large sliding doors of the repair shop and saw another PBR with fresh, dry unpainted resin on a

new .50-caliber gun tub on the bow. Bruce climbed inside
the gun tub and I took his picture. There wasn't anyone
around but us inside the shop. The light fixtures and cobwebs
overhead attached to the metal rafters had fiberglass resin
dust on them from the sanding of fiberglass. So did everything else. The SEAL Quonset hut wasn't far away, maybe
a hundred meters, out the side door of the repair shop and
up and across the street a few buildings toward the main
gate. The repair shop was right by the Bassac River, close
to our docks, and had a wide boat ramp for pulling the
damaged boats out of the water. Needless to say, security
was tight inside the compound. High Cyclone fences with
barbed wire on top surrounded the compound on three sides,
with the river on the north. Sandbag bunkers lined the perimeter and along the river, with sentries on duty at all
hours. Right out the main gate and across a busy Vietnamese
highway was the Binh Thuy Air Force Base.

We walked on over to the SEAL Quonset hut to pick up
our pay vouchers. Hackman, the SEAL administrative personnel, had them waiting for us when we arrived. Hackman
was a second-class petty officer with a yeoman rate; he was
not a SEAL, he just did our paperwork and was attached
to SEAL Team One. He was a wizard at paperwork. "Don't
worry, Hackman will take care of it," was the saying. And
that was true, Hackman would take care of it; he knew the
ins and outs of the military system. He hadn't gone through
UDT/SEAL training, but he sure thought like a SEAL when
it came to paperwork. Everyone got along with him real
fine—of course, we had no choice if we didn't want him
fucking with our paychecks. His boots always needed shining, his greens were always baggy, and there was always
a smile on his face. The only time I ever saw him pissed
off is when the air conditioner broke down in the Quonset
hut.

After going across the street to Disbursing, I drew what
money I thought I would need and left the rest on the books.
Several of us left the Naval Support Facility and crossed
the highway to eat at the chow hall on the Air Force Base,
where they had a real nice chow hall with a large variety

of food. While eating lunch, Bruce talked about a place in Can Tho where he used to go on his previous tour to Nam, saying something about a steambath. Reeves, Panella, Baylett, Bruce, and I decided to check it out later. After eating, we stuffed our pockets with a little something for later, knowing we wouldn't make it back for evening chow. Walking off the Air Force Base, all five of us started hitchhiking toward Can Tho. With all the military traffic, we soon caught a ride with a six-by. I kept an eye on the gooks along the sides of the road; I didn't trust any of them and wasn't going to let any kids get away with the shit they pulled the last time I was in Can Tho.

We soon arrived at Can Tho and climbed down off the six-by. Everyone followed Bruce as he made his way through the busy streets toward our objective. Along one of Can Tho's main streets, he went through a narrow door into a rundown lobby. Several GIs sat around waiting for friends. We paid a mamasan the money she requested and got a towel in exchange, then followed a little gook who was wearing a white tank top, polyester slacks, and a pair of thongs. He led us to the back of the building. He should have been wearing an ARVN uniform and been fighting for his country. Checking the place out, I noticed small booths with curtain doors. Another older mamasan was scrubbing the stained white-tile floor, paying no attention to the GIs walking around her.

Taking off our clothes, we entered a steam room to sit around and sweat for a while. I worried about my clothes the whole time. After sitting there for some time, we went up some stairs and entered a small cubicle each. Each cubicle had a chair, a massage table, and a curtain door. A fan rotated beneath the ceiling. I set my clothes down on the chair and lay on the table with my towel over me. Reeves, Baylett, Panella, and Bruce were in cubicles down the hallway from me. A Vietnamese woman came into the room and started rubbing me down. I didn't trust her at first, but her massaging my shoulders felt pretty good. As she was just about done she said, "You want number-one blow job, you want Miss Quan." I had figured that would be coming up sooner or later. I had to pay a little extra money for "the special." After everyone was finished and had gathered in the lobby, we left the place and walked down the street. My body felt like it had been chased off of Dung Island—no energy. What a morale booster. In the days to follow, the massage parlor would become a favorite place for most of the members of our platoon.

We made it back to the boat-repair facility in Binh Thuy before evening curfew. We found the barracks we usually stayed in and discovered that new mattresses and fans had replaced the ones we had taken. Not everyone in our platoon had nice mattresses yet, so next morning we took care of that problem. Three more mattresses and two more fans were borrowed. By then we had enough fans to keep the whole hootch cool. On the way to the medium, we stumbled across some MSSC engine parts and a complete steering column for Baylett's skimmer. Imagine that, just lying there! So we brought that stuff too.

After regrouping and boarding the medium, we got on step downriver in the direction of Coastal Group 36, Advance Team 71. The closer our boat got to Dung Island, the more the war and killing came back into my mind. A break to Binh Thuy once every two weeks was mandatory for me now, especially after the morale booster steam-and-cream in Can Tho. Even with all the nice equipment and good friends to operate with, my government was going to pay hell in getting me to come back to Nam. I surely didn't think my life was worth losing for some of these slant-eyed bastards. We arrived back at camp in time for lunch and to kick the Seabees' ass in a game of football. Yes, in the mud.

CHAPTER TWENTY

After the game, first squad gathered in the briefing hootch for details on our early morning operation. Fresh intel brought downriver with Mr. Q from Binh Thuy stated that a high-ranking Vietcong organizer lived in a hootch near the east end of Dung Island, inland from the Rach Trang Canal. The Rach Trang Canal meandered north from Ti Ti Canal through 3000 meters of thick mangrove swamp and past a small hamlet called Xom Rach Trang. The canal was small, but we would use the light on the operation, as it had a tighter turning radius. The tide would be up, giving the boat more room in the canal. Intel also stated that the high-ranking VC was supposed to have four Vietcong guards armed with at least three AK-47s and an SKS carbine.

Later that afternoon an Army Ranger helo landed at our camp. Grimes and I climbed on board the chopper for a visual recon of the area of operation. We flew high over the jungle canopy, looking down at Dung Island. It was a scary-looking place. As we flew north, I could see the mouth of the Bassac and the South China Sea to the east, and miles of the Bassac River to the west. Looking back down, I made out the Ti Ti Canal and the Rach Trang Canal we were to use on the op. Orienting my map to the canal below, I even picked out the hootch that would be our objective. We flew over the area a little longer, studying the jungle terrain we would be patrolling through in not too many hours. The objective was about 200 meters from our insertion point, through the thick jungle. We would patrol out a small canal, fifty meters beyond the hootch, that led back out to Rach Trang Canal and the extraction route.

We got underway a little late because we had to wait for the tide to come in high enough to free the light. About 0300 hours we were on step, headed down the Bassac River. At the mouth of the river we turned left and entered Dung Island on Ti Ti Canal without scraping the sandbar. After making it over that obstacle, we still had another 4000 meters to go before we would reach Rach Trang Canal. All weapons were made ready. Several smaller canals entering Ti Ti Canal from both sides showed up on the radar, but there would be no mistake in finding Rach Trang, as it was larger than any of the others. The first 4000 meters of the east end of Ti Ti Canal were about 600 meters wide, and the canal made a large curve to the west. Then the canal narrowed to about 300 meters. At that point we slowed the light to just above idle as Rach Trang Canal was picked out on the radar. The LSSC turned into Rach Trang Canal, which was thirty meters wide. We studied the radar as we moved quietly and cautiously along. The Raytheon 1900-series radar had a two-position range switch; one showed a thirty-two-mile radius and the other showed just a few miles, but with more detail.

Moving another 350 meters up the canal, we passed our extraction site, a small canal entering the Rach Trang. We kept moving slowly along, our weapons trained at both banks in case of ambush. I stayed low behind the ceramic-armor plates, with just the top of my head and my eyes peering over the crew cockpit. After another fifty meters Mr. Q gave the signal to stand by for insertion. It was rare to go so far into Dung Island without hearing any Vietcong warning shots. But the light was a well-designed boat: you would never know there were two Ford 427 Cobra engines under its soundproof covers. With their unique muffler system, they were kept quite quiet.

The light turned to its port side and nudged up against the bank. Grimes and Quan were already on the bow, and with one step they were out of sight, into the thick mangrove jungle in front of us. That would probably be the last time I saw them until first light. On some ops I was lucky to see the man in front of me; the dense jungle and the dark kept me from seeing the front of our squad most of the time. Communication between the members of our squad and platoon was excellent, for the most part, and a detailed briefing before an operation took care of most situations where communication was necessary during patrol. During a patrol, when a situation required passing the word, it was done with arm and hand signals or by word of mouth, whispering very quietly.

We all followed Grimes, myself off the boat last and moving silently into my perimeter position. As the light backed out from our position, a loud crack from a breaking mangrove limb echoed through the jungle. It scared the shit out of me, as I was closest to it. Anybody in the area had to have heard it. The limb must have hung up on the boat, breaking as it backed away from the bank. After a noise like that during an insertion, we usually sat and listened for enemy movement even longer before starting to patrol. If our position had been compromised, we were sure to find out. Without the element of surprise, the squad could not complete its mission. At times like that it might have been better not to insert at all or, at least, to insert somewhere else, but we had already inserted. My heart was pounding as I tried hard to hear the enemy. At times my heart was all I could hear. Every beat of my heart and every breath I took made listening even harder. I worried that if the limb breaking hadn't given our position away, then maybe my breathing might!

The tide was still coming in, and the water filling in the crab holes and moving the vegetation made the most noise now. Damn, the jungle was thick here, the thickest I had seen on Dung Island. After sitting and listening for what seemed like hours, our squad finally started its patrol. My legs and right arm had warmed the mud below me as I lay there. I really hated to get up. Concentrating on Bruce in front of me so I wouldn't get separated from the patrol, I carefully checked out the area behind me. The Vietcong didn't have to place any booby traps in this area; the jungle being so thick was a deterrent in itself. Patrolling was very difficult. At times we crawled on our hands and knees and over the top of the thick crap, trying to make as little noise as possible. Trying to detect enemy movement, we stopped more often because of all the natural noisemakers.

As thick as the vegetation was, we were still very quiet. We patrolled on, one step, then another. I expected the shit to hit the fan any second. Sweat soaked my cammo top and my headband. Our squad stopped again to listen. What a fucked place for a firefight. Grimes was sent out ahead to scout the area out. The rest of us waited silently for him to return. We soon started patrolling again. Then natural openings in the jungle made patrolling a little easier. Grimes had located a trail that led in the direction of our objective. I don't know how he found it in the dark, but we cautiously patrolled down the trail, checking for trip wires and pungi pits as we made our way. We patrolled as slow or slower than we had back in the thick undergrowth behind us. As usual, each man's weapon was trained in the opposite direction from that of the man in front of him.

We soon came across a trip wire. No sooner had we all crossed it safely, than Grimes found another one. We were getting close. Charlie had something or someone to hide in the area or there wouldn't have been booby traps set out. After we crossed the second trip wire without incident, we were inside Charlie's perimeter. I could look up through the thick jungle canopy. The sky was starting to get light, but the jungle floor was still very dark. Birds started sounding off with the first light, not knowing of our presence. We patrolled farther, until another booby trap was discovered. We all crossed it safely and stopped again. It wasn't very far from the last trip wire, maybe four feet. As the sky grew lighter, I could see a pineapple grenade inside an empty GI C-ration can fixed to a small tree. The pin on the grenade inside the can had already been pulled and the can held the spoon in place. The trip wire was tied to the grenade, so when bumped, it would be pulled out of the olive-drab can, causing the spoon to fly off and the firing pin to strike the blasting cap. I didn't care to be sitting this close to it. About twenty-five meters out in front of Grimes was a small hootch built up on stilts and hidden under the jungle canopy. Word was passed back of the danger area.

Grimes and I did not see that hootch from our aerial recon, and it wasn't on our picto map. The hootch that was our objective was a least another hundred meters beyond. We moved in a little closer and set up a perimeter around it. No sooner had I moved into my position when a dog started barking and growling. Everyone froze, but the dog kept on barking. If our intelligence had mentioned this hootch, we might have patrolled in on a different route. But its being there explained the booby traps so far away from our objective—they were a security element for the unexpected hootch. The dog wasn't visible, or Grimes would have used his Model 39 hush puppy on it. As we crouched around the hootch trying to locate the dog, two dark figures crashed open the nipa-palm door and, jumping to the ground, ran like hell toward our objective, the other hootch. Neither figure got fifteen meters from the hootch before being dropped by automatic-weapon fire from the squad.

Doc radioed the light that we had just made contact. Our position had just been compromised. Grimes, Quan, and Mr. Q moved over to check out the bodies while the rest of us set up security to watch our perimeter. To Mr. Q's and Grimes's surprise, the two figures dressed in black pajamas were women. Finding no documents or weapons on the two Vietcong, Mr. Q, Quan, and Grimes went to the hootch to search it. I stayed in my position, covering the way we had patrolled in. The hootch was carefully searched in case it had been booby-trapped. Inside, they found two old sewing machines, lots of material, NVA uniforms, several Vietcong flags, and two short-wave radios. The radios alone were proof enough the two women were Vietcong; it was illegal for South Vietnamese to have a short-wave radio, because they could be used by the Vietcong to monitor South Vietnamese and American radio frequencies.

By then the morning had begun to get pretty light. I don't know what the hell happened to the dog, but it was gone. Panella heard sounds of Vietcong moving toward his po-

sition and alerted us. They were coming from the direction
of our planned extraction route. Bruce heard some movement his way also. The uniforms, flags, and the two radios
were quickly removed from the hootch and passed out for
us to carry. An incendiary grenade took their place. The
sewing machines were too heavy to carry, so were destroyed
and left in the hootch to be engulfed in flames. The sound
of a crackling nipa palm was interrupted by enemy small-
arms fire. We returned the enemy fire with some of our own
as we did what we were trained not to do, extract using the
same route we came in on. This time we had no choice, as
our main and alternate extraction sites were occupied by
Vietcong. As we moved out rapidly, Mr. Q yelled, "Watch
out for the three booby traps." Charles was still quite a
ways behind us, but after he found the two women, he
would want our asses bad. We weren't going to stick around
to give him that chance.

Over one trip wire, then another. Then, *two* trip wires
about two feet apart appeared in the trail. Fuck, I thought,
where did these come from? I'm glad Grimes noticed them
on the way out. How had all seven of us patrolled through
here without tripping them? There was no time to stick
around and find out, Charlie was getting closer and his
bullets cracked overhead. We couldn't see Charlie and he
couldn't see us, but we exchanged bullets anyway as we
continued on. We still hadn't reached the first trip wire, but
Grimes watched for it and I watched our rear as we ran
through the jungle down the trail. Doc was on the radio,
telling the light that we were on our way back to the insertion
point for extraction. Finally, the other booby trap appeared
and we all crossed to the opposite side one at a time. I kept
thinking about the two wires we didn't find on our way in.
That bugged me. It wasn't Grimes's fault, he did his point
job well.

After reaching the spot where we had first found the trail,
we stepped into the thick brush and patrolled as fast and
quietly as we could toward the canal, all of us looking for
an enemy ambush. With less than a hundred meters to go,
we got a good look at the thick jungle we had patrolled

through earlier in almost complete darkness.

The enemy was moving through the jungle behind us. By the sounds, they had split into two elements to try to cut us off. We were moving even faster now, pulling limbs and vines out of our way. Reaching the Rach Trang Canal, we quickly set up a perimeter close to the water's edge. As we waited for the light, we watched the jungle carefully from our hidden positions within the mangroves. The Vietcong could be heard getting closer to our position, as could the LSSC. Doc had a visual on our boat and talked it in to us, using the radio. As the bow pushed up onto the bank, one at a time we boarded as fast as we could. Backing out into the canal, Melfa turned the light and started to get on step as the rest of us fired our weapons into the jungle behind us. I was wishing we had the minigun.

About fifty meters from our extraction site, we started taking enemy fire from the left flank. Shifting our fire immediately, we opened up in that direction, suppressing the enemy's fire. The Vietcong had set up on the small canal we were supposed to extract on. It was lucky we didn't patrol out that way. We proceeded to get the hell out of there with only a few holes in the boat. The light entered the main river, leaving Dung Island to the Vietcong until another day. We had brought the uniforms, flags, and radios out with us. The radios had covers sewn to fit over them. I considered one of them mine since I had packed it out of the jungle.

The radio's cloth cover was blue with sewn red borders. A bird was embroidered on the front with green thread. The bird had red eyes and a red beak with a yellow hammer and sickle on it. Beneath the hammer and sickle was a Vietcong flag. Another bird embroidered on the cover was flying and dropping red, yellow and orange flowers from its feet. The words XUAN-THAM-TINH-Q were also on the cover in red thread. The whole radio was only three-by-six-by-twelve inches. A plastic window was sewn into the cloth to expose the dial. Two small openings exposing the control dials for an on-off switch and a tuning dial were there also. The back was plain blue cloth with the red borders. As I was checking out my new radio, Quan walked over, reached out, and tried to grab it from me. As he pulled, I pulled it back. He got really upset and tried the ''gook holding the M-16'' trick, trying to make me think he would use it on me if I didn't give it to him. I said in a meaningful voice, ''Fuck you, Quan.'' He went and sat down and glared at me the rest of the way back to camp. The radio meant a lot to me, and Quan couldn't legally own it, so he'd probably end up selling it for big bucks as a war souvenir for some REMF.

At first I was freaked out because we'd killed the two women. But after what was found when the hootch was searched, they became just two more gooks for our body count. The incident with Quan really pissed me off. And it was one more reason that my government would never get me back to this mosquito-infested place again. Strasbaugh had told me a story about Quan on one of Second Squad's ops. While engaged in a fierce firefight with Charlie on an extraction, Strausbaugh was on the bow of the medium helping his teammates climb aboard, Quan stuck the muzzle of his M-16 up to Strausbaugh to help him up to the bow. Strausbaugh pulled Quan up with his M-16 only to find out Quan's M-16 was on full auto, and off safe. Strasbaugh threw Quan back off the bow into the mud and wouldn't help him back on board until all the SEALs were loaded first. Quan never fucked with Strausbaugh again. Quan was a good interpreter, but sometimes he forgot who he was working for.

Back at camp we debriefed immediately. We couldn't believe we'd crossed two trip wires without detonating the grenades. Maybe we had patrolled around them, but that was unlikely. Someone up above must have been watching over us. Besides a few torn clothes and a few scratches and bruises from running through the thick jungle, everyone was all right. But my time was coming, I just knew it. It made me feel sick to my stomach just thinking about it.

After the debriefing I skipped morning chow and walked back down to the dock. I was still wet and muddy and my face was still cammoed. As I sat on the dock, I thought things over. The sun was just coming up and the high tide was at its peak. Looking up into the sky, I noticed the only cloud around for miles. It was shaped like a human figure, truckin' across the sky to the northeast. As I sat there, bummed out, wishing the cloud was me, I felt the dock rocking and heard some music. I turned around and Bruce was approaching me with my new radio. He was still wearing his muddy clothes and cammoed face also. But Mongo Jerry was singing "In the Summertime" on the radio. As Bruce sat down beside me, he said, "Look, Young, the fuckin' radio works." Then he pulled out a freshly rolled joint.

We sat there, listening to the radio and smoking the joint as everyone else ate chow. Bruce's presence—and the joint—had snapped me out of my bummer. We listened to the Armed Forces Network, Paul Harvey was doing the talking, as we sat laughing at the cloud moving across the sky.

We had made a pretty good dent in the enemy forces on Dung Island by then. Our body count was climbing and a steady stream of prisoners was being handed over to our intelligence officers. It was always said that the night belonged to Charlie. Well, SEALs were changing that. Not only were we putting a dent in the Cong on the island, but our ops had a psychological effect on them also. Tales of our presence would pass from hamlet to hamlet on the island. The Vietcong wouldn't know where or when we would strike next, until it was too late for some of them.

CHAPTER TWENTY-ONE

With the lack of reliable intel, our squad wasn't going to operate for a few days, so with some free time on our hands, Bruce and I decided to visit SEAL friends up in Cam Ranh Bay who were advisors to the South Vietnamese SEAL (LDNN) training camp. These two guys, Berta and Passyka, had come down to our camp and spent some time with us operating and water skiing. Now they were temporarily attached to that advisory group at Cam Ranh Bay as SEAL instructors while the two full-time SEAL instructors got a break for R&R.

The MST crew took us to Binh Thuy on the medium. From there we caught a helo to Saigon. Half-civilian, half-military clothed, with shaggy hair and scrubby beards, we looked like real slobs. Actually, we felt quite comfortable. Besides, Vietnam was making rags of our clothes anyway. I wasn't out to impress anybody. Bruce didn't care what he wore. More than once I saw him pick up somebody else's shirt in a barracks and wear it till it was dirty, then find another one someplace else. He always wore a different name tag, and sometimes he was even in the Army. It must have been the California hippie in him. His big brownish-red mustache looked like a set of gold jump wings, and his beard hung down to his holey blue and gold tee-shirt. But he sure knew his way around Vietnam.

I don't know what Army officers thought of us along our route, but we got some pretty good stares from some. Maybe they thought we were civilians or something, 'cause they never bothered us. If somebody pissed Bruce off, he would just stare down on them with his hypnotizing brown eyes from six feet, two inches up, eyes on target like a locked-on radar. His facial expression said it all: "You've got one more chance, motherfucker." I was sure glad he was my friend and on my side. As we sat in Tan Son Nhut Air Force Base waiting for a C-130 bound for Cam Ranh Bay, we ran into two SEALs from Golf Platoon with a group of LDNNs waiting for the same flight. The Vietnamese SEALs went through hell week and the whole nine yards. Their training was a little more condensed than ours, and they received on-the-job training in their own country. According to one of the SEALs from Golf Platoon, Berta was supposed to meet them and the LDNNs at the airport in Cam Ranh Bay.

Tan Son Nhut Air Force Base could be a pain in the ass sometimes. Even with our first-priority orders, we still had to experience "hurry up and wait." The large metal building used for a lobby was usually crowded with military personnel of all branches of service from several different countries, most American and South Vietnamese. Civilian personnel were also present, some American and some South Vietnamese. Red, blue, and green chairs in long lines filled the interior of the building beneath rows of neon lights hanging from the ceiling. Most of the chairs faced the main entrance. Immediately upon walking out the front door you were damn near mobbed by the local people wanting to do anything from shine your shoes to haul your ass around. You name it, you could buy it, out the front doors. Just about any kind of transportation you desired was waiting for you there. It was a pain in the ass waiting for the gooks to get done fighting over who was going to take you to wherever you wanted to go. Light yellow and blue Morris Minor taxicabs, motorcycle rickshaws, human-powered rickshaws, bicycle-powered rickshaws, it was all there. Some of these units were taped and wired together, and after riding in one, I felt my chances of survival were better on Dung Island. Every one of the motorized vehicles seemed to need rings and a valve job. They would take off down the street leaving a trail of bluish-white smoke behind them going, "Ring ding ding ding ding ding, ring ding ding." I felt sorry for some of the human-powered rickshaw operators when they hauled some extra-heavy American GI and all his gear around Saigon. I tried to avoid the human-powered ones myself.

Eventually our flight number was called and we gathered our gear and boarded a C-130 transport for our flight to Cam Ranh Bay. As we left the runway, Saigon and all the chaos quickly disappeared behind us. Canals and roads left the smelly city in all directions like spokes from a wagon-wheel hub. Nothing but rice paddies and dikes lay below us, and occasional patches of jungle. Soon the flat, wet land turned to rolling hills and sand dunes. As we circled Cam Ranh, I saw a large number of fuel storage tanks surrounded by a Cyclone fence and barbed wire. When we disembarked the aircraft, Berta and Passyka were there to meet the group. They were surprised to see Bruce and me. Throwing our gear on board a six-by, we set out on our trip to a place called Market Time, a small naval base located in a little valley next to a beautiful white-sand beach. The water off-shore was crystal clear with a sandy bottom. The Vietnamese SEAL training compound was located about a quarter mile from the bay and far away from the other complexes, with a squad of SEAL instructors and anywhere from thirty-five to forty-five South Vietnamese trainees. All the tin roofs had sandbags on them, in case of high winds, I guess. Directly behind the LDNN camp was a mountain with a big rocky outcrop sticking out halfway to the top. Painted on this rock in white paint were the words LDNN SEAL. After so much time in the Delta, I couldn't believe that place: except for a few chuckholes in the road, there was no mud anywhere. I'm sure I could have found some if I looked hard enough, but with a beautiful white-sand beach and large rocks on either flank, it wasn't long before Bruce and I hit the beach. UDT swim trunks was the uniform of the day the whole time we were there, except when we tried to get into the chow hall with them on.

At first I felt guilty lying on the white sand and swimming in the warm, clear water. Maybe I should have stayed back at our camp across the Bassac from Dung Island. I wondered what they were doing back there. It didn't matter, I was here and was going to enjoy every minute of it. The sandy beach at Market Time was a good 500 meters long with a slight curve. It has an even gradient clear out into the water. On either flank of the beach were small mountains with thick vegetation and large rocks. Approximately a hundred meters above the high-water line was the military base, situated in a fifteen-acre area. Barracks and other buildings were lined in rows within the fifteen acres. Between the LDNN camp and the beach was a compound for training German shepherds. Some of the dogs rode around in the bay on the bow of a skimmer and were trained to detect the scent of divers' bubbles left by Vietcong or NVA sappers swimming underwater to set charges on anchored ships. The military used the dogs up in Danang Harbor also.

Over the mountain to the south from this base was another part of the Naval Support Facility with a fiberglass-boat repair shop. Some of the LDNN trainees, divided into squads, were running around with their rubber boats at the head carry. It reminded me of my UDT/SEAL training days, very similar. As one of them was falling behind, a SEAL instructor was yelling at them to keep the IBSs ("inflatable boat, small") together. Most of the LDNNs were good fighters, and SEAL and UDT personnel usually got along well with them. After training, they were highly dedicated to their job and their country. They were great fighting men, not like your run-of-the-mill ARVNs.

Bruce and I climbed around on the huge boulders on the south end of the beach. I wasn't used to not packing a Stoner, and expected to run into Charlie around every corner, but the place was well-guarded and seemed peaceful enough.

Three things were mandatory for Bruce and me while staying at Market Time: number one, no work; number two, don't miss chow; number three, mandatory beach time. We managed to do all three reliably.

After we had been there a couple of days, the SEAL instructors decided a party was long overdue. The Vietnamese trainees carried an IBS down to the bay along with a couple of sets of diving bottles. A few concussion grenades were also brought along. We paddled far out into the bay, sticking our heads into the water from time to time with our diving masks on, searching for a school of fish. Once a school of fish was located, a concussion grenade was sent down to meet them, then two divers would go down with a few gunnysacks and start filling them with fish. The trainees would free-dive down with empty sacks and return to the surface with full ones. I dove to the bottom with my Nikonis underwater camera and photographed the divers at work and all the fish lying on the sand on their sides. Once the IBS was full of fish, we paddled it to shore, pulled it up on the beach, and turned it over. One of the trainees was sent to a nearby village to report the news to the mamasans. That's all it took; within minutes the beach was swarming with Vietnamese ready to buy the fish at a very reasonable price. While the mamasans were buying fish, we were filling the IBS a second time. The mamasans were happy and we were happy—we had enough Vietnamese money for one hell of a party. Have you ever noticed when you're having a good time, time seems to fly by? That sort of thing never happened on Dung Island. Just as we were getting used to Cam Ranh Bay, it was time to return to Coastal Group 36, Advance Team 71.

Berta drove us back to the airport for our return flight. The airport in Cam Ranh was crowded with military personnel waiting for flights out, so it was a good thing we had first-priority orders, enabling us to get on the first flight out. It wasn't long before our C-130 aircraft was lining up on the Tan Son Nhut runway with its landing gear down. After collecting our gear, we proceeded to the helo dispatcher for a flight to Binh Thuy, but no helos were going that way until the next morning, so we caught a cab to the Victoria Hotel for the night.

After checking in, we got inside the elevator to go up to our rooms. I got the same feeling riding this elevator as I did operating on Dung Island—would I make it out alive this time? I expected the cables to snap in a second, sending us to the basement. South Vietnamese safety standards left a lot to be desired. After being jerked around in the elevator, we went to our room, had a short rest and a long joint, and went to the rooftop. I didn't know how old the Victoria was, but by the looks of it, it had been there quite some time. The water in the swimming pool looked very old too. It was a great place to swim if you wanted an infection of some kind. We had a bite to eat and a couple of drinks and took a few pictures of Saigon from the roof.

Bruce and I ended up walking around Saigon taking pictures of buildings, Vietnamese, and Vietnamese statues. Saigon really bugged me; I didn't trust the place. Too many people for me, and most of them gooks. I had the feeling all of them were out to get me. The buddy system was the only way I could enjoy a place like this. With someone with you to watch your ass, and vice versa, it wasn't so bad.

The next morning at 0700 hours our helo lifted off the tarmac and headed toward Binh Thuy. The morning sun reflected off the water on the rice paddies and canals as we gained altitude to about 2000 feet. Rice paddies were built right up to the city's edge from all directions. It reminded me of the Emerald City in the Wizard of Oz; Saigon even had the little munchkin people. Every direction I looked was rice, the only landmarks being Saigon, roads, and a few larger rivers and canals. The rivers and canals ran in all directions, and the farther away from the smelly city we got, the fewer roads were visible. Our journey took us over My Tho, a small city on the northernmost branch of the Mekong River. From My Tho we continued south and flew over Vinh Long, a small town on another branch of the Mekong.

Where the Mekong River enters Vietnam from Cambodia, it slows down and widens out. It then splits into two main channels by the city of Chau Phu. The southern branch flows southeast, flowing by Binh Thuy and Can Tho and finally emptying into the South China Sea just past our camp at Dung Island. This branch of the Mekong is called the Bassac. The northern branch flows more east-southeast, and it splits again just upstream from Vinh Long. Farther downstream the main channel splits again and flows east. All the main channels eventually end up in the South China Sea, forming the Mekong Delta along the way. This system is one big fuckin' river. Its headwaters start up in China, then flow through Burma, Laos, Thailand, Cambodia, and finally end up in South Vietnam. By the time the river made it to Dung Island, the water had been used by just about everything you could imagine. From washing clothes to the family sewer, it all drifted past our camp at Dung Island. I wondered how far upstream you would have to go before the water was clear. The Bassac had the color of a freshly mixed glass of Nestle's Quik.

I could see the Bassac River ahead of us now. We started to descend toward the Tactical Helo Support Base. Soon we were directly above the Naval Support Facility. As we continued descending, I saw the boat-repair building, the EOD bar, and the SEAL Quonset hut. After passing over the busy highway, we set down on a corner of the runway. Grabbing our bags, Bruce and I leaned out of the way of the rotor blades as the pilot cut the engine on the chopper. Looking back, we both waved to say thank-you. The pilot looked familiar. Maybe we had used him on an op in the past.

Crossing the highway to the Naval Support Facility, we proceeded to the SEAL Quonset hut. Mr. Walsh had been in Binh Thuy on business the last couple of days and needed a ride back to our camp too. He had requested a helo, but none was available in our direction. He had tried to get someone to take him down in a boat, but that didn't work out either. Sometimes a guy had to hang around for a couple of days for transportation. It seemed easier to get a helo when we had more men on hand than just a couple of us. I guess the Army didn't want to send a helo on an eighty-mile round trip for just three men, unless we were all officers. Well, one thing led to another, and before long I found myself looking for an alternate means of transportation. I soon came up with the answer. Mr. Q and Mr. Walsh were just too nice not to have a jeep. If the fuckin' Navy wasn't going to provide our officers with a jeep, then I was. I left the SEAL hut to look around the facility for a jeep. I found two, an olive-drab Navy one and a sky-blue one with the letters P.A. & E. on the side of the hood. Both had the keys in them, but the blue one looked like it was in better shape. Besides, I was getting sick of olive-drab. That color always made me want to stick my finger in my mouth and throw up. Both jeeps were parked right outside the disbursing office where we got paid every two weeks. Returning to the SEAL hut, I informed Mr. Walsh and Bruce that I had found a ride. I didn't tell them what kind of ride. I had them wait outside the gate on the highway while I rounded up our transportation. After they both were well outside the gate, I walked right up to the blue jeep, got in it, started it, turned it around, and drove toward the gate. Shit, man, the dude on security at the gate even saluted me as I drove out of the Naval Support Facility.

Turning toward Can Tho, I noticed Mr. Walsh and Bruce standing along the road. Bruce jumped in the backseat while Mr. Walsh jumped in the front. As I went through the gears, getting out of the area, I saw that the jeep had a full tank of gas. "Nice jeep, Young," said Mr. Walsh with a big grin. We drove off down the dusty road toward Can Tho. From my rides with the Seabees up to Binh Thuy, I knew the road pretty well by then. This was the "hat route," as we now called it.

I couldn't have picked a better jeep: full tank of gas, good rubber, nice soft top, pretty blue, but I couldn't figure out what P.A. & E. stood for. I had seen other blue vehicles just like it around, but they were few and far between. On the left side of the jeep, just inside behind the driver's seat, a large fire extinguisher was mounted on the body. The fire extinguisher had a long, flexible bell-shaped nozzle on it, and by bending it outside the jeep, toward the street, Bruce began to surprise the zipperheads as they walked along the side of the road. The loud whooshing sound along with the white smoke surrounding the victims scared hell out of the unsuspecting gooks. Finally, Bruce took the fire extinguisher off its mounting bracket so he could use it on both sides of the road. After driving through several smaller villages and surrounding several Vietnamese in a white cloud, the extinguisher finally emptied. What a bummer— made us wish we had a couple more. It had emptied before we even reached Soc Trang.

Mr. Walsh wanted to stop in Soc Trang at the Phoenix House and visit his CIA officer friend who fed us intelligence about Dung Island. Besides, it was chow time, and we knew they had an outstanding chow hall. After lunch and a short visit, we continued on toward Long Phu. That was the part of the ride I liked best. Not only did the countryside change, but so did the people: the countryside actually looked the same as anywhere else in the Delta, but being less populated made it seem different. I was enjoying the ride with Mr. Walsh and Bruce, and felt like I could have driven forever with my good company. The only thing missing was being able to smoke a doobie in front of Mr. Walsh. I didn't think he would have minded, but I had too much respect for him, and besides, I didn't want to take that chance.

The ferry just happened to be on our side; that was a first for us. Since it was empty, I drove our new jeep up onto it and parked. The Vietnamese ferry pilot remembered me from before and greeted us warmly.

Soon we were on our way again, swerving from side to side dodging the chuckholes and Vietnamese foot traffic in the road. Very few vehicles had any reason to travel that road, so we had it all to ourselves. After driving through Long Phu and down the last straight stretch toward our camp, we drove slowly through the village outside our gate. The Vietnamese villagers stared at us as if they hadn't seen a jeep before. Maybe they just liked the color. The Vietnamese sentry opened the gate for us as we approached. Through the gate, around the Seabees' equipment, past the metal buildings, a short turn to the right, and we were honking the horn at the front door of our hootch. Baylett stepped outside and yelled, "Hey, guys, Young got a jeep." Everyone inside the hootch came outside to check it out. Weber said, "What does P.A. and E. stand for?" Nobody had a answer.

While we were on the way from Binh Thuy, Baylett and Panella were packing to go on R&R in Hawaii. Panella had relatives there, and his girlfriend was going to meet him. They would ride up to Binh Thuy with some Seabees the following morning. As much as I didn't want to be in Nam, it was good to be back at our camp. Little did I know, first squad had an operation the next morning.

CHAPTER TWENTY-TWO

That night's briefing was short. The platoon had very little reliable intel, so the following morning first squad was taking the LSSC across the river to Tron Island, one of the many that made up the Dung Island area. Our mission was simple enough—capture a few civilians and try to collect intel from them worth operating on. Interrogating civilians was also part of the Phoenix program. If we chose a place previously known to have Vietcong movement, Vietnamese living in that area should know what and where Charlie was and what he was doing. Although the civilians' lives would be jeopardized if they talked to us, their information might give us a chance to get rid of some of the Vietcong in that area. Sometimes, getting information out of the civilians was difficult, but when they talked they usually had a few horror stories to tell us. Everywhere the Vietcong went, they had to make contact with the locals just to survive. Taking—by force, if necessary—food, clothes, information about South Vietnamese and American troops, or recruiting new Vietcong members, increased their chances of survival.

Mr. Q, Grimes, Quan, Bruce, Doc, and I were involved in this mission. Grimes carried his beloved CAR-15, Quan and Mr. Q carried M-16s, Doc carried his M-16, the medical gear, and the PRC-77 radio, Bruce carried his M-16/XM-148 combo (there was no way anyone was going to take that weapon from him), and I carried Baylett's M-60.

The M-60 machine gun could be used as an offensive or defensive weapon. It had controlled accurate fire and was one hell of a great ambush initiator. It fired fully automatic only, and was air cooled. The M-60 used the 7.62 NATO cartridge

(.308 in the civilian world). Initially weighing in at twenty-three pounds, the M-60s we used were completely stripped of all unnecessary weight. We mainly fired the thing from the hip position, so dragging all that unnecessary equipment, like the bipod, front and rear sights, longer barrel, and butt stock through the jungle was just a waste of energy. I would rather carry that extra weight in ammo. Paying attention to small details like this could mean the success or failure of a mission, even the difference between life and death. Some SEALs preferred to carry the M-60 the way it came out of the box, but not me. The only extras we used on the M-60 were a nylon carry strap and a rubber boot like the helo door gunners used to replace the original butt.

The M-60 was gas-operated and belt-fed with a disintegrating metal link belt; the muzzle velocity reached 2800 feet per second. Four types of ammo were available: ball, tracer, armor piercing, and incendiary. A hundred rounds weighed approximately seven pounds, and the basic load for our platoon was 450 rounds. The M-60 fired from the open bolt position and had a two-position safety—safe and fire. Maximum range was 3725 meters, but maximum effective range was 1100 meters. We didn't have to worry about that in the thick jungles of the Delta.

The M-60 was a very dependable weapon, especially when modified to our standards. If it was kept clean, there usually weren't any problems. SEALs carried the linked 7.62 ammo three different ways. The most popular method was to wrap it around the upper body and hook the ammo together by the loose ends. Another way was using a rucksack frame with a large ammo pouch attached to it, the ammo being clipped together in one long belt and stowed in the pouch. A flexible 7.62 ammo feedway was attached to the M-60 and the ammo pouch, feeding the ammo over the user's left shoulder. These aluminum flexible feeders were used by door gunners on some helos, and on our minigun on the medium. The other way was to use a specially-built metal container that attached to the weapon. That was the way Baylett had his set up. One of the main reasons for stripping the M-60 of all the unnecessary cosmetic pimp shit was so SEALs could carry more ammo. Using the M-60 with the rucksack had one drawback: if the weapon started running wild, it was hard to break the ammo link to stop the firing.

With at least two men on R&R at all times by now, we continued to rotate squads and men as needed for the particular missions. Tron Island was the second largest island in the string of islands in the middle of the river. By saying Dung Island, I referred to all of the islands in that group. From the air or looking at a map, they appeared to be one. The light would use Ti Ti Canal, one of the main canals in that area, to get us to our insertion point, again from its mouth on the east end. Our objective, after inserting into a small canal on Ti Ti's south shore, was several hootches. After reaching our objective 500 meters inland, we would set up an LP (listening post) at first light; if conditions were favorable, we would question any inhabitants in the area. After the questioning had been completed, we would extract south to the Bassac, taking any Vietnamese with us we felt needed more questioning. It was not known if the inhabitants of the hootches were VC, and that's why we wanted to set up a listening post, to check that out first instead of walking into something we couldn't handle. The medium would pick us up at the extraction point, 6000 meters downstream from our camp. Once everyone was safely on board, the light would be radioed to extract out of Ti Ti Canal, where they would be waiting on standby in case our extraction had to be to the north. We would wait on standby in the river until the light was safely out of Ti Ti Canal.

At 0200 hours, all geared and cammoed up, first squad boarded the shallow-draft light and got under way down the Bassac. We knew of some Vietcong activity in the area because Charlie used Tron Island as a staging point to cross the Bassac River south of our camp. The tide was rising— it had to be in order for our boat to cross the sandbar at the mouth of Ti Ti. Staying to the south shore, we continued on toward Ti Ti. The main river channel from camp to Ti Ti was over 1500 meters wide. As Ti Ti Canal was located on the radar, we slowed down and maneuvered over the sandbar toward the mouth's west shore. We knew from experience that the river was deeper toward that side. The medium was to stay at camp monitoring the radio until after we had inserted, then it would come downstream from camp and wait near the south shore of the Bassac until the radio call for extraction.

After safely maneuvering over the sandbar, the light stayed in the middle of Ti Ti Canal and Melfa slowed the boat down to just above idle. We still had about 7500 meters to go before our insertion point. As the jungle began to close in on either side of us, the dark morning seemed to get even darker. Four thousand meters up Ti Ti Canal we located Rach Trang Canal on the radar. Directly across from the Rach Trang Canal, we turned ninety degrees to the south to make a fake insertion. All weapons on the boat had already been made ready as we crossed the sandbar. The light slowly moved its bow up onto the canal bank. We waited for about a minute before backing off into the canal again and continuing on up Ti Ti. The canal had narrowed to about 200 meters or less at that point and was straight for about 2500 meters ahead. Both banks were covered with thick triple-canopy jungle growing right out into the canal. At just above idle, the light moved slowly up the straightaway. I felt a little safer operating on Tron Island because the Bassac River to the south wasn't too far from our insertion point. I figured if our squad got into a bad situation and I became separated from the others, I might be able to evade the enemy and make it to the south shore to hide in the thick vegetation. With the next incoming tide I could swim upstream to camp. The 6000-meter swim wouldn't be too hard, as the Bassac damn near flowed upstream on the changing tides. I'm sure that if any of us got separated from the squad, the medium and light would be cruising the river and canal to look for us. Tron Island was still enemy-controlled territory.

At the end of the straightaway, Ti Ti Canal made a bend to the left. We made another fake insertion at that point on the north shore. Fake insertions or not, they still scared the shit out of me. We were still very vulnerable. I expected Charlie to throw a grenade into our boat or fire an RPG-7 at us at any time. To make things worse, as we nudged up against the thick vegetation the bow snapped a limb and a *crack* echoed through the jungle. Crouching lower in the light, we waited, weapons trained at both flanks and straight ahead. After another minute we backed out into the main channel and continued.

The canal made a bend back to the right, then straightened out again for another 2500 meters. Ti Ti Canal was a natural canal, not a man-made one. It narrowed to about a hundred meters, closing the jungle in on both sides even more. The insertion canal was located on the radar; Mr. Q gave the signal to stand by for insertion as the light turned toward the south bank. The insertion canal went south about half-way into Tron Island, near the island's narrowest point. Our radar had picked up the canal and clear across to the Bassac, which made it easy to pick out our insertion point. The distance from there south to the Bassac River was twice as narrow as the rest of the long island; heavy triple-canopy jungle grew on the insertion side, rice paddies filled the center of the island, and a thin fifty-meter strip of nipa-palm jungle rose along the Bassac shoreline. The distance between Ti Ti and the Bassac was approximately a thousand meters.

The light cut its throttles and drifted into the small canal as far as it could go. The mud bottom stopped it. Grimes went over the bow first and made a quick check for booby traps. The rest of us followed and set up a perimeter on both canal banks as the light backed from our position. The light would go downstream, where the canal widened, and wait in the middle of the canal in case we needed it. At that point the medium was alerted that the insertion had taken place; it moved downstream from camp and waited.

After waiting quietly for several minutes, watching fireflies and putting up with the mosquitoes, Grimes climbed up onto the canal bank to look for a patrol route inland through the thick jungle. The rest of us waited in the chest-deep water. Being dropped off in an area where we weren't welcome made for a scary, lonely feeling. Actually, we were at one of the safest places to be on a mission: we had the canal behind us, preventing an enemy from circling around in case we got into a firefight, and the muddy canal banks gave us good cover and protection from enemy bullets.

After a few minutes Grimes returned to the canal and started patrolling upstream. Maybe the jungle was too thick and noisy, or maybe too many pungi pits and booby traps had been detected; I didn't know, I just followed. My breathing and the mosquitoes seemed to make more noise than the natural jungle sounds. The incoming tide made a little noise filling in the holes we left in the mud and moving the vegetation around. The few natural jungle sounds were to our advantage, covering our movement as we patrolled up the canal. A few meters at a time, stop, listen, move up a little more. These fuckin' mosquitoes had to be bothering Charlie too. Waiting for more natural jungle sounds to blend in with our movement, we would move ahead a little more. I heard it starting to rain on the jungle canopy above. An occasional raindrop would make it through the thick leaves and branches above and strike my head, but the rain sounds covered any noise we made, so patrolling in the chest-deep water was a little faster. I kept the M-60 out of the mud and water and the muzzle pointing toward our rear. The M-60 wasn't much heavier than my Stoner, but with its 7.62 ammo, I could tell the difference.

We had patrolled about 200 meters in a little over an hour, so we stopped to listen for enemy movement again. The canal was getting shallower and narrower. Each time I lifted myself up out of the water, I had to do it slowly to let the water drain from my ammo pouch without making any more noise than the falling rain. We never really knew where or when we might run into the Vietcong. Our last operation would testify to that. Charlie might have been watching us at that very moment, ready to initiate an ambush.

Stopping at times to listen, we patrolled about fifty more meters, until we reached a danger area where the canal came out of the jungle and into an open rice paddy. We set up a perimeter along the jungle treeline to wait and listen some more. That was the name of the game, wait and listen. After about a half hour we slowly climbed back down into the canal, one at a time, and moved farther inland through the rice paddies. By staying down in the canal we had cover and concealment instead of exposing ourselves in the open. After fifty more meters, the canal made a sharp ninety-degree right turn. Grimes was sent out again to check out a dike that continued south. By standing up, I could look over the sides of the canal banks, but there wasn't much to see except for the silhouette of the jungle against the dark early morning sky behind me. Reeds about six feet high lined the canal banks on both sides of us. The rain had stopped, leaving the dike trails damp. That would make patrolling on the dikes quieter.

Grimes crawled back to the canal and stuck his head through the reeds where the dike started. We had about 200 more meters to go before we reached another small jungle area. Along that treeline were three good-size hootches. The canal we were in made a big circle to the right, then back to the left near the treeline and the hootches. According to the picto map back at camp, one of the hootches was on the west side of the canal and the other two were on the east side, near the south end of the dike. Covering each other, we climbed out of the muddy water one at a time, through the reeds and onto the dike. Bruce helped me up. Wrapping each other's fingers together worked better than grabbing each other's wrists. This way, even with our muddy hands, we had a more solid grasp.

The left side of the dike was also lined with reeds. After waiting quietly, crouched down for a couple of minutes, we started to patrol again. The early morning was still, and not many sounds were heard in the middle of the rice paddy. Soon we were within sight of two of the hootches, which were between us and the same canal that we had patrolled in on earlier. The other hootch was across the canal to our right about a hundred meters, back against the treeline. We spread out along the tall, thick reeds a few meters apart and quietly disappeared into them, hiding ourselves. I took up a position where I could see through the reeds to the hootches and back down the dike behind us, the way we had patrolled in.

No sooner had I settled down than the mosquitoes started crawling all over my face and hands, in my nose and ears, sucking up that good American blood. Compared to the local Vietnamese, I must have been a delicacy to them. I could feel other weird bugs crawling over my legs as I lay on the water-soaked bottom of the reeds. To stay warm, I curled up my legs. I couldn't hear Bruce, who was just a few meters away from me, and I'm sure I was just as quiet. I felt all alone, but secure with the cocked M-60. A light mist about three feet high moved over the rice paddies and made it harder to keep an eye on the hootches. We waited and listened. Some kind of animal crawled around behind me in the reeds. It didn't sound big enough to be a human. The morning moved on with no sign of light to the east yet. No movement or sounds from any of the hootches either. No dogs to give away our position, and no visible Vietcong guards. Rather than lie out there for nothing, I would have preferred to stay at camp, not operating, until we received some fresh reliable intel to operate with. But maybe the patrol wasn't going to be for nothing; the operation wasn't over yet. Extraction from that area on Tron Island probably would have to be back at the light, which was waiting on Ti Ti Canal. It was still closer to our position than the Bassac River. We were in a bad area to run into a larger enemy force because it was a long way in either direction to be extracted by boat. Four or five hundred meters might not seem very far, but traveling through thick mud and jungle can really slow you down.

Finally, the signal to move came down the line from Mr. Q, ending up at me. We moved in the direction of the two hootches not far from our position. I was glad to be moving again; it was getting cold in the bug-infested water. Security was set up to cover the front element of the squad as it passed the two hootches and took up position in the canal. They covered us as we cautiously moved closer to meet them. As I quietly slipped past the two hootches, I heard movement and coughing inside. Mr. Q must have figured on passing these Vietnamese by and hitting the hootch closest to the Bassac River. The rear element of our squad set up security at the canal, more like a large ditch there, while the rest crossed to the other side one at a time. I stayed low to the ground, looking up against the sky to get a better silhouette of anyone who might try sneaking up behind us. The front element set up security for us as we crossed the canal. Once on the other side, I again crouched low to the ground, looking up through the thick reeds behind us, trying to detect movement. Looking to one side or the other of an object that looked like a gook, not directly at it, gave me a better chance of detecting movement.

Grimes had been sent to check out the area to our south, and had been gone a long time. Sometimes I thought he was never coming back. He always moved very slowly, checking for booby traps and a safe route for us to follow. We all had been trained to walk point, but Grimes was one of the best in our platoon. Being rear security did have its advantages, because there was less chance of tripping booby traps while patrolling. But being the last man in the patrol while being chased off the island wasn't any picnic either, especially if we had captured a gook the Vietcong wanted back real bad. Fire superiority or not, it always scared the shit out of me.

It wasn't as long as it seemed before Grimes motioned to us and we were following him again. Like a long snake, we twisted through the thick reeds and into a thick nipa-palm area. Larger trees stuck up through the nipa-palm canopy and long vines hung down to the jungle floor, making silent movement more difficult. We patrolled about 200 more meters to the south through that shit, not knowing what we would run into around the next clump of vines. Grimes would check out the area ahead, then we would move up behind him. Move up, squat down, wait, move up again. This went on for a long time until we reached the treeline that gave way to more rice paddies, dikes, and two more hootches. As we lay on the damp ground under cover

and concealment inside the treeline, we noticed there didn't
seem to be any VC guards or mouthy dogs around. We had
an excellent view of the hootches and rice paddies. Except
for the mosquitoes, no movement could be detected at all.
After sitting awhile, watching the hootches and surrounding
area, we started patrolling again. We didn't want to get
caught in the open rice paddies at first light, so we walked
right between the two hootches and out onto a large dike
that led in the direction of the Bassac.

At night or in the early morning darkness our visibility
was limited, so we relied on our hearing as well. Being as
quiet as possible while moving allowed us to hear noises
outside our patrol. Stopping to listen a lot was essential to
avoiding an enemy ambush. Doc radioed the light and in a
low voice told it to start withdrawal from Ti Ti Canal. They
were a long way from friendly forces, and our extraction
would surely be at the riverbank of the Bassac. Because we
were so close to our extraction site, I felt a little relieved.
We had not been detected by any enemy forces yet, but the
operation wasn't over.

We patrolled on down the dike until it split into smaller
dikes leading in different directions. Staying very low to
the ground and several meters apart from each other, we
crossed several smaller dikes. We were out in the open, and
that wasn't a good idea, but we still had the darkness on
our side. Everyone in the element kept track of the person
in front of him and behind him so no one could get separated.
Charlie knew that Americans like to travel the easiest way
possible, that's why he booby-trapped the trails and paddy
dikes. That was a good reason for us to stay to one side of
the dike now, patrolling down in the rice; booby traps could
be anywhere. The going was a little harder, but the dike,
being higher than us, gave us some concealment and protection. Mud dikes have a tendency to absorb bullets with
less pain than humans. At the south end of the rice paddies
was another small hootch. Fifty meters beyond the hootch,
through thick nipa palm, was our extraction site on the
Bassac.

In the far distance behind us we heard machine-gun fire

and several explosions. It came from the direction of the light. We crouched below the dike while Doc radioed the light to see if everything was all right. Since there were no other friendly forces in the area except the light, the sounds had to come from Ti Ti Canal. The light soon radioed back that they had taken Vietcong small-arms fire and had silenced Charlie with the .50-calibers, M-60s and a few 40mm HE rounds. Everything was all right, and they were continuing their extraction.

We were only fifty meters from the hootch at the end of the rice paddies by then, and we heard some activity inside. The excitement over on Ti Ti Canal must have woken up the occupants. Mr. Q gave the signal to set up security around the hootch. Quickly, with great caution, everyone moved into designated positions. In seconds the hootch was surrounded and taken under our control. After entering the hootch, Quan and Mr. Q immediately started to interrogate an old papasan and mamasan. The eastern sky was starting to lighten by then. I covered my two sides of the hootch and the perimeter behind me, thinking about the fifty meters to our extraction site. Doc had radioed our position to the medium and told it to stand by. No weapons, no documents, no Vietcong. The two Vietnamese were too old to fight for any cause. They claimed to know nothing. To Quan it didn't matter whether they were VC or not, he interrogated them in the same way he interrogated any other Vietcong suspect, but without harming them. He meant business and wanted them to know who was in control.

Mr. Q and Quan decided it was worthless to question the two any longer. Not wanting the Vietnamese to know which way we left the area, Quan told them to lie facedown in the hootch and not to go outside for a while or they would be shot. With the fear of God put into them, it didn't take them long to hit the deck. Within seconds the squad had slipped into the nipa palm and was heading toward the Bassac River.

We patrolled cautiously toward the extraction site, checking for booby traps in our path and watching carefully to our flanks and behind us. Once at the river, we set up security along the bank. We crouched down in the mud and water along shore, looking back into the nipa-palm jungle the way we had come. Thick vegetation grew all around us, giving us excellent concealment. Doc radioed the medium for extraction. We waited patiently. Soon the boat was visible. Doc guided it into our position using the radio. The MSSC crew was manning the weapons, steel pots on their heads, flak jackets wrapped around their bodies. As the bow moved into our position, we began to maneuver toward it.

The wet and muddy squad boarded the boat, one man on the starboard side and one man climbing over the port side until all were on board. The medium backed out into the river and the stern was turned toward the bank in case the minigun needed a workout. We slowly pulled out into the middle of the river to wait for the light. The medium had kept up radio communications with it throughout the entire operation. The light had made it out of Ti Ti Canal and was heading upriver on step to meet us.

The sun was just starting to rise, and made the muddy river look as orange as the clouds scattered above it. I peeled the wet ordnance tape off the bottom of my jeans and threw it into the river. It was great for keeping the bugs and leeches from crawling up our legs, but it could only last so long under the wet, muddy conditions. Finally the light pulled up along our starboard side. The crew told us that they had received incoming rounds from the bank of Ti Ti Canal and returned the fire instantly. The incoming rounds stopped within seconds. Whether any Vietcong were killed or not was unknown, but all the light's crew was okay.

Sometimes, after the Mobile-Support Team personnel inserted us on an operation and were waiting on standby to extract us, they got into trouble themselves. It happened more than once while I was in-country. The MST crews were highly trained and handled such situations just fine. The men of the MST group were an added reason for the success of SEAL missions.

Mr. Q gave the word to head back to camp, so we pushed the two boats apart. The medium and the light got on step upriver, and we were back at camp in minutes.

CHAPTER TWENTY-THREE

After arriving back at camp, we assembled for the mission's debriefing. Mud and water still dripped from our clothes. We went over the operation as to what went wrong, what went right, what we should have done, and what to do under similar circumstances on the next operation. Debriefing after each operation improved operating techniques; fine-tuning the squad or platoon after an op made us better SEAL operators. The boat had taken us up Ti Ti Canal over 7000 meters, inserted us at the designated insertion point, and we had patrolled over a thousand meters through Charlie's backyard without being detected or firing a shot. There were no Vietcong KIA nor were any prisoners captured, but the mission was successful. We brought back intel about that part of Dung Island and came back with no friendly casualties. If there had been a large Vietcong force in the area, we would have detected them. The presence of booby traps would have been a good sign that Vietcong were in the area. We found none. Booby traps were usually located close to Vietcong activity like hootches, trails, dikes, etc. The MST crew members of the light might have blown away a few VC on Ti Ti Canal when the light was ambushed, but that could not be confirmed, other than that the incoming enemy rounds stopped when the MST crewmen returned the fire.

After the short debriefing, I began to strip down the M-60 I used on the operation, and cleaned it thoroughly. After my weapons and operating gear were cleaned and stowed away, I grabbed a towel and a bar of soap and headed to the shower. I hung my towel on a nail and, since my clothes were already wet and muddy, I walked right into

the shower, clothes and all. The gasoline engine that ran
the pump on the tanker trailer behind the shower didn't
provide hot water, but at least we had clean water. I slowly
turned in circles, washing off the mud, and then slowly
peeled off my wet clothes and washed them out. Finally
stripped down, I took off my diving watch and set it on a
small shelf by the shower head. I grabbed the soap and
began to wash the cammo paint from my hands, face, and
the back of my neck. After all the soap was washed off, I
wrung out my clothes, wrapped my towel around me, and
walked back across camp to our hootch. Even when our
clothes had been washed and cleaned they still had that
moldy, mildew smell to them. Weird things would grow in
our jungle boots if they were left unused for any length of
time. They reeked of moldy mildew also.

I put on UDT swim trunks and hung up my wet jeans
and cammo top to dry. About a half hour passed. Fuck,
where is my diving watch? I wondered, walked back over
to the shower and stared at the empty shelf where I had put
it. "Fuckin' gooks," I yelled. The South Vietnamese side
of camp was to the right of our shower, separated only by
concertina wire strung to mark the boundary. One of the
slant-eyed little bastards thought one of us would leave a
bar of soap behind, and after we left the shower, crossed
the barbed wire and checked out the shower. You couldn't
leave a fuckin' bar of soap lying around. Well, I'll never
see that watch again, I thought as I walked back to my
hootch. I asked myself, Why am I putting my ass on the
line for this country of worthless gooks? I didn't have an
answer to my own question. For a few minutes I wished I
was stationed with a UDT team or a Seabee team somewhere. Everytime I got pissed off at the gooks or our squad
got into a world of shit with Charlie, I wished I was somewhere else in the world. It really didn't matter who I was
stationed with or where I was in the world, a bar of soap
was a valuable item to some people. I had no one to blame
but myself for being in my situation. I calmed down and
went to morning chow. The day had just begun for most
people, but for first squad the workday was now over. Get

some chow, some rest, and forget about the gooks for a while. Everytime I looked at the white band of skin around the suntanned arm where my watch had been, I got mad again. God help the gook I catch wearing my watch!

After filling out a theft report with Mr. Q, I climbed into my rack to try to get some rest, but the Seabees working around camp made sleeping impossible, banging on the new building and driving their equipment around camp. I got out of my rack and, to keep ourselves occupied, Reeves and I took a ride around camp in our officers' jeep. How far could we drive in our three-acre camp? Plenty, in between the hootches, down to the helo pad, back over to the gate, down to the river. Then we got stuck in the Bassac mud. All four wheels were buried past the axles. The jeep's frame was sitting on the mud, and the tires just spun. Reeves and I walked back across camp to find one of our Seabee friends to pull out the jeep with their six-by. After returning to the jeep, the Seabees joked around and gave me a bunch of shit while they freed the jeep from the mud. They said they wanted to leave it in the mud until the next high tide came in.

Bruce, Panella, and Baylett were water skiing, so Reeves and I walked down to the dock to wait our turn. Meanwhile we decided to go for a swim, being careful to watch out for broken glass and sharp pieces of metal that littered the muddy bottom around the dock. We swam out into the Bassac, then back to the dock. When the tide was in full, you couldn't touch the bottom of the river while hanging on the end of the dock. Reeves and I started hiding from each other under and around the fifty-five-gallon drums that supported the dock. The slimy bottom felt weird oozing up between my toes when I did touch the bottom. A real eerie feeling. Then Reeves grabbed my foot when I wasn't expecting it and scared the shit out of me. If I saw Reeves coming in my direction, I would slip under the muddy water and wait until he walked into me and then grab his legs. We named this game "Bang Bang." When sneaking around one of the fifty-five-gallon drums and running into someone, we would say "bang bang" and scare the shit out of each

other. At times, for a split second, I would get the same
excited-but-scared feeling that I felt sometimes on Dung
Island. It seemed kind of crazy to have full-grown men
playing Bang Bang, but it was great for the morale.

While we were playing around the dock, waiting for our
turn on the skis, a Vietnamese man floated into the camp
in a small sampan. The poor little guy really looked stressed
out, and he seemed to have a story to tell. Reeves and I
escorted him to Mr. Q. Quan interpreted the story as Mr.
Walsh, Reeves and I listened. Seems that a group of Vietcong was running around Dung Island demanding rice and
harassing the small villages. The little Vietnamese shook
with fear as he told his story. The Vietcong had just left
his village. The people there hadn't wanted to cooperate
with Charlie, so the Vietcong picked several people from
the village and cut off their heads.

Mr. Q asked Mr. Walsh to get second squad together for
a quick briefing. Reeves and I went back down to the dock
to call in the guys from water skiing. Quan and the little
Vietnamese looked over a picto map together. He showed
Quan where the village was and where the Vietcong usually
hung out. It seemed to be the first time the Vietnamese man
ever saw a map. He offered to guide second squad into the
village using the safest route. Second squad had a short
briefing on the situation and then geared up for the operation.
They were soon on their way to Dung Island on the medium.

Second squad was gone for most of the day. When they
finally returned to camp, they brought back a Vietcong
prisoner. He hadn't given up easy. Second squad got into
a fierce firefight with the Vietcong and couldn't get into the
village where the decapitated South Vietnamese were supposed to be. During interrogation the VC suspect admitted
to being one of the Cong involved in the VC terrorist group
on the island, so he was turned over to our intelligence
personnel in Soc Trang. I don't know what the problem was
with the intelligence personnel or the South Vietnamese
gooks in charge of putting that Vietcong away and throwing
away the key, but he was soon released and running around
Dung Island again.

A few days later second squad was back on Dung Island engaged in another firefight with the same group of Vietcong. I felt a little sorry for Quan having to operate with first squad then second squad back to back. But after all, it was his country, and he was getting paid top dollar working with us SEALs, not counting under-the-table benefits. In fact, working with us was keeping him out of the South Vietnamese Army. Anyway, second squad brought back a few Vietcong prisoners, one of whom was the same Vietcong they had captured a few days earlier. That really pissed off second squad, but once again the prisoners were turned over to the intelligence personnel in Soc Trang. Sometimes I felt like taking a few of those people on a couple of dick-dragging SEAL operations, then maybe they would do their job a little better. Some of them were getting paid mega-bucks for being civilians in a combat zone, they had super-secure places to live, with anything they needed to get their jobs done. Maybe I was in the wrong business.

Well, the little gook who had been captured twice was once again running wild on Dung Island, cutting off civilians' heads and harassing the villagers for food and supplies to keep the Cong rolling. Being so far from North Vietnam and not being able to be resupplied adequately, what else were the VC supposed to do to get the stuff they needed to fight for their cause? But *twice* captured, *twice* set free?

The Vietcong terrorism continued on that part of Dung Island, so this time the whole platoon was deployed to suppress the VC a third time. Again we got into a fierce firefight with the Vietcong, which led to many Vietcong KIA. One of them was the little fucker who the intel personnel had set free. This operation was not pointed directly at the little fucker; he just happened to be in the wrong place at the wrong time and collected a few bullets from a Stoner. We had walked into a Vietcong camp and eliminated eighteen of them on one operation. We continued on to a safe extraction in the early morning darkness, the enemy in hot pursuit all the way. Fire superiority, the element of surprise, and the early morning darkness had killed eighteen of the enemy and brought all of us back alive. We put a dent in the Vietcong activity on Dung Island and the success of that mission put some of the South Vietnamese people's minds at ease for a while, but for every one gook we eliminated, two or three more seemed to take his place.

After chow that morning I wrote a several-days-late letter home to my parents. "Don't worry, Mom, I'm just fine. I'm getting plenty to eat and I'm keeping my head down." After I sealed the letter, I walked out of our hootch to fetch a glass of water from our rain collector. Turning around as I put the glass to my mouth, I just about choked. The Seabees had picked up our jeep with a crane and set it on top of a huge gravel pile. There was no way to drive it down. The Seabees laughed all morning while the jeep sat atop the gravel pile. Finally the crane operator lifted the little blue jeep off of the gravel pile and set it down carefully by our hootch. I walked over to the crane operator and said, "Wait till the next football game, motherfucker." He knew I was just joking.

After morning chow a few of us decided to do a little water skiing. I hadn't been skiing in quite some time. Using Baylett's M-60, then using "his" boat, seemed strange. Just because he was in charge of the skimmer didn't make it his, he just acted like he owned it. He was having a good time in Hawaii on R&R anyway, might as well have fun with the skimmer while he was gone. Reeves grabbed the rope and skis, Bruce grabbed his M-16/XM-148 and my Stoner, and I grabbed some extra gasoline for the forty-horse engine. We all regrouped down at the dock. Trying to get Doc or Sitter out of the bar to go water skiing was like trying to pull their teeth. The bar was just an alternate duty station to them. They had to get in their mandatory bar time, and nobody except maybe a Vietcong attack or a walk to the pisser could get them off the barstools.

The tide was near halfway out, and a longer wait would cause us a delay. The skimmer was too heavy for three of us to drag through the mud if it was high and dry. The part of the dock closest to shore was already beached on the mud bank. Luckily, our skimmer was still floating, tied at the end of the dock. We proceeded up the Bassac River

with Reeves driving, Bruce skiing, and me sitting on the
bow shooting movies with my triple-lens Bolex. We pulled
Bruce out into the main channel and then up the river about
a mile before turning back to camp. We always tried to stay
within sight of the base camp in case we ran into trouble
and needed some assistance.

We cruised back past camp, then Reeves decided to try
to pull Bruce up the Long Phu River. Bruce swung to the
outside left as Reeves made the sharp right turn, and we
left the southeast corner of the camp behind as we proceeded
through the small village. The village people gathered along
shore watching us speed by with Bruce dragging behind.
At the far end of the village Reeves turned the skimmer
around in the narrow river and headed back toward camp.
Bruce was a good skier and managed to make the tight turn
also. I was wondering what the village people were thinking
about as they continued to gather along the riverbank. Some
of the younger kids jumped into the water to absorb our
wake, and some of the older men grabbed the smaller sampans so they wouldn't get swamped. Bruce weaved from
side to side as he was dragged back out into the Bassac.
We made a wide circle and Bruce dropped the rope and
slowly dropped down into the water next to the medium.
Then it was my turn.

I used two skis, as I wasn't as good a skier as Bruce or
Reeves. Before I joined the Navy, I had tried water skiing
only once, and did pretty good for my first time. The second
time I got on skis was on the Bassac River in Nam. Hell,
I was just glad to get my turn. Up the river we went again,
cooling off gooks in sampans with the spray of water off
the skis as we went by. Some of the sampans were so heavily
loaded down with bananas, wood, nipa palm, and people,
I thought they would sink from our wake.

Back in the States we have safety laws as to how many
people or how much weight you can load into a boat. In
Vietnam it's as much or many as could be squeezed in
without sinking. I saw some sampans traveling the South
Vietnamese waterways that were unbelievable: everything
from water buffaloes to six-by truck parts, and very little

freeboard left on the boat. One small wake or a slight breeze
would surely have swamped them. One thing I did admire
about the Vietnamese though, they could take nothing and
make something useful out of it. If *they* threw something
away, one thing for sure, it was garbage. That's your basic
South Vietnamese I'm talking about.

After Reeves had his turn at the skis, we beached the
skimmer. Running the skimmer at full speed, Reeves
rammed the muddy shore and all on board held on tight.
This method was used by Baylett on many occasions, successfully docking the skimmer far up onto the mud next to
the medium. The tide was at its lowest, so we secured the
boat to the shore with the long ski rope. We still had to walk
up through the knee-deep mud to reach the riverbank. It
seemed kind of funny packing a Stoner in one hand and
water skis in the other. We checked in with Mr. Q to see if
he had anything lined up for us, then hit the chow hall for
lunch.

Walking through the chow line didn't take too long. There
was never a very long line because there weren't many
Americans stationed at our camp. The assistant cook who
was helping to serve the chow was not the most appetizing
person in Nam, but he was a hell of a nice guy. He was always up early in the morning getting breakfast ready for the
troops. In the afternoons he would ride his bicycle around
camp dressed in a white tee-shirt, cutoff green military
pants, wearing his unshined military boots with civilian
socks pulled halfway up to his knees. We depended on him to
hide some of the good food in the back of the reefer for us so
no one else would find it. Like the corpsman, we always
wanted to keep the cooks on our side. But that day primo food
heated up out of an olive-drab can was the meal. After being
dragged behind the skimmer all morning, I had worked up an
appetite. Usually, all the meals at our camp looked and tasted
the same. It didn't matter to me that day, I was hungry.

A few days before our platoon had left the States, Mr.
Q got all of us together in the SEAL-team air department
for a briefing. One of the things he said that always stuck
in my mind was that anyone caught smoking pot would be

sent back to the States. It didn't bother me then because I had never smoked pot, I knew I never would smoke it, and so I had nothing to worry about. But after the many, many nights of not sleeping, drinking every night until my guts ached and I couldn't see straight, I broke down and tried it. The good feelings, good night's sleep, togetherness with my comrades, its effects as a morale booster, and being relaxed in a combat zone, overcame my ability to follow Mr. Q's orders. I only regret two things about it—disobeying one of my officers whom I respected, and having to hide in different parts of the camp to smoke. That was a mission in itself. Pot didn't make me any worse a SEAL. In fact, it made me a better SEAL operator because I was in better mental shape. As I said before, never did I or anyone in the platoon ever smoke pot before or during an operation. I had too much respect for the men of my platoon, who counted on me. But after a tough operation, I deserved a hit on a doobie, just as some of the other guys deserved a chug from the old whiskey bottle.

Some of the places we smoked at night were the dock, in the medium, up in the thirty-foot machine-gun tower, inside the new metal buildings the Seabees were building, or inside some of the sandbag bunkers around the camp's perimeter. Even up the river while water skiing.

I respected my peers in the platoon and looked up to them, but they did what they had to do and I did what I had to do to survive. Everyone has his own way of dealing with everyday life in a combat zone, whether it be whiskey, pot, or religion. No two humans are the same. In a SEAL team, working together as one is one of the most important issues. But without individuality it won't work either.

CHAPTER TWENTY-FOUR

It was now 18 September 1970. Baylett and Panella had been back from their R&R for a few days. The platoon still hadn't gotten haircuts, but I could feel the bad vibes coming. I have to admit that haircuts were long overdue. I wasn't going to be the first to suggest it. Some of my teammates did have fresh haircuts, but on their own. I think it had something to do with their rank and how long they had been in the service. If LePage hadn't been sent back to the States, we probably would have had haircuts long before. He would have made sure of that.

After morning chow the Seabees invited us to join them in a game of softball. After losing to us so many times, you would think they would've known better than to ask. I pitched for the SEALs, and yes, it was in the mud. Home plate was closest to the shoreline of the Bassac River. That way balls wouldn't be hit out into the river so much. An area alongside the garbage ditch was first base, second base was a sandbag, and third base was the top of the fifty-five-gallon drum we used as a pisser outside the bar door. The top of the drum had been cut out and a wire screen covered it. It was buried in the ground up to about an inch from the top. Needless to say, nobody slid into third base.

The game had been going for a while and the Seabees were up at bat. Time-out was called so Baylett could recover the softball that one of the Seabees had knocked over the barbed wire fence into the claymore-mine area that guarded the perimeter. Baylett had safely recovered the ball and was on his way back to the game when Mr. Q approached us. "I have some bad news to pass on to you guys," he said. "Two men from UDT-Thirteen just got killed up by Danang and several other members were wounded.

"I heard a squad from UDT Team Thirteen was on an early morning operation to place haversacks of explosives on some Vietcong bunkers. The Army had planted some sensing devices in the area to detect enemy movement, but the devices weren't working. After the explosives were positioned and the fuses pulled, the squad started to patrol away from the bunkers. The team hadn't gone very far from the bunkers when either the corpsman or a man named Palma stepped on a mine—or the Vietcong command-detonated it.

"Several people were wounded," Mr. Q continued. "Banfield was seriously wounded by shrapnel from his heels to the top of his head. The biggest pieces of shrapnel were embedded in the radio on his back. The radio saved his life."

Palma and Banfield had both been in my training class, along with Weber and Reeves. A sick feeling came over me. Palma and Banfield had joined the Navy together, went through the same boot camp company, went through the same UDT/SEAL training class, and ended up on the same UDT team. If one of them had dropped out of UDT/SEAL training, the other one would have dropped out also. They also recovered the Apollo Thirteen astronauts together, got on the same UDT platoon deployed to Vietnam, and damn near got killed together. If that wasn't the buddy system, what was? They were best friends and were well liked in their training class and in the teams. Palma was a great loss to Banfield and the rest of his team members. Panella, Strausbaugh, Weber, and Reeves had just returned to camp from visiting them in Danang the day before. Reeves and Weber had helped them get their gear together for that particular operation before they left Danang for our camp. During training they had really liked to party on our days off. I remember the Schlitz Malt beer being carried into our barracks and the drinking getting started. After a few beers and a little card playing, everyone would get crazy.

The UDT training barracks was a good place to stay clear of on the weekends if you wanted some rest. Between the partying and Schroeder from Class 54 riding his Harley-

Davidson into our barracks all the time, nobody could get any sleep.

The bad news about Palma and the corpsman ended our softball game. Weber, Reeves, and I went to our hootch and, sitting on our racks, started talking about our training days, the good times and the bad times. Reeves reminded us about one of the members of our training class who had killed a cat that hung around our barracks. He then threw the cat in San Diego Bay, which was close to our barracks. It pissed off some of the people in our training class, and Monday morning one of them told the instructors. The guy who killed the cat damn near got kicked out of training, and everyone in the class was lined up and given weird haircuts by the instructor. Everyone was really mad at the cat killer because not only did the class receive crazy haircuts, but also we had to do extra push-ups all week. Personally, I wasn't mad at him because he killed the cat, since I hate cats anyway, but I was pissed off because if one guy fucked up, the instructors made the whole class pay for it. While some of the guys got Mohawks, mine was the doughnut. Shaved around the head with the very top of my head shaved too. After training was over for the day, I ran to the PX to buy myself a hat, any kind of hat. I ended up at the San Diego Sports Arena that night for the Ringling Brothers Circus, and it was the only time in my life that I never took off my hat during the national anthem. A few days later the instructors lined us up and shaved our heads down to nothing again. We had better not have shaved it off ourselves.

Palma was the first casualty of Class 53. The Vietcong would have to pay the price for that. Weber's stomach had really been bothering him, and he hadn't been feeling very well most of the time. Doc thought he might have an ulcer. There was some talk about sending him back to the States. Fuck, I thought, why couldn't I get sick? Then someone yelled "chow time," and we all proceeded to the chow hall for lunch. The word was passed around, all SEALs had to have haircuts after chow. Rather than have the Seabee barber get hold of us, Weber and I trimmed each other's hair. Shit, first the news of Palma and the corpsman, then haircuts.

What next? I thought. Weber and I cut off just enough hair to keep Mr. Q off our backs; it was still pretty long by Navy standards.

If everything went right, Weber and I would be going on R&R soon. We had talked about Hawaii in the past. One thing was for sure, I never wanted to get so far away from home again. The South Vietnamese people had better get their shit together soon because I didn't plan on returning to fight for them again if I made it home alive.

Mr. Walsh had taken the jeep to Soc Trang to visit with the intelligence officers. We still needed to paint it. The day seemed to drag on with not much to do at times and, when we were limited to our three-acre camp, things got pretty boring at times. That evening a few of us gathered around one of the sandbag bunkers with our guitars. None of us could play very well, but the music sounded good to us. Every once in a while a parachute flare would be sent into the sky at the outpost upriver from us. It reminded me of the night not too long ago that the Vietcong attempted to overrun it. I hoped that wouldn't happen to our camp; I always kept my Stoner clean and ready just in case.

Besides the .30-caliber Browning machine guns positioned in bunkers around the camp's perimeter, and the .50-caliber Browning up in the tower, the camp had two 81mm mortars. The mortar weighed 107 pounds, was smooth bored, and had just four basic parts: base plate, bipod, barrel, and M-4 sight. The M-4 sight could be adjusted from zero to 150 millimeters left or right. One turn of the elevation handle would raise or lower it ten mils. Several projectiles could be fired from the 81mm, including illumination, white phosphorus, and antipersonnel. The kill radius of the antipersonnel was twenty to twenty-one meters. The Seabees were trained to use the mortars in case of an attack by Charlie. The claymore mines located in different positions around our camp would be detonated from the sandbag bunkers.

The Seabees stationed at the camp had pretty good duty. They worked five and sometimes six days a week. The metal buildings they were constructing were nearing completion, and it really pissed me off knowing the gooks would end up with them. While we were living in rat-infested plywood hootches, they were getting new metal buildings with concrete floors. It still wasn't clear to me why I was risking my life for them in Vietnam. I was told I was freeing these people from Communist aggression, but it was sure hard trying to help people who wouldn't help themselves.

After dark that night I decided to check my rat trap and found a nice fat juicy rat in it for the snake. I took the trap over to the snake cage. Grimes was already there, and he opened the cage door for me. With the trap inside the cage, I opened its doors and released the rat. The rat ran into the cage, then ran around sniffing his new environment. The cage door was shut and secured after I removed the trap. Melfa held a flashlight on the rat as it continued to curiously sniff its way around. The cage floor was covered with dirt, and a few tree limbs were scattered around for the snake to crawl on and hide under. Several of us gathered around the front of the cage and watched the rat in the beam of the flashlight through the screen window. The snake had curled up in a back corner of the cage after the rat crossed its body several times. With the light shining on the snake's head, we could see his tongue flicking in and out. It was waiting for the moment to strike. The rat continued to run around the cage, crossing over the snake's body several more times and stopping for less than a second to sniff a snake turd on the cage floor. The cage was totally dark inside except for the small beam of light shining on the rat. The beam of light was pointed at the snake once again, then back to the rat. The confused rat sniffed its way back and forth across the cage, getting closer to the snake again. I don't think the rat liked what it smelled. Suddenly the snake's head shot into the beam of light and grabbed the rat in its jaws. The snake curled its body around the rat so tight we could hear bones popping as the rat's eyes bugged out. The snake squeezed its prey until the rat's nose stopped twitching. After a minute or so the snake uncurled its body and dislocated its jaws, then pushed the limp rat into its mouth head first. Then it lifted up its head and moved it back and forth, so the rat slid down its throat until only the hind legs and tail were exposed. The snake used its body to help pack in the rest of the rat. Its jaws came back together, and the rat was nothing more than a lump behind the snake's head, on its way to becoming another snake turd. Then the snake slithered off to the back corner of the cage and curled up, looking like it had a bad case of heartburn. The flashlight was turned off and I walked to the chow hall to restock my trap with food. If I didn't catch four to six rats a night, I would get discouraged. After placing the baited trap back inside one of the sandbag bunkers, I returned to my hootch for the night.

CHAPTER TWENTY-FIVE

I was awakened the morning of 27 September 1970 by the sound of a helo descending toward the helo pad. As I left our hootch, two high-ranking naval officers—one a lieutenant commander SEAL, the other a lieutenant from NILO (Naval Intelligence Liaison Office)—an older gook, with bare feet and dressed in black pajamas, and three other SEAL team members exited the chopper and ran out of the way of the rotating rotor blades. Mr. Q and Mr. Walsh were at the helo pad to meet them. The four officers and the gook went directly to the briefing hootch.

Fuck, here we go again, I thought. Something had to be in the works if two high-ranking officers were hand-carrying intelligence directly to the platoon. The other three SEALs, from Kilo Platoon, were Blackburn, Peterson, and Miller, who were stationed at RachGia. They had gone through UDT/SEAL Training Class 54. Some members of our platoon had been in their class, so they decided to spend their in-country R&R at our camp. I could think of a lot better places to spend in-country R&R than on the Bassac River near Long Phu. But when you have as tight a bond as SEALs and UDT personnel, it really doesn't matter where you are.

Blackburn didn't have very many good things to say about being stationed down in RachGia. He and Peterson and Miller were glad to get away from that defoliated hellhole, even if it was only for a few days. I told him he should have gone to the white-sand beaches of Cam Ranh Bay and got the hell out of the Delta region.

The two officers with the gook were in the briefing hootch with Mr. Q and Mr. Walsh for a long time, while the Army helo pilot and copilot waited down by the chopper. The pilot was the same one who had given Reeves and me our "ride for life" up the Bassac a while back. I didn't care to ask him for another ride. Eventually the visiting officers had finished their business, climbed on board the chopper, and disappeared into the western sky, leaving the gook with us. We headed for the chow hall for breakfast. Hot cereal, toast, fake milk, and the only thing that tasted real—sugar. Orange juice, mixed from powder concentrate to hide the taste of the Vietnamese water, was used to wash everything else down.

After leaving the chow hall, I was approached by Mr. Walsh. He said, "Your squad's ambush has been canceled for tonight, Young. Something else has come up." A queasy feeling stayed with me the entire day as I worried about what might be in store for us. It wouldn't have been so bad if our officers had just come out and told us what to expect, the way they did for most of our ops, but their silence gave me the impression that something really big was up. I tried to do things to occupy my mind, but everything I did seemed to be operation-oriented, like checking over the Stoner and ammo, making sure I had enough grenades and fresh ord-nance tape. I didn't even know what we were going to do, but I was ready for just about anything.

The gook turned out to be a Vietcong battalion com-mander who had Chieu Hoied (surrendered) during the past week and knew everything that was going on in the secret zone of Quan Long Phu District. Mr. Walsh and second squad left early that afternoon on the light for a coastal raid on a tax collector to verify the Chieu Hoi's information. Later second squad came back, leaving the Vietcong minus a tax collector and his three bodyguards as well as all the taxes he had collected. The Vietcong battalion commander's intel seemed to be reliable. During the next two days the Army's courier helo, which had a daily flight over Quan Long Phu District, took Mr. Walsh along for aerial reconnaissance of our next target, chosen based on intel brought by our new Chieu Hoi.

I was in our bar on September twenty-ninth when Mr. Walsh approached me. "Young," he said, "we have a briefing at 2000 hours tonight." But he wouldn't discuss any details about the operation until that time, and the suspense was killing me.

Our Chieu Hoi was in the chow hall all the time. That guy could pack away more food than any other Vietnamese I'd ever seen. During the last few days everyone took to calling him "Porkchop," since that was his favorite American meal. Quan and Mr. Walsh had been interrogating him morning, noon, and night ever since the operation against the tax collector.

After noon chow I decided to clean out the ammo bunker. It reminded me of walking into a cave. The metal box used for ammo storage had so many sandbags stacked on and around it that it looked like a small mountain. Some of the wooden crates that had contained ammo cans were empty, some were half full. I threw out the empty ones and consolidated the others. I finally got the bunker squared away by storing grenades, LAWs, and claymores on one side, and all ammo, sorted by caliber, on the other. After finishing, I closed the door and secured it with a huge lock. If any SEAL needed ammo or explosives, the key was readily accessible through Mr. Q and Mr. Walsh.

The evening came too quickly, and I really didn't want the day to end. At 2000 hours the door of the briefing hootch slammed shut. Fifteen SEALs and Quan were ready for the briefing on the next morning's op.

"Okay, listen up," said Mr. Q as he started the briefing. "The situation is, we have fresh intelligence on a major Vietcong munitions and weapons-repair facility. On and off there are up to two dozen Vietcong in the area of this facility, with at least ten Vietcong there at all times. Thick nipa palm and mangrove triple-canopy jungle cover the entire area. The facility is well hidden. One small canal is located approximately one hundred meters from the facility, to the east. It runs north toward the Bassac River.

"The weather will be overcast with no rain expected. The Vietcong have welders, torches, generators, and just about anything needed to repair weapons and construct booby traps. The Vietcong carried this equipment into the jungle in pieces and reassembled it at the facility. Since there are no roads or major canals nearby, the only other way to get heavy machinery there is by helicopter. We all know Charlie doesn't use helos." After a short hesitation, Mr. Q continued. "The Vietcong are heavily armed with AK-47s, RPG-7-B-40 rockets, and other small arms. The repair facility will be heavily guarded and well booby-trapped. Several of the Vietcong's own men are killed each month by their own booby traps in this area." Now I knew why my gut had ached all day. "This operation will be conducted in the southeastern section of Quan Long Phu District, just north of the prisoner-of-war operation we went on earlier in our tour. Because the Vietcong and NVA move through this area quite often, any number of enemy forces could be there. The Vietcong have had this area to themselves for quite some time, and absolutely no friendly forces are in the area. Our air support will be two OV-10 Broncos from Binh Thuy. We will also be using two Army slicks for our transportation to and from our objective.

"As you all know, Blackburn, Peterson, and Miller have volunteered to go on this operation with us."

"That's one hell of a way to spend your in-country R and R," said Panella. Everyone in the briefing hootch laughed.

"The mission, men, is to capture and destroy. We will bring back prisoners, documents, and weapons, and destroy the rest. Time of departure will be at 0530 tomorrow morning. Our insertion by helo will be in this small clearing,'' he said, using his pointer to show the landing zone on the picto map. ''We will patrol west to this canal, set up the security element to cross, cross the canal, and continue patrolling to the weapons facility. In case we cannot use this LZ for inserting or extracting, there is an alternate LZ two hundred meters to the east. Upon reaching our objective, we will enter the facility with great caution only after Grimes and Quan have checked out the area. If enemy contact is made, we will try to gain fire superiority and take command of the place, or maneuver back to the LZ for extraction. We will extract by helo from our main LZ or our alternate LZ, depending on enemy forces. If anyone gets separated from the platoon, patrol to the Bassac River—to the north— or the South China Sea, not far to the east. A recovery boat will cruise these areas in an attempt to recover you. Are there any questions up to this point?''

''Do I have to go, Mr. Q?'' I asked jokingly. This brought another laugh from the team members.

''Yes, Young, you have to go too,'' Mr. Q said.

Using helicopters usually means a daytime operation. I didn't care for helo ops. Helos are not quiet machines, so they tend to blow the element of surprise, especially if you don't insert right on top of the objective. If we had to patrol any distance from the landing zone to our objective, Charlie would surely run or set up an ambush. Sure, a helo comes in low and fast at jungle-canopy height, drops through a small hole in the jungle barely wide enough for the rotor blades, and inserts us into Charlie's world, but I liked to have the element of surprise on our side. Since both squads were going on the op, we'd need two choppers, but the landing zone and the alternate landing zone were only big enough for one slick at a time, giving Charlie lots of time to figure out what he wanted to do—run or stick around and fight. I didn't think he would want to give up the repair facility without a fight.

Mr. Q continued the briefing. ''Mr. Walsh, Panella, Young, and Reeves will carry the Stoner machine gun with their basic ammo load. Sitter and Bruce will carry the M-16/XM-148 combo with their basic load, and myself and Grimes will carry our CAR-15s. Strausbaugh, Baylett, and Blackburn will carry the M-60 machine guns, and the rest of you will have M-16s. Since we are using two Army slicks for transportation, we will use two PRC-77 radios. One will be carried by Doc and the other by Shannon. We will carry four haversacks of C-4 plastic explosives, and two LAW rockets. Sitter, Bruce, Miller, and Strausbaugh will pack the C-4; Young and Panella will pack the LAWs. Patrolling order will be as follows: Grimes, Quan, Porkchop, Mr. Q, Doc, Mr. Walsh, Strausbaugh, Sitter, Panella, Shannon, Peterson, Miller, Baylett, Blackburn, Bruce, Young, and Reeves. Everyone will carry standard grenades and pop flares. Young, Panella, Miller, and Baylett will handle prisoners, so make sure you guys have at least three handcuffs each. Any friendly wounded will be transported back to the LZ for extraction. Standard arm and hand signals will be used, and Doc will be the primary radio man. The call signs for the two Army slicks will be 'Free Ride One' and 'Two,' and our call sign will be 'Wet Back One.' I will be in command of the operation and third in our patrol, and Mr. Walsh will be sixth in the patrol and second-in-command. Are there any questions up to now?''

"How come we have to use Army slicks in daylight instead of the medium under the cover of darkness?'' Doc asked.

"Because the facility is reported to have 82mm mortar rounds buried in the jungle floor every square meter and is ringed by two mine fields which include buried as well as trip-wire booby traps. In addition to that, it's too far for us to patrol to from the river or South China Sea, and I feel we have a better chance if we drop right in on them. Besides, extraction by helo is quicker from this area, especially if we have prisoners and captured equipment. As I mentioned earlier, this place is hell even for their own men. Are there any more questions?''

There were no more questions, so everyone left the briefing hootch except Mr. Q, Mr. Walsh, Doc, and Shannon.

Most of us went directly to the bar, figuring a couple of cold ones wouldn't hurt anything. The operation wasn't too far from our camp to the southwest, about a twenty-minute chopper ride, and it was one of the platoon's biggest ops so far in our tour. Hell, our intel was good and fresh. We even knew some of the names of the gooks who ran the munitions facility. Porkchop had told Mr. Walsh that a South Vietnamese outpost with a 105 Howitzer was being paid by the Vietcong to shoot dummy rounds into the area of the Vietcong munitions facility. That way the Vietcong could recover the 105 projectiles, saw them open, and remove the explosive for use as booby traps and grenades. The Vietcong was supposed to have one hell of a pile of 105 projectile rounds stockpiled at the munitions facility.

As he sipped his beer, Reeves said, "Well, Young, if we have to go, we might as well go together." He had a big grin on his face. Doc walked in and took over the bartending. He didn't look too happy about the operation himself.

I looked back over at Reeves and said, "Maybe after we get back from the operation tomorrow we'll paint the jeep." Hell, the Seabees always had plenty of olive-drab and gray paint around. After a couple of beers we returned to the hootch, where Bruce was brewin' up a batch of tea over a can of Sterno. It was beginning to rain quite hard outside, and several people from the platoon began to filter into our hootch.

Sometimes the time spent before the operation was harder on me than the operation itself. But once the boat left our position after inserting us, or the helo flew away leaving us in a thick wall of green vegetation, things didn't seem to be so bad. At least while on the operations my mind was occupied with my duties and gave me little time to think about anything else. Even being engaged in combat with Charlie seemed to bother me less than thinking about it before an operation.

I died several times as the hours slowly passed until I was all geared up and ready to go, cammofaced, jungle-booted, and waterproof. We stood around Bruce's rack, the top one of a three-high stack, at the far corner of our hootch. His head was positioned toward the corner, and he used the two-by-four around the top of the wall to store his odds and ends. You could find everything from M-79 HE rounds to 35mm film cans full of pot sitting on his shelf. Some men in our platoon knew Bruce smoked pot and wanted to bust him. All they had to do was climb up to his rack, reach over to his shelf, and open one of his many film cans.

After we finished Bruce's tea, we raided the chow hall and then returned to our hootch for the night. The morning's operation wasn't far away. I climbed into my rack and tried to get some sleep.

CHAPTER TWENTY-SIX

The night went by, minute by minute; 11:34, then it was 12:05, 1:40, then 2:00. I don't know what was keeping me awake more, Bruce's tea or thinking about our next operation. Was I sleeping between the times I rolled over and looked at the clock? I couldn't answer that. Trying to sleep that night, I set up a lot of security around a lot of hootches and crossed a lot of canals in neck-deep water. Thinking about riding that chopper on a combat operation didn't help either. I kept remembering the five SEALs who were killed the day before I arrived in Nam. All night, thinking about them, I rode that chopper all the way to the ground. They had to be alive until they hit the ground, didn't they? I tried not to think about that, but I couldn't get it out of my mind. When I woke up in the morning, I was lying in a wet, sweaty bed. I was worn out all night fighting the operation I hadn't even gone on yet.

September 28, 1970. I was up and ready to go. I checked

over my Stoner and the rest of my gear. I took a can of flat black paint and sprayed over the red warning label on the LAWs Panella and I would carry. The platoon stood around in the hootch finishing up the last-minute face cammoing and morale boosting. The night was over for me, and things didn't seem so bad. Weber had been sent to the hospital in BinhThuy a few days earlier. I was thankful for that.

I had been careful of what I ate that morning. A simple burp or fart could give our position away. I had laughed about it back in training, when the instructors told us that, but I wasn't laughing anymore. Then I could hear the two slicks coming. I slipped on my UDT life jacket and secured it around my body, fitted on my Stoner vest full of fresh ammo and grenades, then checked my Smith & Wesson revolver one more time to make sure it was loaded. I grabbed my Stoner and followed my teammates down to the helo pad.

Mr. Walsh called out our names and we sounded off with the gear, ammo, and special equipment we were assigned. The sounds of the two Army slicks grew louder, and then they were visible. Soon they were circling the camp, judging the wind direction from a yellow smoke grenade that Mr. Walsh had thrown out. The first chopper descended into the wind and set down on the helo pad. The second chopper landed in the grass not far from the helo pad. Mr. Q, Bruce, Panella, Grimes, Doc, Quan, Peterson, Blackburn, and I climbed on board the first helo. Mr. Walsh, Porkchop, Strausbaugh, Sitter, Shannon, Miller, Baylett, and Reeves climbed on board chopper two.

The first chopper lifted off and, nose down, headed southeast. The second chopper followed close behind. Staying a safe distance apart, we gained altitude and moved into position side by side. I sat in the port door next to the door gunner. I was on the deck, but my feet hung outside the door. My legs weren't long enough to touch the skids unless I slid forward. We continued southeast about 1500 feet above the jungle canopy. Reeves was sitting in the starboard door of the other chopper, Stoner lying across his lap like a guitar. We exchanged waves like we hadn't seen each other for a while. We were on our way to a real game of Bang Bang.

To the north stretched the full length of Dung Island, the Bassac on either side. I could see the muddy brown Bassac mixing with the clear blue-green waters of the South China Sea. Very few rice paddies were down below now, just triple-canopy jungle with a few canals here and there. Then both helos started descending toward the jungle. Inside the chopper, Mr. Q was looking at a waterproofed picto map of our operating area. He was kneeling between the pilot and copilot, pointing toward the landing zone. Soon we were barely above the jungle canopy. Mr. Q gave the signal, and everyone locked and loaded his weapon. The second helo had dropped back behind us quite a ways.

The slick I was riding slowed down and started to drop into a small clearing in the jungle. Holding to my Stoner with one hand and the helo with the other, I slid my ass to the side of the helo until my feet touched the skids. The Stoner was cocked and off safe, ready to retaliate against any incoming enemy rounds. The helo had to hover above the ground because of vines and vegetation too tall to allow it to land. Mr. Q gave the word and we all jumped to the ground. Fuck, man, I didn't want to get off that chopper. But as usual, my SEAL training worked like clockwork.

After jumping to the ground, we immediately set up a perimeter to secure the LZ for the second helo. The first helo got the hell out of the way while the second one dropped into the jungle hole. There wasn't any room for pilot error, as the rotor blades barely cleared the thick green jungle walls. I had found some good cover and concealment to hide myself, but I couldn't see far beyond the thick green wall of the perimeter. As the second slick hovered, the rest of the SEALs jumped to the ground and took up their positions. Shannon ran over by me and hit the ground. The slick lifted through the jungle hole and took off in the direction of the first one, toward the South China Sea. Using both radios, an immediate radio check was made with the helos to ensure they were in working order.

Nobody moved, everyone was quiet. I listened to the

sound of the helos until they could not be heard any longer. I felt secure with my Stoner and the other fourteen SEALs with their firepower. The leaves and bushes were wet from the morning dew and smelled of mold. The ground was soft and damp. We had been delivered to Charlie's back door, alert and dry.

I stayed as still as possible, listening for signs of Vietcong who might have been sent in our direction to see if anybody had gotten off the choppers. Sometimes the Vietcong sent out scouts to alert the main force of trouble. With our firepower and training, we were definitely trouble to any Vietcong or NVA.

Soon the insects, then the birds, came back to life. Sometimes I thought the mosquito was the South Vietnamese national bird; they were nearly everywhere I went in Nam. After a while Grimes and Quan were sent to check out the area in the direction of the munitions facility. After about ten minutes or so they returned looking puzzled. Mr. Q, Mr. Walsh, and Grimes studied the picto map very carefully. Soon they realized we had inserted into the wrong area. Doc looked a little pissed off as he was told by Mr. Q to call back one of the choppers. Personally, I was ready to abort the mission. Hell, Charlie wasn't dumb, he already knew someone had inserted in the area.

The sound of the chopper grew louder, and the next thing I knew, Mr. Walsh and his picto map were climbing on board for an aerial recon of the area. The chopper climbed out of the jungle again. Taking advantage of the chopper's noise, the rest of us set up a better perimeter. I could hear the helo flying around, looking for the correct LZ. I'm sure Charlie could also hear and see it. There would be no element of surprise on this operation. I'm sure Mr. Q had his reasons for continuing the op, but I sure couldn't figure them out. I felt the safety of the entire platoon was being jeopardized.

Soon, Mr. Walsh returned and everyone assigned to his chopper climbed on board once again. The other chopper had been recalled. As it hovered above the foliage, the rest of us helped each other on board with our weapons on safe.

Both door gunners were alert and ready for anything that might come up. We were airborne again, moving to our correct LZ.

Just as planned in the briefing, Mr. Q's chopper descended into another hole in the jungle, not far from the one we had just left. At least reinserting us with the two choppers saved valuable time. One at a time the helos inserted us. As before, everyone ran to cover, and we had the LZ secure. The new area looked exactly like the last place, but the smell was different.

After the choppers were far away and we had waited for some time, normal jungle sounds did *not* reappear. There was no lack of mosquitoes, though. The sky was overcast and the ground was soft and damp. I noticed Vietcong footprints and alerted Mr. Q. After a while Grimes and Quan were sent out in the direction of the objective. The place was just too quiet. It had an eerie feeling to it. I expected to hear machine-gun fire from Grimes and Quan as they scouted the jungle ahead. They had been gone a long time before Grimes finally returned. He had located the small canal, and Quan was waiting by it for the rest of us.

One by one we started patrolling toward the canal in the proper order. Pork chop was out in front with Grimes and Quan; Reeves and I were last to follow. After the front of the platoon reached the canal, we set up security while Grimes crossed to check out the other side. Reeves and I guarded the rear of the element. The area was as quiet as a grave. After Grimes returned to the canal, he signaled us across to his side. One at a time we crossed the canal in waist-deep water. Once everyone was safely across, we began to patrol on a very well-traveled, heavily booby-trapped trail. The jungle was still motionless and quiet, but the trip wires across the trail proved the enemy was near.

I stayed crouched low to the ground as I patrolled. The barefoot prints in the trail were being replaced by American jungle-boot prints from the men in front of me. Reeves and I watched the rear and both our flanks very carefully for a possible rear attack. We patrolled forward a few meters then stopped to listen. This went on for a few minutes until we were just outside the facility.

We had already stepped over and around several trip wires and pungi pits. There were more out ahead of us. Stepping over a trip wire on a muddy trail loaded down with ammo and grenades was something in itself, especially when fifteen of us crossed the same wire one at a time. I made damn sure Reeves saw everything that was shown to me, and anything else suspicious. Everyone in the platoon stayed far enough apart so an enemy ambush wouldn't get us all. In the thick undergrowth we kept an eye on the man in front and the man behind us; Reeves watched our rear.

We stopped to listen again. Not a sound! Just the fuckin' mosquitoes and my beating heart. I was crouched low to the ground, checking out the green wall of jungle to the patrol's right flank. I looked forward and saw Bruce and Shannon crouched, covering their fields of fire. I looked back at Reeves crouched in what seemed to be the lowest spot he could find in the trail, his Stoner pointing in the direction we had just come from. Flashing back to the picto map at the briefing, I knew we were damn near on top of our objective. We stayed in that position for a long time. I figured Grimes was checking out the area ahead. I couldn't see anyone in our platoon any farther than Shannon to the front of our element; twelve men were ahead of him.

Finally the signal was passed back for the security element to move forward. That meant we were at our objective. I signaled Reeves we were moving again, then turned back to look at Bruce and Blackburn. Blackburn stood up to patrol forward, then Bruce. As I stood up to start patrolling, I looked to my right flank again. Without any warning, an explosion near the rear of our patrol picked me up and threw me in the direction I was looking. I landed facedown in the mud on my Stoner, several feet from where I had been standing. My actions were several seconds behind what was actually happening. I felt a burning sensation in the back of my left shoulder. Reeves crawled over to see if I was okay. I could hear machine-gun fire through the ringing in my ears. The LAW had been knocked off my back and was sticking out of the mud beside me. Well, at last the silence had been broken.

The two Army slicks along with our air support were immediately scrambled. Enemy tracers streaked over our heads through the jungle as Reeves and I lay side by side. Leaves and branches came down around us. We lifted our Stoners together and laid down a volley of automatic weapons fire in the direction of the incoming rounds. A quick situation report was needed to evaluate the wounded.

Six other SEALs were also wounded. Shannon had his back and radio full of shrapnel, Strausbaugh was lucky he was so short, since he had a strip torn open down the top of his head, and the rest had assorted holes and cuts everyplace but where it counted. The explosion had been a command-detonated mine in the trees which had blown off the top half of one tree close to the rear of our patrol. Mr. Q started moving the other wounded SEALs back out toward the LZ for med-evac. He sent Mr. Walsh with Grimes and Blackburn into the weapons factory to quickly search it and blow it up, because I knew he didn't want to come back here again.

The front element went through another mine field and got inside the munitions facility. Blackburn set up his field of fire to cover everything out front, while Mr. Walsh and Grimes searched the entire area. It was packed with explosives. The VC were manufacturing grenades, claymore mines, and dismantling bombs and 105 Howitzer rounds as a source of their explosives. The place had enough tools and equipment to stock a small army with weapons for a long time to come. As Grimes and Mr. Walsh finished their quick search, ten Vietcong came strolling down the trail into the factory with little caution. Blackburn opened up with his M-60, killing several. The rest fled. Before Mr. Walsh put the C-4 explosive packs in place, there was one of the biggest damn explosions I ever heard coming from their direction. The men in the helos overhead thought all the SEALs down below were dead because so much shit came flying through the air it nearly knocked out one of the helos. I felt the concussion rush through the jungle and pass over me clear back where I was. More crap came flying through the air. Enemy rounds continued to saturate our perimeter. The Vietcong had command detonated a 105 Howitzer round which was sitting in the well in the center of the factory. The shrapnel knocked the hell out of Blackburn and Mr. Walsh. The blast only got part of Grimes, since he was standing in Mr. Walsh's blast shadow. He received only shrapnel in the legs. The concussion knocked them all down. Grimes picked up Mr. Walsh, who stood with his Stoner pointing straight out over the back entrance to the factory. Grimes was crawling toward Blackburn when two more Vietcong opened up and shot out Blackburn's arms from under him. Without hesitating, Mr. Walsh cut the two Vietcong down before they had a chance to do any more damage. Grimes dragged Blackburn toward the LZ while Mr. Walsh moved ahead to provide security for them. Two more Vietcong jumped out of the nipa palm, and Mr. Walsh killed both of them before they had a chance to get off a round. Reeves was ordered to move forward and help Mr. Walsh. I watched him crawl off into the jungle in their direction.

Enemy rounds continued to pour into our position. By now it seemed that everyone had been wounded except Mr. Q, Reeves, and Quan. Still, everyone able returned the enemy's fire. Reeves finally reached the front of our element, then crawled farther toward the munitions facility. As Reeves got close to the facility, he saw Mr. Walsh, Blackburn, and Grimes coming across the mine field.

Mr. Walsh looked like one of the walking dead, bleeding badly from the head and other parts of his body, but he kept moving as Reeves grabbed Blackburn's M-60 and helped Grimes drag him through the jungle. As they returned to our position, enemy tracers streaked over our heads through the jungle. I took over Reeves's position and continued to deliver a maximum rate of fire from my Stoner into the surrounding jungle. Enemy rounds continued to fly through the area. I kept my head down. Bruce was trying to figure out where the enemy rounds were coming from so he could retaliate with his 40mm HE. My shoulder still burned and it was bleeding.

Reeves was firing at the enemy's position as sweat ran down his forehead and burned his eyes. It was difficult for him to see. He didn't stop firing his weapon until it was empty. Then he switched to Blackburn's M-60 and emptied it. Doc was still talking to the helos on the radio and crawling around tending to those wounded worst. He passed Blackburn up, thinking he was dead. I still couldn't see the little bastards, but by firing my Stoner into the green jungle walls to our flanks around me, I continued to try to suppress their fire. Word was passed back for me to secure the LZ so we could try to get the wounded out. By the rate of enemy fire coming our way, I knew that wouldn't be easy.

Firing my Stoner to my flanks all the way, trying to suppress the enemy's fire long enough to reach some safe cover, I moved slowly back toward the canal. I couldn't see the VC, but it seemed like he could see me. Suppressing the Cong's fire seemed impossible. How many of those little fuckers are out there? I wondered, as I stayed low and crawled through the mud toward the LZ. Thoughts of the booby traps in the trail preyed on my mind. The smell of burned gunpowder filled the air. Tracers flew in all directions. Why in the fuck did we even come to this place? I thought.

I finally saw one of the little fuckers who was shooting at us. He was trying to move around behind us, toward the LZ. He disappeared behind a bush and I knew he had come out the other side, but I didn't think he knew my position. Sure enough, he came out the other side, moving rapidly. Tracers from my Stoner streaked through the jungle and disappeared into his body. He fell face first over his AK-47. My Stoner barrel smoked from the heat of the full automatic fire. I dropped back down to the ground and changed to my third box of ammo. I only had a few rounds left in the second box, and didn't want to run out of ammo in a tight situation. I felt more secure with a full ammo box in the Stoner. I heard more sounds of Vietcong trying to cut off our only exit, so I had to get to the LZ as quickly as I could. I fired into the jungle toward the noise and continued to crawl back down the trail. Soon I was staring at a trip wire right in front of my nose. I lifted up and fired my weapon into the jungle and then jumped to the ground on the other side. My teammates were firing their weapons into the jungle behind me and slowly bringing the wounded my way.

Finally I reached the canal. I could still hear some gooks, out ahead of me this time. Bruce was bringing one of the wounded SEALs up close to my position. I pointed to the trip wire. Bruce lifted him over the wire and laid him back down to the ground. I crawled back to Bruce and helped him drag our wounded comrade toward the canal while I continued to fire bursts into the enemy's positions. At least where the fuckers *seemed* to be. Again I heard gooks across the canal. I looked at Bruce and said, "I'll fix their ass." I took the LAW rocket off my back and laid over on my side. I set down my Stoner and cocked the LAW by opening it. I made sure nobody was directly behind me, and then lifted my body up far enough to point the LAW toward the enemy's position. As I squeezed the trigger mechanism, enemy rounds came into our position. I squeezed the trigger harder. Nothing happened. I dropped back down to the ground. I looked at Bruce and he looked at me. Again I lifted up to squeeze the LAW's trigger while Bruce covered me with his M-16/XM-148 combo. I squeezed that fucker as hard as I could. Still nothing from the rocket. That wasn't the first time that the LAW didn't work for me in a tight situation.

Not wanting to drag around a cocked LAW rocket or take it out on a helo, I threw it downstream into the water of the canal and watched it sink out of sight. I looked at Bruce and said, "Charlie can have that one." I grabbed my reliable Stoner and jumped into the muddy canal. Bruce covered me as I pulled myself out of the canal on the opposite side using the available vines and tree limbs. I hosed down the jungle around the LZ away from my teammates. Bruce brought the wounded SEAL across the canal and stayed inside the treeline from the LZ. The rest of our platoon was nearing the canal, and I could hear the two slicks circling our position, their door gunners helping me secure the LZ. I could hear Mr. Q back on the other side of the canal keeping control of what was left of the platoon. Back toward the munitions facility, acting as rear security, Reeves was at the far end of our platoon.

I returned to the canal and left Bruce to cover the LZ. Crossing the canal again, I joined my teammates and led them back to the canal. Once there, I continued to fire to our flanks while Reeves fired his weapon back toward the weapons facility, giving Charlie little chance to stick his head up behind us.

I helped the wounded across the canal and back to the LZ. My hands, Stoner, and clothes were soaked with blood from my wounded comrades. My left shoulder still burned and was beginning to ache like hell. All I could think about was, Let's get the fuck out of here! Finally, most of the worst wounded were near the LZ, and Doc called in the first chopper. To help keep Charlie down, both door gunners were firing their M-60 machine guns to their flanks. I helped carry Mr. Walsh and some of the other wounded to the hovering chopper, while everyone able fired their weapons into the jungle to help cover the helo's retreat. Blackburn was left behind with the rest of us. After the first helo was safely out of the way, the rest of us set up a perimeter around the LZ to cover the next helo.

Charlie knew he had hurt us bad. The second helo came in fast, at treetop level, and started to drop into the LZ. Those of us able fired our weapons outside our perimeter to keep Charlie down while the chopper descended. Seeing us firing our weapons, the chopper pilot chickened out and started lifting up out of the LZ. Doc grabbed the radio and yelled at the fucker to get back down and pick us up. I think the pilot knew Doc was serious. We continued to fire out into the surrounding area as the helo descended again. We carried Blackburn over to the hovering chopper and loaded him first. Firing our weapons behind us, the rest of us climbed on board, Mr. Q and I boarding last.

As our helo lifted up out of the LZ, the enemy opened up to try to bring the chopper down. Enemy rounds were popping through the aluminum sides of the helo as we returned fire. Vietcong tracers streaked out of the jungle toward us as we climbed out over the jungle canopy and headed northwest.

CHAPTER TWENTY-SEVEN

Once we were clear of the area, Blackburn was laid in a better position on the deck. We had managed to bring out all our weapons and explosives, leaving nothing behind except for the faulty LAW rocket at the bottom of the canal. The door gunners stared at us in disbelief. The chopper pilot looked as if he had shit his pants, but he was glad to be alive and out of that area. If Doc hadn't assured him on the radio that it was okay to pick us up, I think he would have left us to the mercy of the Vietcong.

Doc was tending to Blackburn, who was now unconscious. The deck of the helo was covered with blood from our wounded. I sat in the starboard doorway, my feet hanging outside. It wasn't long before we caught up with the other helo. The pilots had already radioed Binh Thuy that wounded were on the way. Then Blackburn was coming to. He started kicking and thrashing around inside the helo and damn near kicked me out the door. I laid across him, holding him down, while Doc gave him a shot of morphine. I held him down until he quieted down. He didn't seem to know who or where he was. His glossy eyes stared into the overhead of the helo. While we were flying for Binh Thuy, air strikes were called on the munitions factory.

I didn't know how bad our helo had been hit by enemy fire, but I sat there looking out the door at the jungle below and thought about the five SEALs who were wasted in the helo crash. I looked over to the other helo flying beside us. I wondered how Mr. Walsh was doing. He and Blackburn seemed to be the worst wounded. Looking down again, I saw our camp on the Bassac, but we continued on to Binh Thuy. As we landed, I saw Weber standing by the ambulances. I was glad he hadn't been on this operation.

As the helos shut down, the pilots walked around the aircraft checking the damage and counting the bullet holes. Weber helped his wounded teammates on board the ambulances. Mr. Q stayed in Binh Thuy, and those of us who weren't seriously wounded returned to camp on one of the helos with the weapons and gear. By the look of my teammates, I was the least wounded. Back at our camp, the MST crew and a couple of Seabees helped us unload the helo while we told them what had happened.

All the weapons and gear were laid out on the cleaning table by the time the slick took off to return to Binh Thuy. I peeled off my wet, muddy, bloody clothes and put on my UDT swim trunks. With the cammo still on my face and hands, I started helping the others clean the weapons. With over half the platoon in the hospital, the camp seemed deserted. It took quite a while to clean everyone's weapons.

After all the weapons and gear were squared away, I looked around camp for the Seabees' corpsman. My shoulder was still burning and I wanted him to check it out. He discovered a small piece of shrapnel embedded too deep in my shoulder for him to dig out. He was afraid that the shoulder would be damaged even more if he tried. He cleaned the wound, gave me a tetanus shot, and told me to have it looked at in Binh Thuy. After that day's operation, I swore I would never come back to Nam to fight again— that is, if I made it home alive. I learned that the air strikes on the munitions facility after we extracted had missed their target. That really pissed me off, as I knew the Vietcong would continue their operations in that area.

With only three and a half more months left in my tour, I was beginning to know Charlie pretty well. We had hit his positions on Dung Island hard in the past, now it had been our turn to get hit. It looked like the platoon would be shut down for a while. The invisible shield our platoon had had around it, which stopped us from getting hit, had been broken. There was no posing for the cameras with VC prisoners on this operation. Going into that operation with just a squad of SEALs would have been disastrous. The mission should have been aborted after we inserted into the wrong LZ, blowing any chance of surprise.

I would not look forward to another daytime helo operation. I felt safer deep within enemy territory at night on the medium than on any helo operation during daylight hours.

I thought about the shrapnel in my shoulder and wondered what else had flown past my body without hitting me. I was lucky to be alive; the whole platoon was, as far as that goes. I wondered how Mr. Walsh and Blackburn were doing. They had graduated from the same training class, now they lay in the hospital together.

If anybody could pull through, they could. Blackburn was a big son of a bitch, and it looked like his in-country R&R had just been extended. He had been quite the hell-raiser in Class 54. The instructors would lay a little shit on him, and he would give them shit right back. He could take anything the instructors could dish out and a little more. He was a great morale booster for Class 54. Mr. Walsh had been the honor graduate of that training class, and was known as "Iron Nick." He could survive just about anything and come back stronger than ever.

By now everyone in my training class had been hurt either in training or in Vietnam; Palma had been killed. My combat experiences were hardening me, I could feel it, but I still felt it wasn't worth losing my life over gooks who didn't want to help themselves. Still, I kept my thoughts to myself; that was a wound in itself. Everyday life in Nam was a booby trap for me, and I got the "glad that operation is over" feeling, yet at the same time I couldn't wait to go out again and blow Charlie away at his own game. Even though Charlie was small, swift, and seemed to be invisible, the bullets from my Stoner were faster, especially if I had the element of surprise on my side.

As the days slowly went by, the wounded returned from

the hospital. Except for a few ambushes from the boats, very little operating was conducted over the next couple of weeks. Mr. Walsh was the last one still in the hospital. He had been temporarily blinded because of his head wounds. The doctor wanted to send him back to the States, but he didn't agree. He would stay on with Juliett Platoon.

The day Mr. Walsh got out of the hospital, he went to the Binh Thuy Air Force Base and found First Lt. Alan Dillman, an Air Force forward air controller who was a friend of his from the Air Force Academy; Mr. Walsh had graduated from the Air Force Academy but took his commission in the Navy. First Lt. Dillman was attached with the 22nd Tactical Air Support Squadron which flew recon missions only at night. Mr. Walsh and Lt. Dillman took off that night in an 0-2 aircraft and found the weapons factory. He called in an air strike with a flight of AT-37 fighters. Another friend of Mr. Walsh's from the Air Force Academy, First Lt. Mike Armstrong, was in charge of the AT-37's which flew out of the Bien Hoa Air Force Base just north of Saigon. First they bombed the place and counted ninety-one secondary explosions off their first bombing run, then wall-to-wall napalm, followed by 20mm and 7.62 strafing. Air strikes continued, aimed at the munitions factory, until the whole area had been saturated with rockets and bombs and all the aircraft had expended their payloads. That was the one time in Nam that I didn't mind all that American taxpayers' money being spent. The air strikes must have made it hell in the area around the munitions facility. I'm sure they slowed the Vietcong down, but the flow of weapons and supplies to the Vietcong would continue. They would relocate their facility, and the process would start all over again.

The silence and smell of that operating area would haunt me for a long time. Charlie had the element of surprise on his side that time. The munitions facility had been in operation there for a long time and was a vital strategic facility for the Vietcong and NVA in the whole area. Even with all our firepower, we hadn't been able to overcome the enemy. It was difficult to determine how many Vietcong were there at the time of the operation. After the second air strike, I would be surprised if any Vietcong could have survived, no matter how deep they were dug in.

Payday found our platoon on the way to Binh Thuy riding on the MSSC. Weber still had stomach problems, and they were getting worse every day. He was going back to the hospital, and Reeves was going on R&R to Australia. Weber and I still planned on Hawaii for our R&R, which was scheduled for November 3rd. On R&R the platoon's married men usually met their families in Hawaii. That was as close to home as the military would let them get while serving in Vietnam.

The tide was at its highest and the river was bank to bank. The water surface was glassed off and the medium cut through it smoothly leaving a neat wake behind. The mid-morning sun beat down on us as we lay on the medium's canvas top with our shirts off collecting the rays. A peaceful moment in a hellhole. Our boat wove in and out of debris picked up from the riverbanks by the high tide. Looking toward shore, one could see the reflection of the compact green jungle wall on the glassy surface. The muddy water looked like a mirror until our wake disturbed it. Looking at it at an angle, one couldn't tell if the water was muddy with the reflection of the blue sky and white clouds. But looking straight down it was obvious. Everyone on board had his private spot to sit or lie down on the boat. Very little conversation was conducted as the medium cruised at three-quarter speed up the river. Everyone was lost in his own thoughts, that is until the medium developed engine trouble and Melfa shut them down. One of the MST crew members went aft and opened both soundproof engine covers, as we sat dead in the middle of the Bassac about ten miles downriver from Binh Thuy. The problem was discovered but couldn't be fixed until we reached Binh Thuy. Melfa started one of the engines and we moved upstream barely above idle. I was glad the engine problems happened there and not in the middle of Dung Island on an operation at two o'clock in the morning.

It seemed like it took an hour to go one mile, but as soon as the tide started going out, our progress would be even worse. We were making very little headway. Not long after the engines broke down a large sampan pulling a barge came upriver behind us. As the sampan neared our port side, Mr. Q motioned to the Vietnamese on board it to pull over. The gook maneuvered his large sampan up alongside our boat and Reeves and I were told to search it. The little fucker was more than happy to show us around, he had nothing to hide. The Vietnamese man was then asked if he was going as far as Binh Thuy. He was going farther than that. He was then asked if he would take Reeves and me to Binh Thuy and drop us off. He seemed glad to have the company.

Reeves and I stayed on the sampan and shoved off from the MSSC and got under way. The sampan was moving a lot faster than the medium. We were to get help from the Naval Support Facility and send a boat downriver to recover the MSSC. The sampan cut through the water just as fast as it could go pulling the barge. It bounced around from the wakes of other South Vietnamese boats crossing the river in front of it. Reeves and I sat up front near the bow with the Vietnamese steering the vessel in an open cabin behind us. I looked back downstream. The medium was now a small dark dot on the horizon of the wide brown Bassac. Large cumulus clouds lined the background toward the South China Sea.

The closer to Can Tho we got the more boat traffic there was. Mamasans washed clothes along the shores, not taking the time to look up from their duties. Naked kids with dark brown bodies jumped into the muddy water and swam around. I took pictures of Reeves sitting in front of the cabin with the Vietnamese steering behind him. Reeves had filled his curved-stem pipe with pot and had it hanging out of his mouth. The gook was smiling and his teeth and mouth were smeared with betel nut. There was a lot of contrast between tall, blond, blue-eyed Reeves and the skinny, wrinkle-faced dark-haired and complexioned Vietnamese. By the looks of the gook's weathered face, he had been running the Bassac for years. I sat next to Reeves as he lit the pipe. The trip upstream was a great opportunity for us to light up, and we took advantage of it.

After a couple of bowls we had red eyes and big smiles on our faces. We offered some to the Vietnamese, but he declined. Trying to strike up a conversation with him was impossible as he understood no English and we understood very little Vietnamese.

Binh Thuy wasn't far away now. Reeves and I kicked back and had one more bowl. I could see the docks at the Naval Support Facility now. All along the south shore of the Bassac, inside the facility, were large rocks used for riprap, to stop the wakes from passing boats from eating away the shoreline. A long floating dock with a tin roof paralleled the shoreline. It had a flexible hinged ramp off the west end that went up to the shore. The Vietnamese pulled in close enough to the dock that we could jump off the bow. He looked a little nervous, probably because he was in a restricted area. We had assured him it was all right, but he nervously eyeballed all the boats and equipment around the area as he backed away from the dock. Reeves and I stood on the dock and waved to him as he got under way again, then reported the disabled MSSC at the SEAL quonset hut. A boat was immediately dispatched downstream to recover it. Reeves and I sat around and waited for the medium to arrive.

After a while we walked back down to the dock to see if our boat was getting close. A light from Kilo Platoon was just arriving, and two men who'd been in the training class with Reeves and me were aboard. We helped them secure the light to the dock. Staudinmire and Garces were glad to see us. They were a great surprise because Reeves and I hadn't seen them since we left the States. Staudinmire had red hair and a long bushy red beard. Garces was from a Mexican background. He was short, had dark hair, and was serious about everything he did. He had already had a three-year hitch in the Army Airborne and after his Army enlistment was up he joined the Navy. What a crazy fucker.

As we stood on the dock and talked, I saw the medium approaching, being towed by another boat. When it finally arrived, Reeves and I helped secure it to the dock. Reeves collected his bags from the medium and everyone went straight to the SEAL Quonset hut to collect their pay vouchers. Before anyone had a chance to leave, Mr. Q said, "Be back here at 0900 tomorrow morning and stay out of trouble." Doc asked if anyone wanted to go into Can Tho with him, but we said we might meet him there later. I wanted to go to the PX for some film. Doc and Sitter went out the main gate to hitch a ride to Can Tho.

Binh Thuy and Can Tho were supposed to be a secure area and only the MPs were supposed to carry weapons. But, not trusting any gook, I always packed my Model 15 Smith & Wesson. I always kept it concealed, but I would rather have been in trouble for packing it than follow the rules and be dead. With a weapon, at least I would have a chance of surviving an attack. After all, I was in Vietnam, not downtown San Diego. You never knew who or where the enemy might be. Besides, I thought carrying a pistol was better than packing around a frag grenade the way some SEAL Team members used to do.

Reeves' flight to Saigon wasn't until the next morning so we ended up in Can Tho for our routine steam and cream and had a few beers with Doc and the guys at our favorite bar.

Next morning, about 0845, we all came staggering into the SEAL Quonset hut. Doc's eyes looked like two piss holes in the snow and the knees on his cammo pants were all bloody. It wasn't like Doc not to be squared away and looking his military best. He must have really hung one on after Reeves and I left him at the bar.

After all of Juliett Platoon poured in we walked to the dock to board the medium, which had been worked on throughout the night. We untied it, shoved off, and proceeded down the Bassac at a slow speed to let the twin Chevy's warm up. Behind us, standing on the dock, Reeves waved good-bye. That's the last I was to see of him for about ten days. He was soon out of sight on the flat horizon to the west.

CHAPTER TWENTY-EIGHT

Doc had found a comfortable spot in the corner of the medium with his head lying on a curled-up flak jacket. His feet were up on a minigun ammo can. The medium got on step, heading for home. We worked hard on our operations, but we played hard too. Doc was living proof of that.

We really got away with a lot of shit sometimes. I guess most people thought it really wasn't worth fucking with us for some of the things we pulled off. Most people just left us alone. Our platoon was lacking LePage, Weber, Mr. Walsh, and Reeves now. LePage wouldn't be back, Reeves was on R&R, and Mr. Walsh and Weber were in the hospital.

The medium stayed on step all the way down the Bassac. Soon the camp was in sight off in the distance, and not much later I was sittin' in our chow hall eating lunch. The Seabee cook could put out one hell of a meal if he wanted to. It all depended on what side of the bed he got up on in the morning.

Mr. Q was setting up a briefing for an ambush that night. It was time to uncover some more mysteries of the Vietcong's movement and sanctuaries. We were to conduct the ambush from the medium. Everyone was still a little shook up from the September 30 operation. Mr. Q, Bruce, Doc, and I would go on this operation, plus Melfa and two other MST crew members. An ambush was about the only type of operation Doc was able to go on until his knees healed. He didn't want to chance an infection crawling around in the mud and water in his condition. That didn't make Mr. Q very happy, because, as a first-class petty officer,

Doc was supposed to set an example for the rest of the platoon. Nothing was said to Doc about it, though; Doc normally had his shit together. Mr. Q relied on Doc for a lot of advice about the missions we went on. With Doc's SEAL experience, he was a great asset.

At 1400 hours we had a short briefing on the night's operation. That gave us plenty of time to prepare. The MST crew made the medium ready by filling it with gasoline from the fifty-five-gallon drums stacked along the shoreline. This was always done using a hand pump which was inserted into each drum, one at a time. The crew also loaded all the ammo cans for the General Electric minigun, two .50-caliber machine guns, and the two M-60 machine guns. Two M-79 grenade launchers and ammo were also loaded on board, and the medium's two radios and the radar were checked out. A cooler of freshwater was also added.

The medium was hard to beat. Designed strictly for SEAL operations, you didn't see many of them around. Not all SEAL platoons had Medium SEAL Support Craft—or Light SEAL Support Craft. There weren't very many made. There seemed to be an unending supply of PBRs (patrol boat, river) around. I saw them everywhere I went in Nam, along the waterways inland and along the coast. The medium and the light had a higher top speed than the PBRs, and the medium could carry more men and equipment.

At 2200 hours everyone involved climbed on board, and the medium backed out into the Bassac. It wasn't long before we were on step into the dark night. The radar and the starlight scope led the way. I sat on the bench seat on the starboard side, watching the camp's perimeter lights disappear behind us. No one talked; we were all lost in our thoughts. We were soon around the west end of Dung Island and heading back down the Bassac toward the South China Sea. I wondered just how many Cong there were on Dung Island.

We soon reached the eastern end of Khem Bang Co Canal. Our weapons were cocked and put on safe and we proceeded down the canal. The Khem Bang Co Canal was a natural canal that separated Con Coc Island from Dung Island. The canal was anywhere from 400 to 200 meters wide, and our ambush site was at the narrowest point, near the east end of the canal where it made a right turn to the northwest. We picked out our site on the radar, and the medium moved into position on the south bank of the canal. The engines were turned off. We were partially hidden by the vegetation that grew into the water. Limbs and vines hung over the top of the medium, and we had an excellent view of the canal; to the right, back out to the Bassac, and to the left, back into Dung Island. The narrow point in the canal was an excellent place for Charlie to cross. We took turns studying the canal with the starlight scope. The night's ambush was conducted in the vicinity of Xom Ba Keo, a small village on the island, near where the Vietcong were harassing the villagers for rice and had cut off a few South Vietnamese heads. It was considered to be a hot area of the island, and both banks of the canal were heavily boobytrapped with pungi pits, grenade trip wires, and homemade Vietcong claymores.

No warning shots were heard as we entered the canal, but that didn't mean Charlie wasn't watching. For all we knew, he was in the thick jungle beside us. It was overcast that night, making it difficult to see through the starlight scope. Without enough ambient light, the picture was less intensified. Our weapons were left on safe while we were on the medium. Stay quiet, wait, listen. Fireflies flickered through the medium and through the vegetation beside our boat. Sometimes they even looked like eyes peering out of the jungle. Mosquitoes dug into our flesh. Time crept by as we waited silently. An ambush could make for a long night.

As time went by we continued to pass around the starlight scope, checking out the entire area 360 degrees around us. I anticipated the little fuckers would show up any time. The suspense was killing me.

Around 0130 in the morning, about the time I thought we might be sitting out there for nothing, a noise was heard up the canal from us, a hollow wooden sound like a pole hitting the side of a sampan. We waited, listening into the dark. Very quietly, we made our weapons ready. Doc had the starlight scope glued to the canal upstream. My fingers were going numb gripping the Stoner. A long time went by. Then Doc spotted a small sampan coming from a small canal on the south shore, about 200 meters upstream from us. Two Vietnamese were in it. We waited until the sampan entered the middle of the canal. They had over fifty meters between each canal bank. Maybe they have a supporting element on the bank, I thought.

With a push of a button, the medium's engines were started. We pulled out of the vegetation and sprinted toward them at top speed. The two Vietcong suspects, wondering where the hell we came from, turned the sampan around and paddled as fast as they could in the direction they had come from. As we closed in on them, Doc yelled, *"Lai dai,"* meaning "come here" in Vietnamese. They paddled harder toward shore. Doc yelled one more time. They ignored him. Doc opened fire on them, and everyone on board immediately followed. Both gooks jumped into the water twenty-five meters from shore. Two concussion grenades were thrown into the water. They had to have been hit, the sampan was riddled with holes. A quick search of the sampan came up with nothing but blood from the gooks; they had been hit.

We looked around the water but saw no bodies. There was no way they could have survived the concussion grenades. We waited for a while, hoping one of them might surface. We stayed low, behind the walls of the medium, and also watched both banks of the canal in case a larger enemy force was setting up an ambush for us. Maybe if we had let the two go by, a larger force would have exposed itself.

After a short time we tied the sampan to the stern of the medium and towed it back out to the Bassac and back to camp. It could be used on a clandestine operation in the future. Sometimes we dressed in black pajamas and used a sampan for insertion. The sampan would be left behind after the mission, and the element would extract another way. Using sampans, Communist weapons, and dressing like the

Vietcong, made it easier to penetrate enemy areas undetected. Operations like that were rare, but SEALs were flexible in choice of clothes, weapons, transportation, tactics, and areas of operations. This attention to detail made for the success of many SEAL missions. You couldn't always tell what Charlie was up to or what to expect from him next. He was very unpredictable. That's one reason we had to be unpredictable and flexible.

This ambush hadn't been a big operation. At least the Cong knew somebody was out there besides himself, and that had a psychological effect on him. He never knew where we would be next or what to expect from us. For the time being, his movement in that area would be dampened.

A few days passed. A couple more ambushes were conducted from the medium on different parts of the island. Some were more successful than others. One morning I was awakened by the sound of a helo circling our camp. It was 10 October 1970. Another helo operation, I thought, as I rolled out of my rack to check it out. Mr. Walsh was running from the helo with Reeves. Mr. Walsh had been released from the hospital, and Reeves had returned from R&R. I welcomed them both back to the sun-fun capital of the Bassac. Mr. Walsh said Weber wasn't doing too well and might have to be sent back to the States.

Why in the hell couldn't I get sick? I thought. I was sorry Weber wasn't feeling well, but sending him back to the States sounded great to me. We were close friends, so if anything had happened to Weber, I would have a hard time dealing with it. I had a stack of mail I was collecting for Weber. I sure missed him.

Mr. Walsh was looking real good and he was already talking about operating. Reeves had a real good time in Australia and gave me the address of some friends he met who I could stay with if I decided to go there. But my decision depended on what Weber wanted to do.

That same day, Mr. Walsh planned an ambush for Sitter, Baylett, Shannon, and himself using the medium. I helped them gear up and cammo their faces that night. They boarded the medium and disappeared into the dark in the direction of Dung Island. After sitting at the ambush site several hours with no results, Mr. Walsh decided to cruise a few canals in the medium and try to make contact with Charlie that way. Finally, some poor gook fired his weapon to warn his comrades. The medium opened up with all its weapons in the direction of the shot. If there was anything left of the poor fucker who fired the shot, he deserved to live. The medium returned to camp just about sunrise. Those of us sleeping were awakened by all the noise the ambush party made as they entered the hootch.

I helped them clean their weapons and gear and then we all went to chow. During chow one of Mr. Walsh's intelligence-officer friends showed up from Soc Trang. Mr. Walsh and the officer left the chow hall to talk. It wasn't long before Mr. Walsh returned and approached Bruce and me. "The Military Police are looking for that jeep in the Soc Trang area," he said. "It's an American civilian contractor's jeep. We have to get rid of it, and quick. Next time, Young, get a military jeep."

What should we do with it? Bruce suggested we dump it in the Bassac, but there were too many people at the camp to do that. Someone would talk. The only thing left to do was drop it off someplace. I was sure glad Mr. Walsh was friends with Lt. Doug Moran, the naval intelligence liaison officer in Soc Trang. Mr. Walsh had driven the jeep to Soc Trang on several occasions, so the intel officer could have told the Military Police.

After talking the situation over, we decided the best thing to do was drive it to Soc Trang and drop it off. We arranged for a Seabee to drive to Soc Trang with a six-by, and I would follow in the jeep. It was too late to change the jeep's numbers and give it a paint job. Bruce and I went through the jeep and removed any gear that was ours. We also wiped off our fingerprints from any part of it we might have touched. The gate was opened at our camp and we hauled ass toward Soc Trang. The children, pigs, and chickens scattered out of our way as we drove through the village outside the camp. We didn't slow down for anything.

A couple of hours later, we finally approached Soc Trang.

As we entered the city, the road came to a stop sign where the intersection teed off. I pulled the jeep to the side of the road by a concrete wall. Bruce and I wiped off the last of our fingerprints and jumped onto the six-by that was standing by. The six-by pulled out into the busy street and made a left turn. I looked back at my blue jeep and then down the road behind us. I felt like I had just lost a good friend, but a Military Police jeep was just reaching the intersection. The MPs noticed the blue jeep and turned in beside it. They hadn't seen us because of the concrete wall. "Fuck, Young, that was too close," Bruce said.

We took the six-by on into Soc Trang to waste a little time before going near that intersection again. A blue jeep in Vietnam wasn't an easy thing to hide. After a while we got the balls to drive back by the intersection on the way back to camp. The blue jeep was gone. We continued on to our camp. We knew how lucky we were. During the next few days I expected the M.P. to show up at any time or Mr. Q to say, "Okay, Young, you have to take a little ride to Soc Trang and meet these guys."

But nothing ever happened. I never heard another word, nor did I ever borrow another jeep.

CHAPTER TWENTY-NINE

The platoon wasn't going to operate for a few days because the medium needed to be worked on. So Bruce and I got permission from Mr. Q to go to Saigon, but we were to be back at camp in four days. Since the medium had to go to Binh Thuy for the work, we threw our gear on board for the ride upriver. Once in Binh Thuy, we caught a ride on an Army slick to Saigon and later that day found ourselves kicked back at the Victoria Hotel. I was nervous as hell the whole time I was in Saigon. I trusted the enemy on Dung Island more. At least I knew what to expect from them.

The next morning Bruce and I went to the MAC/V headquarters and found the top-ranking SEAL in Vietnam, an easygoing officer named Clemente who was in charge of all SEAL platoons. Bruce asked him if he would cut us some orders to Subic Bay in the Philippines. He looked at Bruce in a funny way and then said no. Bruce wouldn't give up, and asked him to reconsider. We told him we weren't going to operate for a few days and our platoon was the one that just got shot up pretty bad. Finally, Lieutenant Commander Clemente gave in and authorized us to leave Vietnam. I couldn't believe it. It's a good thing he knows Bruce, I thought. It felt great getting way from the blue-jeep area for a while. Bruce and I thanked the lieutenant commander and returned to the Victoria to collect our gear. A half hour later we were sitting in Tan Son Nhut Airport waiting for a flight to Cubi Point Naval Air Station in Subic Bay.

Subic Bay was the main headquarters for Underwater Demolition Teams in the West Pacific. I wondered what Mr. Q would have thought if he knew Bruce and I were on our way to the P.I. After we waited a couple of hours, our flight was called out over the loudspeakers. We boarded a C-130 transport and were soon airborne, looking down on South Vietnam. Then the South China Sea appeared as we flew to the east. Bruce and I looked at each other with big grins on our faces.

The afternoon of 9 October 1970, we stepped off the C-130 at Cubi Point. We went directly to the air terminal and phoned the UDT headquarters. A jeep was dispatched, and Bruce introduced me to the UDT person who picked us up, a petty officer named Shere. He drove us back to the far side of the bay, set us up with an air-conditioned room in the UDT barracks, and got us a chow card. After settling in, we walked over to the UDT compound, where we ran into Abney, another friend of Bruce's. Abney was assigned to the swimmer delivery vehicle (SDV) platoon. The SDV was a small submarine designed to carry swimmers faster, farther, and with less exertion than is possible by swimming. But it can also carry more than just swimmers. Abney was just getting finished working on one and showed it to us in detail.

The SDVs used by the Underwater Demolition Teams frequently vary in type and modifications because of rapidly improving technology. All, however, have the same basic characteristics and major components: some method of ballast, a propulsion unit consisting of motor, propeller and shaft, a hull, and gauges to indicate depth, direction, time, and status of the SDV. All SDVs used by UDT are of the wet type, that is, the diver is in direct contact with the water and must carry an independent life-support system. The disadvantages of wet units include the greater amounts of maintenance and training and the increased possibility of detection by skilled operators using finely-tuned sonars. When utilizing SDVs with closed-circuit scuba, an additional disadvantage is the necessity for very precise depth control and the inability to take evasive measures into deep water. Using closed-circuit scuba, you can't dive below one atmosphere—or thirty-three feet—because you are breathing pure oxygen. The dangers of severe electrical shock, acid burns, and an explosion from hydrogen gas are always present. These hazards can be minimized if good engineering practice and sound judgment are utilized. Two types of the many SDVs the UDT teams used were the Sea Horse II and the Trass III.

The Sea Horse II was 14.5 feet in length, a two- to three-foot beam, and four feet in height. Surface speed was 3.5 knots and submerged speed was 3.0 knots. It was capable of diving to a depth of a hundred feet, and had an operating time of three hours. It was powered by a 1.8-horsepower electric motor, and its power source was a 25-cell, 48-volt lead-acid battery. The reinforced-fiberglass hull was completely open and contained three waterproof chambers: the forward sphere, which is a permanent buoyancy tank; the battery case in the center; and the motor case in the stern.

A removable buoyancy air chamber can be mounted over the battery case.

The Trass III was seventeen to eighteen feet in length, and its beam was two feet, five inches. Its height was four feet, five inches. Surface speed was 3.5 knots and submerged speed was 3.0 knots. It could also dive to a depth of a hundred feet, and had a surface endurance of sixty miles, fifty miles submerged. Its power was a 2.6-horsepower electric motor with a power source of four 12-cell, 24-volt lead-acid batteries connected in series, for a total of 96 volts.

The Trass III can be thought of as a larger and more sophisticated Sea Horse II. Four waterproof chambers were contained within the open fiberglass hull of the Trass III. Two 160-cubic-feet air cylinders were mounted under the SDV. The airline from one small air cylinder was connected to the two large cylinders, and this entire system provided ballast air, in addition to breathing air, for the operator and three passengers.

If a water leak occurred in any waterproof case, operation had to cease immediately and the craft had to be surfaced and recovered quickly, or it would sink. Even with all ballast systems fully charged with air, the Trass would not float if even one waterproof case filled with water. On a combat mission it would be difficult to surface in enemy-controlled territory.

Operating an SDV required that safety precautions be followed quite strictly: do not exceed the operating depth of the SDV; check frequently to be aware of any decompression as soon as the situation exists; divers had to wear an extra depth gauge and compass due to the possibility of SDV instrument failure. A safety boat with a standby diver was always highly desirable, especially during training evolutions. Because of the speed of the SDVs, tracking by bubbles could be difficult, especially in dirty water and under conditions of reduced visibility.

Abney was one of the Navy's best SDV drivers. He understood the arrangement of the ballast system, the purpose of the trim tank, and the surfacing air chamber. The

Trass III was navigated essentially in the same fashion as the Sea Horse II. Once the craft had been trimmed, the trim-tank controls were not utilized except for an emergency ascent. Normal ascent and descent were accomplished by use of the surfacing air-chamber lever. The electrical system had to be watched closely on the Trass III.

After Abney's intensive lecture on the SDVs, he suggested we go into Olongapo City and party. Bruce and I didn't have any civilian clothes with us, so after Abney secured for the day, we returned to the UDT barracks to get fixed up. We had gotten liberty cards, which were needed to get on and off the naval base, from the officer-in-charge of UDT. After showing the Marine guard our cards, we crossed a bridge into Olongapo City.

Several small sampans with beautiful Filipino women on board were in the water by the bridge. "Give me money," they called out.

"Watch this," Abney said. He took a couple of pesos from his pocket and threw them into the black, smelly water. A few young boys dove into the water and recovered every peso. I don't know how they found them in the filthy water.

First stop was the money exchange. This was at the first building across the bridge on the right side of Rizal Avenue. Rizal Avenue started at the bridge at the main gate to the naval base and continued the entire length of town. The avenue was lined with bars, bar girls, shops, and an occasional restaurant. As we walked downtown, I had the feeling I was still in a combat zone. I felt uneasy following Abney and Bruce around as we made our way through the crowd of sailors and Filipinos.

Jitneys lined the streets waiting for passengers, sailors from ships anchored in the bay maneuvered in and out of their favorite bars. Bar girls stood in the doorways and grabbed at us as we walked by. "Hey, buddy, buy me drink. You wanna fuck?" Same old shit. At least they looked a lot better than the Vietnamese bar girls. Abney seemed to know where he was going. He only stopped to tease a few bar girls on the way. The girls would listen to him for a minute, step back, then say, "I know you, motherfuck. You UDT, you stationed here."

Finally we reached our objective, the U and I Club, a favorite hangout for UDT. The drink of the day was Mojo's, and any fleet sailor that walked into the bar was thrown back out. I felt right at home. We had a few drinks and kicked out a few fleet sailors, and then Abney took Bruce and me to the Bayview Club.

A huge Filipino woman called Mama Rosa sat inside the bar door. It was customary for UDT personnel to kiss Mama Rosa's big breasts as they entered her bar. We sat upstairs on the balcony with our feet up on the railing and chugged down a few beers. Then, after smothering my face into Mama Rosa's big breasts again, I followed Abney and Bruce to the Cherry Club a few doors down the street at 1340 Rizal Avenue. Fully air-conditioned, floor shows nightly, best combo, beautiful girls. I was beginning to have a good time.

After a few beers at the Cherry Club, we decided to go upstairs to the Pin Up Hotel. Air-conditioned rooms, private bath and toilet, hot and cold water, foam-rubber mattresses, and piped-in music. Sounded good to me, so we each rented a room.

After arriving on the third floor, Abney showed Bruce and me a little secret known by only a few UDT personnel. Down a hallway on the third floor, a ladder that was fixed to the wall led to a hatch on the roof. The bottom of the ladder was at least seven feet up from the floor, so nobody would use it. Abney made sure nobody was watching us, and one at a time we jumped to the bottom of the ladder and climbed up and out the hatch and onto the roof. The roof was of the corrugated-tin type and very slick. One false step and you would slide off the side and into the alley behind the Cherry Club. On top of the roof at one end of the building was a tall, square, concrete water-storage tank that supplied the hotel and bar with drinking water. A ladder fixed to the side of the concrete water tank went another twenty feet up to the top. We worked our way along the top of the roof, being very careful not to slip. Once we reached the ladder, we climbed to the top again. We seemed to be on top of the tallest building in Olongapo City. The top of the water tank was level. A wooden cover covered an inspection hole that was about three feet by three feet square. We took off the cover and then our shoes. We then sat around the hole soaking our feet and looking over Olongapo. It was dark and the lights of the city really stood out. We could see down Rizal Avenue its entire length in both directions. Subic Bay and the Cubi Point Airport far beyond were visible too.

As good a time as I was having at Subic, I couldn't get my mind off the war zone. The next afternoon I was walking from Olongapo City back to the naval base. Bruce had stayed back in town. After crossing the bridge and going through the main gate, I walked toward the UDT barracks. Looking down the street in front of me, I noticed a fleet sailor walking in the same direction, wearing a coat with a big green frog embroidered on the back of it. I walked a little faster to catch up to him to get a closer look at his coat. Around the frog were the words UNDERWATER DEMOLITION. Fuckin' blackshoe, I thought. Nobody I knew in the teams would be stupid enough to advertise like this.

I walked up beside him and said, "Hey, man, are you in UDT?" He said, "Yeah, what about it?" I said, "That must be pretty neat." All the time we were getting closer to the UDT barracks. I bullshitted him as we walked, trying to keep the conversation going. I didn't let him know I was in the teams. We soon reached the UDT barracks. No sign outside the barracks announced UDT, they were just four-story concrete barracks. I asked him if he would come up to the fourth floor with me to meet some of my friends, knowing what would happen to him if he did. He hesitated for a moment and I thought he was going to say okay, but then he said, "I don't have time, I have to get back to my ship." Nothing I could say could convince him to come into the barracks. Maybe he had figured me out or something, but all of a sudden he didn't want anything to do with me.

As he started to walk off, I grabbed his shoulder with my left hand, and as he turned around, I embedded my right

fist in his face. He flew back and landed on his ass. I stood
over the top of him and said, "I'm in SEAL Team One,
and that's the UDT barracks, asshole. What gives you the
right to run around with that stupid-looking coat?" He just
looked up at me, still sitting on his ass. I asked him to come
upstairs to meet some of my friends in UDT again. He still
didn't want anything to do with that. I said, "Give me that
fuckin' coat, asshole," and I began to rip it from his body.
The coat was handed over. As he stood up, I said, "Get
your blackshoe ass back to your ship before I drag you
upstairs." He turned and proceeded at a fast pace in the
direction of his ship, not looking back.

We had to earn the UDT frog patch or the SEAL patch
through months of rigorous training, it wasn't just handed
to us. I took the asshole's coat upstairs into the UDT barracks, showed it to some of my teammates, and told them
where I got it. We got some K-bar knives and cut the coat
into small pieces and it ended up in the shit can.

The three days Bruce and I were in the Philippines seemed
like only a few hours. I don't remember getting very much
sleep. Then I was looking down from our C-130 flight and
saw the last of the Philippines I would see for a long time.
Our flight was designated for Danang, but it was the only
flight we could get to Vietnam for several days. We would
be late getting back to our camp as it was. I'm sure Mr. Q
was wondering where the hell we were.

I sat in the C-130 looking out a starboard window watching for the first signs of Vietnam to appear over the horizon
of the South China Sea. It wasn't long before Bruce and I
were walking into the air terminal at the Danang Air Force
Base. We couldn't catch a flight to Saigon until the next
day, so we called the UDT compound and a jeep was dispatched to pick us up. Seemed like everyplace we went
there were friends and places to stay. Bruce and I waited
outside the air terminal looking for a jeep with someone
dressed in cutoff military greens with a frog patch on his
shoulder. Bruce spotted the jeep first. Driving the jeep was
a man named Pfanzelter, who had graduated from my train-

ing class and was stationed in Danang with UDT Team 13. We threw our gear into the jeep and jumped in for the ride back to the UDT compound located on the south side of Danang harbor near Monkey Mountain.

The only mud I saw was around the rivers and harbor; the rest of the area was mountains with thick vegetation. This was not the Vietnam I was accustomed to. We stowed our gear in the UDT compound and were taken on a tour of the area. We soon found ourselves at China Beach. While sitting on the beach, a group of American girls walked by, the first round-eyes I had seen in months. I know it wasn't polite to stare, but I couldn't help myself. They seemed to be well guarded by some higher-ranking Army types.

We returned to the UDT compound and borrowed a jeep, legally this time. Bruce and I wanted to see how far up Monkey Mountain we could drive. The road was paved, and the higher up the mountain we drove, the better the view. Sure didn't look like Vietnam. When we reached the top of the mountain, the road was closed. A tall Cyclone fence with barbed wire unraveled along its top surrounded a radar installation. We turned around and started back down the mountain.

The view of the South China Sea and Danang Harbor was fantastic. American ships were stacked in the harbor like cordwood ready for the stove. The smoke-filled air over the city of Danang reminded me of Tijuana, Mexico. The muddy waters of the Danang River turned to a blue-gray as it entered the harbor, then to a turquoise-blue as the harbor entered the South China Sea. The surrounding mountains were dark green, contrasting with the blue sky. As our jeep came around a corner, we found a monkey sitting in the road, and had to stop. It quickly ran off the downhill side of the road, disappearing into the thick vegetation. We continued down the road until we reached a big round rock with graffiti painted all over it. Names of GIs and their units and the words BOOM BOOM painted in big red letters. I took a few more pictures, then we started down the road again. A huge white hospital ship with a red cross painted on its side stood out from all the other ships in the harbor. It seemed to be the only white object in the entire area.

Our stay in Danang was short. The next morning the sound of a C-130 Hercules transport's engines winding out made me realize it was time to leave Danang. The C-130 shook around and vibrated until we were finally airborne on our way to Saigon. Once in Saigon, there were no flights to Binh Thuy until the next morning. Another night was spent at the Victoria Hotel. Another day in Saigon, looking at gooks wearing one-way mirror shades, civilian clothes, and riding around on Honda-55 step-throughs. Why the hell weren't they fighting for their country?

I still couldn't get my mind off what Mr. Q might be thinking. For being late getting back to our camp, I was expecting the worst from him. We had been AWOL for a few days already, not counting leaving Vietnam for part of that time. Early the next morning we were Binh Thuy bound, riding on an open-door Army slick. We were lucky to arrange transportation back to our camp that afternoon from Binh Thuy. As we climbed out of the chopper with our gear, several of our teammates were there to meet us. Mr. Q was one of them.

As the helo left the area, Mr. Q asked, "Where the hell were you guys?"

Bruce answered, "We had transportation problems getting back, sir."

"First squad has an operation early in the morning, briefing at 2200 hours," Mr. Q said. That was it, not an ass chewin' or nothing. That sure surprised the hell out of me. I found out from Reeves that only two operations had been conducted since we'd been gone. After one hell of a good time traveling around the Philippines and Vietnam, there I was, back at the salt mines.

CHAPTER THIRTY

That night after chow, Mr. Q, Bruce, Panella, Grimes, Doc, Quan, and I assembled in our briefing hootch. Mr. Q had received some fresh intel on a meeting of high-ranking Vietcong officials that was to be held the following morning in a small hootch near Xom Ong Tam. This small village was located near the northwest end of Dung Island. Mr. Q pointed out our insertion, extraction, and alternate extraction points on the picto map. Those areas were always stressed so all involved in the mission could memorize them. No special gear other than the normal prisoner handling gear was to be carried on this operation. Extra UDT life jackets were always taken along for prisoners. Time of departure would be 0100 hours, and our estimated time of contact with Charlie would be at first light. The same two OV-10 Broncos from Binh Thuy would be our air support. The hootch at our objective was reported to be guarded by up to five Vietcong with automatic weapons. With the element of surprise on our side, that shouldn't be any problem. Rain could be expected in the early morning hours also. That was to our advantage; we usually welcomed any natural noisemaker in the jungle. Nobody had any questions, so the briefing was considered completed.

We left the hootch to get our shit together. My equipment had been checked out earlier that day but I went completely through it again. I wrapped fresh ordnance tape around the butt of my Stoner. That could be used as part of the prisoner handling gear or to keep the leeches from entering my clothes. After rechecking my gear, I left the hootch to find my fellow freaks. Smoking a joint would allow me to sleep better that night. After working hours, when it was dark, the heads in our camp weren't hard to find. Most of the straights were usually in the bar. I found a small group of SEALs and a few Seabees down at the dock. As I approached, they looked nervous. Then I heard one of the group say, "It's okay, it's Young." The doobies were relit and passed around again.

I was not the perfect SEAL the way some SEALs thought they were, but I did my job to the best of my ability and coped with the job's special demands to the best of my ability also, but in my own way. I took my job seriously, or I probably would have been killed on an operation long ago. The men in my platoon counted on me as I counted on them. They had their ways of dealing with their life, I had mine. I was good at what I did, in the field and off the field.

I returned to my hootch and hit the rack. I didn't sleep, because all night my mind was inserting into a dense wall of green vegetation as thick as cobwebs. I seemed to be stuck there like some kind of insect, unable to get out or away from its enemy. I'd been briefed, I had my assignment, I'd checked over my gear, I'd smoked a joint, I still couldn't sleep. The mosquitoes buzzed outside the mosquito net that hung around my rack. Someone forgot to light the mosquito coil, I thought. No special gear, five guards with automatic weapons, departure at 0100 hours. I could watch the clock rotate, getting closer to cammo time. Insertion, extraction, rain could be expected, no questions. The clock continued to rotate like the rotor blades on an Army slick.

I was soon standing on the plywood floor, barefoot in my jeans, sliding on my blue and gold tee-shirt. Next I slipped into my jungle boots, sockless. Over the blue and gold went my standard issue cammo top. Some guys wore tiger stripes, I saved my money for other things. Ordnance tape was passed around to seal off the bottom of our pants. I used my share and then some. UDT inflatable life jacket was put on next. Soon it was my turn to use the mirror to cammo my face. I used the dark face paint first, then the green. My face, ears, front and back of my neck, and the back sides of my hands were covered. There was no exposed skin that wasn't covered with cammo. Next came my K-bar knife and Model 15 Smith & Wesson on a belt around my waist. Then my Stoner vest with ammo and grenades. I picked up my Stoner and was ready for some more fun on my routine deployment to Southeast Asia.

First squad assembled at the dock for Mr. Q to inspect us. We boarded the medium one at a time after our inspection. I sat in the same place I had sat in the medium since I'd been there. That spot on the bench seat seemed to have my name on it. As the twin 427 Chevy engines warmed up, a radio check was made to make sure all the radios were on the right frequency and operating properly. It started to rain. Soon the medium was in gear and on step moving upstream on the Bassac. Watching the perimeter lights of camp disappear in the dark, rainy night seemed to be the thing to do. Everyone on board knew his duties and special assignments and knew what was expected of him. Soon we would all be green faces in the nipa palm.

Using the radar and the starlight scope, we continued toward our objective. The Bassac water slapped off the aluminum hull of the medium as it sped through the water on step. Melfa knew where we were going, not only because he had studied the picto map, but also because he had taken us to Dung Island on the medium several times before. The medium was well-tuned and was running well. No one talked. It was hard to see the man sitting next to you in the dark night. The rain clouds blocked out most of the ambient light.

We stayed in the main channel while Mr. Q kept a close eye on the radar, looking for a small canal that led back into Dung Island. The tension was growing. On the radar Mr. Q finally picked up the canal we wanted. It turned east into the island. The canal protruded about a thousand meters into Dung Island and then teed off. The right channel of the canal went southeast about 2500 meters to the intersection of Ti Ti Canal, and the left channel ran northwest about 2500 meters until it grew so narrow that only a small sampan could pass through it. Then the canal opened up again into the Bassac.

The medium slowed, its bow dropping down into the water. It turned to starboard and entered the canal. All weapons were made ready, a distinct metallic sound, a feeling of power. The tension grew even stronger. The medium slowed down even more, to just above idle, a good target for a B-40 rocket. Even a lousy shot probably wouldn't have had any problem hitting the medium with the 80mm-shaped charge Chinese Communist Type 50 heat grenade. This rocket was usually fired from the Type 56 launcher, a copy of the Soviet RPG-2 recoilless antitank grenade launcher. The rocket had a base detonating fuse, a 40mm stabilizer shaft with a fin assembly of six flexible fins, and a black powder propellant charge in a moisture-proof cardboard and aluminum container. This rocket was capable of penetrating up to seven inches of armor plate if hit head on at a zero-degree angle. We had captured several of them. Just knowing those weapons were in the area had an effect on us. I, for one, was terrified while cruising the canals at low speed.

The heavy rain covered the sounds made by the quiet medium. The visibility was poor, next to nothing. Thank God for our radar. Over the sound of the downpour, the wake from the medium could barely be heard lapping against the shores of the canal. I stood up slowly, turned around, and got down on my knees where I was sitting, ready to return fire. Mr. Q was still glued to the radar. I'm sure that didn't do anything for his night vision.

The canal narrowed to about a hundred meters wide. Thick nipa palm and triple-canopy jungle lined both banks. It was so thick it sometimes seemed like we were in the bottom of a dark green canyon. As we got closer, the tee intersection was clearer on the radar. We moved toward it slowly. Another canal showed up on the radar to our port side. The medium turned ninety degrees to the port for a fake insertion. The bow nudged up against the bank and we came to a complete stop. After a few seconds we backed out into the canal and continued on toward the intersection.

We soon reached it and made a left turn. Moving slowly

up the canal, Mr. Q continued to study the radar looking for the insertion point. It wasn't long before he identified a very small canal on our starboard side that entered the canal we were on. He signaled us to prepare for insertion. The medium turned to starboard and slowly moved into the small canal until it was stopped by the muddy bottom. Grimes was already up on the bow, and he quickly slipped over into the muddy water and thick vegetation. As quiet as possible, each of the rest of us followed one at a time off the bow of his proper side. As the medium backed away, a perimeter was immediately set up to secure our position. A head count made sure everyone had successfully inserted. The muddy water and the rain soaked our clothes. The tide was on its way out. The wind moved the triple-canopy jungle back and forth, making the nipa palm leaves rattle against each other.

We stayed in our position for a while, listening for enemy movement. Then Grimes was sent out to inspect the area toward our objective. The rest of us waited quietly for him to return to our position. My position was near the canal that the medium was on. I stared out into my field of fire to detect any unnatural movement. It was hard to hear anything over the pounding rain, but the natural noises made me feel a little more secure, covering any noise we might make.

It wasn't long before Grimes returned. He told Mr. Q we had inserted into the wrong canal. Not again! I thought. Doc radioed the medium to come back to our position. I stayed in my position, watching into the dark jungle, waiting for the medium. A gook would have to damn near step on me before I would be able to see him.

Our boat had not been far away and didn't take long to return. Doc guided it into our position using the radio. One at a time we pulled ourselves over the bow and back into the medium. We took an immediate head count again to make sure we had all extracted safely. Head counts were very important on insertions and extractions, especially if it was dark. The medium backed out and headed farther up the canal to find the correct insertion point. It didn't take

long before the medium made another turn to the starboard
and I was lying on the jungle floor again, soaking up the
rain and mud with my body.

The medium moved back down the canal to stand by for
extraction. That could have been anywhere from a few seconds to a few hours. It all depended on if and when we
made enemy contact. That was the squad's first wrong insertion by boat, but there were so many smaller canals
entering the main canal in that area, it was hard to tell which
canal was the correct one. It was very important that we
did insert into the right canal, as it was the only one that
led to the objective. The Vietcong rarely expected anyone
to enter their territory by canal, which was one of the reasons
we patrolled in through the canals in the first place: They
were quieter, usually had less vegetation and fewer booby
traps.

With our support boat gone, we were all alone again.
After a short time Grimes was sent out again to check out
the area. He came back a few minutes later and signaled us
to follow. I was the last man to drop back down into the
canal, covering our rear as we silently moved farther into
enemy territory. We had to stay close together because of
the dark, rainy night. One step, then another. Stop, wait,
listen, move ahead a little more. Grimes never knew what
he would walk into. An enemy ambush could be disastrous
for him or anybody near the front of the element. For everyone in the squad.

The water in the canal was chest deep, but I held my
Stoner above the muddy surface as we patrolled. We had
about 200 meters to go to reach our objective. Using the
pounding rain to our advantage, we moved right along,
stopping only for short periods while Grimes inspected the
canal in front of us. After patrolling up the canal about a
hundred meters, we stopped for a long time to listen. I
crouched up against the canal bank looking back into the
dark in the direction we had come from. I could taste the
cammo paint running down my face with the rain. At least
there weren't any mosquitoes out. I looked like part of the
jungle myself. I felt like it too.

After a while I was signaled to follow again. We patrolled for what seemed like hours to go the next hundred meters. Finally the objective was reached. We moved into positions around three small nipa-palm hootches, staying back far enough to wait till first light. One hootch was on the right bank of the canal and the other two were on the left. We would lie low in the mud and rain of the canal until it was just light enough to see. I could hear someone coughing and moving around in the hootch closest to me. I tried not to move at all in my position. Only my eyes moved from behind the vines and bushes that concealed me. I looked for Vietcong guards. I looked and listened for Vietcong guard dogs. I checked out the area within my field of fire. My face dripped with water, some sweat, some rain. Personal discomfort was always present.

Just before daybreak the rain let up a little. I noticed a small flicker of light in one of the hootches. I could make out detail within the surrounding jungle now. It was time. The signal was given, and we rushed toward the two hootches to our left. I dropped to the muddy earth on the left (closest) side of the first hootch, covering its left and right side. The rest of the squad moved into position. A second later two dark figures ran out the back of one of the hootches toward the jungle. Panella and I opened up with our Stoners. Flaming muzzles lit the dark morning. The tracers from my Stoner disappeared into the back of one of the gooks. He immediately dropped to the mud face first. The other gook was seriously wounded but kept on running toward the jungle.

Doc radioed the medium that we had made contact and to stand by. We started taking enemy fire from the hootch on the other side of the canal. We returned the fire to try to overwhelm it. Two dark figures ran to a large mud-log bunker along the canal bank, slipped in, and were out of sight in a second. Mr. Q signaled Panella and me to cross the canal and cover the bunker. I slipped into the canal once more, waded across, climbed out on the opposite side and took up a position behind a large tree trunk. My Stoner was trained toward the bunker entrance. Grimes searched the

body of the dead Vietnamese that Panella and I had wasted
while Mr. Q covered him. Soon the rest of the squad crossed
the canal to my side. They had searched both hootches and
recovered weapons and Vietcong documents. Meanwhile
Quan was near the entrance of the bunker, trying to persuade
the occupants to surrender. But we had to work fast and get
out of the area before Vietcong reinforcements showed up.

The two gooks inside the bunker didn't respond to Quan's
orders. Quan tried again. *"Lai dai, Lai dai,"* he yelled.
Still nothing. I kept looking behind us and around the area,
expecting more Vietcong to show up in a second. We had
been completely surrounded before in just a matter of a few
seconds. Grimes threw a concussion grenade into the entrance of the bunker and quickly took cover. The blast shook
the ground clear back to where I was. Grimes returned to
the bunker entrance. Sounds of someone moving around
inside could be heard. Quan yelled again for the assholes inside to come out. The bunker must have had passage-
ways inside which the Vietcong were hiding in. I don't
know how anyone could survive a blast like that in a con-
fined area. In our part of Vietnam, due to the high tides
from the South China Sea, the Vietcong couldn't dig too
deep without getting flooded out, so bunkers had to be built
mostly above the ground.

The two gooks inside the mud-log bunker refused to come
out. Part of the bunker had already been collapsed by the
first grenade. Quan told them this was their last chance. I
guess the two inside told him to get fucked—at least they
answered him. Quan didn't look too happy, but he signaled
Grimes to throw another grenade inside. Grimes already had
one ready and did. Grimes and Quan again took cover.

The second blast shook the earth again and collapsed more
of the large bunker. Grimes and Quan returned to the bunker
again. It must have been reinforced, with several different
compartments inside. Movement could still be heard. I
couldn't believe it. Grimes finally threw a tear-gas grenade
through the entrance and into the bunker as far back as he
could. They took cover again and everyone waited. The gas
drifted out of the entrance and through the mud of the

collapsed area and came in my direction, adding to my discomfort. Coughing could be heard inside, and soon the two gooks had crawled to the bunker's entrance. Grimes and Quan had their weapons trained on their heads. Quan reached down and dragged one of them out. Grimes pulled the other one out.

The two Vietcong were a mess. Not much left for a field interrogation. Grimes had his foot on one of the gook's shoulder blades and was handcuffing him. Quan was searching the bunker, and Mr. Q had control of the other prisoner.

Each hootch received an incendiary grenade, and we started our extraction, moving out back down the same canal that we had patrolled in on. I was the last man to slide down the muddy bank into the canal. I covered our ass as we patrolled toward our extraction site. The three nipa-palm hootches were really popping and crackling. They were soon out of sight behind me.

The water in the canal was really low compared to when we patrolled in on it. Where the water had been chest deep, it was only ankle deep. We moved along rapidly but trying to stay quiet. I pointed my toes into the mud, and sinking up past my knees, I pulled them out of the mud with my toes pointed, trying to avoid the suction sound. After we had covered about a hundred meters, we stopped to listen for enemy movement. Our two prisoners had been blindfolded and gagged with ordnance tape. They were scared and weren't giving the prisoner handlers any problems. The sound of the three hootches burning echoed through the jungle from behind.

We started out toward the mouth of the canal again. As we moved along, Grimes studied both banks of the canal and out in front of him for signs of enemy ambush. I guarded our rear, Stoner's muzzle pointed in that direction. We finally reached the mouth of the canal. Moving to each bank, we quickly set up a secure perimeter in the vines and vegetation and radioed the medium to move toward our position. I could hear the medium running toward us, it wasn't wasting any time. A visual was made on the medium, and Doc radioed them to maneuver toward the mouth of our canal.

The bow moved up on the mud about thirty meters from our position. The MST crew was ready for action, flak-jacketed and metal helmets on.

Prisoner handlers and prisoners first, one at a time we waded out through the mud to board the medium. The mud was waist deep there, making walking difficult. Mr. Q and I were the last ones to wade out to the medium and climb on board, our teammates covering us all the way. Doc started tending to our prisoners as the medium backed off the mud bank and started out the canal toward the main river. We wanted to interrogate them as soon as we reached camp. They lay on the deck with the ordnance tape still around their eyes and mouths and the plastic handcuffs secured tightly around their hands. They showed no signs of resistance, and if they tried to move, Quan would kick them in the ribs.

The danger wasn't over yet, not until we reached the Bassac River, so everyone on board kept his weapons trained toward both banks of the canal until we finally entered the Bassac. Our weapons were then unloaded and made safe.

CHAPTER THIRTY-ONE

After the medium reached the Bassac River, we got on step toward camp. It only took us a few minutes to get back. Mr. Q, Quan, and Grimes started interrogating the prisoners while the rest of us cleaned our weapons and muddy gear. After the gear was squared away, I went to morning chow. As usual, I hadn't had time to wash off the cammo paint or to take off my wet, muddy clothes. But not wanting to fix my own breakfast later, I ate with the Seabees. As I sat in the chow hall eating, I heard a helo circling our camp.

I quickly finished eating and ran out of the chow hall toward the helo pad. Helo landings at our camp were kind of rare, and one could be the most exciting thing that might happen around camp for days. As I approached the helo pad, the chopper had already landed. Weber ran from the port door, and two high-ranking officers behind him were still sitting in the chopper. The engine had been shut down and the rotors were beginning to slow down.

Shit, here we go again, I thought. Our two prisoners had already been interrogated and placed in prisoner-holding boxes awaiting transportation to Soc Trang. Mr. Q, Mr. Walsh, and the two officers went directly to the briefing hootch. It was good to see old Weber again. He said his stomach was feeling a little better and he was ready to operate again.

The officers spent the longest time in the briefing hootch before they finally came out. Since the bar was so close to the briefing hootch, Mr. Q took them inside for a beer. A short time later they were back in the helo, the rotor blades rotating faster and faster, the helo fuselage vibrating and jerking around until it finally lifted from our pad and, nose down, headed out over the rice paddies, circling to the northwest.

Mr. Walsh said, "Pass the word to the platoon, we have a briefing at 1800 hours." Like before, Mr. Walsh wouldn't discuss any details. Weber had brought the mail down from Binh Thuy and was passing it out. Weber and I sat around the bar most of the day playing cards and writing letters home. Mr. Walsh entered the bar later in the day and told Weber and me we had been advanced to Third Class Petty Officer. Usually, to become a petty officer one has to be in the Navy for a specific length of time and pass two written exams, one on military leadership and the other on one's rate, in my case gunner's mate. But we were given a "Ho Chi Minh Advance," which meant we didn't have to take the written test. I had an idea it had something to do with the POW-camp operation our platoon operated on a while back.

To kill some time, Bruce and I went through the gate at camp for a walk through the village, leaving the security of our fenced-in booby-trapped perimeter behind. We walked about 75 meters into the village. On our left, sitting on a bamboo platform hanging over the river, was a pig. It had been tied to a tree next to the platform the entire time our platoon had been in-country. Since it was a small pig, never once did I see the pig moved anywhere else. It ate and slept on the platform its entire life.

As always, the local kids started coming out of the wood-work and to hover around us like flies. As we walked along, more and more kids gathered around us coming from the river, the nipa-palm hootches, and down the road in front of us. Bruce and I passed out some gum, which made things worse. Finally we reached the nipa-palm hootch at the far end of the village next to the river. This is where Tu Lin's family lived. Bruce and I had brought some C-rations along for the family.

The old man was glad to see us, or glad to see the items we had brought him from camp. The people standing all around us couldn't speak any English but seemed to know what we were saying. There must have been seven or more people living in their small nipa-palm hootch. After taking a few photographs, we said our good-byes and returned through the village back to our secure perimeter of sandbags and machine guns.

I spent the rest of the day watching the Seabees work on the metal buildings, putting in sliding glass windows and hanging doors. Nice place for the gooks someday. I couldn't get the night's mission briefing out of my mind. I knew something was up: all us SEALs would be operating to-gether. Not long after evening chow, I found myself in the briefing hootch with my fellow SEALs.

"Our platoon has received fresh intelligence on another POW camp," said Mr. Q. "The Vietcong have two Ameri-cans who have positively been identified, and about thirty or so South Vietnamese prisoners in this camp. The two Ameri-cans are army officers. A South Vietnamese outpost was attacked and overrun by the Vietcong two years ago. The two have been prisoners ever since. A Vietcong who surrendered has positively identified them from eight photographs laid out in front of him. The Vietcong used to work at the POW camp.

Whether they're the same two Americans who we tried to liberate on the last POW operation is not known. This POW camp is located several miles due west of our camp.'' That really got our platoon talking. Without freeing the two Americans, we would never know if they were the same two or not. Even though the POW camp was miles from the last camp we hit, they very well could be the same two men.

The trouble with an operation like that is that too many people want to get involved. The bureaucracy involved in setting up the operation involved too many people and too much time. By the time SEALs got the intel and the date and time to conduct the operation, it was probably already too late; the Vietcong had probably moved the Americans to another area. But if an operation like that was successful in freeing even one American, the rewards would be numerous. All supporting units involved would get a few medals too. But rescue operations didn't really need all the supporting units and setup time. They should be simple and to the point, and not designed to make men think of promotions, medals, and their image. Especially the men who weren't going on the actual operation. The intel on the Americans should have been handed directly to Mr. Q, and our platoon should have lined up the necessary supporting units and figured out when the mission should be conducted. Hours or maybe even days of bureaucratic bullshit were keeping American POWs from the possibility of freedom.

The Vietcong POW camp was quite a ways south of the Bassac and too far from any major waterways to use our boats, so this operation was to be conducted using two Army slicks as our primary transportation to and from the objective. Air support was to be two Army gunship helicopters. Extra Army slicks would be on standby to evacuate freed POWs, South Vietnamese or American. Everyone in the platoon was eager to go. Our platoon could have been ready to operate in five minutes or less. No shit. With all our weapons and special gear. We could have cammoed our faces en route to our objective if we had to. But another bureaucratic night had to go by while the big shots from up above figured out how to start their clocks. The mission would begin at sunrise the next morning. Fuckin' helos! Everybody on the ground would know we were coming.

"Like the last POW operation, this is a priority mission, and the information you receive inside this briefing hootch should not be repeated. Don't even talk to your Seabee friends about it," Mr. Q said. SEALs didn't talk much about clandestine operations to anyone anyway. Talking to the wrong person could put lives and the mission in jeopardy. The mission briefing went on. Finally Mr. Q asked, "Are there any questions?" No questions were asked, so we left the briefing hootch to check the gear for the operation.

That night I had problems sleeping. Not because I was worried about the operation, but because I was ready to get under way right then. Maybe we could free the two Americans this time. That thought repeated in my mind all night until early the next morning, when I was standing around our helo pad with my platoon, all geared up and ready to operate. The two Army slicks were circling camp, judging the wind direction from the yellow smoke grenade we had thrown out. A few Seabees watched us from a distance. The expressions on their faces gave their thoughts away. None of them knew where we were going or what our mission was, but they did know something big was up because our whole platoon was mounting up for the operation.

A few minutes later my legs were dangling from the port door of an Army slick en route to our objective. An Army gunship was on each flank. Looking down on the South Vietnamese countryside, I saw mostly rice paddies with an occasional treeline following the banks of canals and waterways. Paddy dikes crisscrossed the entire area. Small villages were scattered throughout the countryside also, most being along the canals and waterways.

I was practically hypnotized as the helo shook and vibrated, its engines staying at a constant RPM. As far as I could see, the ground was green and wet. Our chopper started descending. The chopper with the other half of the platoon had dropped back and started to descend also. I snapped out of my trance, leaned forward and looked out the chopper door. In the distance I saw an area of jungle completely surrounded by rice paddies. It looked more like a big bamboo thicket or willow bushes with lots of vines. The signal was given to make our weapons ready. I cocked my Stoner and pointed the muzzle in a safe direction.

There was no mistake in our landing zone this time. Both helos quickly moved in and landed near the southeast corner of the overgrown perimeter, our air support covering us. I jumped from the chopper into ankle-deep grassy water and ran to the higher vegetation for cover and concealment. The rest of the platoon did the same. As the helos left our position, we immediately took a head count to make sure everyone had inserted. Everyone kept concealed and waited and listened for signs of enemy movement.

I was crouched, half lying in the bug-infested, wet, waist-high grass, watching the choppers move off in the distance until they disappeared. Doc and Shannon had already checked their radios with the helos after we had inserted— just a couple of prearranged clicks with the radio mikes, and the choppers returning the same. That way no words were spoken within the platoon. My jeans and cammo top were soaked on my left side, and the fuckin' mosquitoes had found me already. Very few places stuck up above the water floor. The ones that did were mud, still soaked from the high tide from the South China Sea. I kept my freshly WD-40'd Stoner up out of the water so it would stay dry. I kept my position, looking and listening for the enemy. Grimes moved out ahead, then signaled us to follow.

We followed him, one at a time, into the thick, light green, reeded jungle. Reeves, packing his Stoner, was rear security, and I patrolled just in front of him. Grimes soon found a trail through the thick reeds. The area looked like a young bamboo forest with lots of vine, bushes, and small trees; nothing grew too high. The trail led into thicker vegetation, toward the POW camp. Some places along the wet, muddy trail we had to crawl on our hands and knees, other places we patrolled in the crouched position. Wooden poles used for bridges crossing small ditches and wet areas were everywhere. We came across one trip wire, then another. Each time after crossing, we stopped to listen for the enemy.

All the tops of the brush and bamboo above the trails were tied together so they wouldn't be visible from the air. We patrolled again until Grimes located our objective. The signal was given and an immediate assault on the camp was executed. We moved into our positions only to find the camp freshly abandoned. The sound of the choppers arriving must have sent the Vietcong and the prisoners in the opposite direction. Fresh campfires were burning and gook footprints went in all directions. Mr. Walsh, Mr. Q, Grimes, and Quan searched the interior of the camp while the rest of us kept the perimeter secure. No cages were found in this area. It looked like the cooking and eating area to me. The Vietcong commandant's sleeping area was also located. As on all the trails, the tops of the bamboo were tied together. A short wave radio was found here. The Vietcong weren't far away, I could feel it.

After Mr. Q was finished with the search, our platoon moved into a long line through the camp and we laid low, listening for the enemy. Everything seemed too quiet. Mr. Q told Doc to call in the two helos for a fake extraction. The word was passed back by arm and hand signals to stay in our positions. From my position I could see a short way down several trails. The interior of the camp was like the hub of a wheel, the trails like spokes leading in all directions. Reeves had taken along an instamatic camera wrapped in two plastic bags. I watched him take several pictures inside the compound. I could hear the helos now, getting louder as they approached the landing zone far back behind us. It was easy to see why the Cong had run in the opposite direction. The two helos made their fake extraction with the gunships covering them. They then flew off to the east.

All was quiet again, except for the fuckin' mosquitoes. They were thick. We lay very still and quiet, expecting Charlie to come back to camp and set up shop again. Soon the area was quiet as a grave. Maybe he would fall for our trick. It wasn't long before the dead-quiet morning was filled with Vietcong talking. First one, then another voice from a different direction. Soon gooks were talking from all around our perimeter, out beyond our visibility in the thick vegetation. The voices grew closer. The platoon was tense, weapons off safe, waiting for the first signs of the Cong.

Visibility was very poor as I scanned the vegetation for Charlie. I could only see three to four feet into the thick shit. It reminded me of places I used to play when I was a kid. I could hear and feel my heart pounding. I moved only my head and eyes slowly, looking into my field of fire. The gook noises grew louder. Soon I could hear what sounded like a single gook walking in the mud off to my left flank. The sound of his feet squishing through the muddy trail grew louder. It sounded like he was moving around to Grimes's position. I could look down the long line of our platoon lying quietly in the mud on both sides of the main trail right in the POW camp.

Grimes looked ready for anything, his CAR-15 pointed down the trail in front of him. The gooks around us still talked. Obviously they thought we had left. The sound of the footsteps grew louder. Twelve feet in front of Grimes a muzzle of a Soviet 7.62mm M1944 carbine poked out from behind the bamboo, followed by a little Commie gook dressed in black pajama shorts with no shoes or shirt. The gook turned toward Grimes, not knowing he was there, and his eyes opened wide when he finally noticed Grimes. A quick burst of fire from Grimes's CAR-15 sent the little fucker to his knees and then facedown in the mud, his chest cavity full of .223 holes. Grimes could almost reach out and touch him.

All the gook voices and sounds of movement that had surrounded us stopped immediately. Grimes crawled toward the gook, keeping his muzzle pointed at him at all times, and poked him in the head with his weapon. No response. Grimes picked up his carbine and opened the bolt. Shit, it didn't even have a cartridge in the chamber. The magazine was full but the gook didn't even have his weapon loaded. Grimes passed the weapon back down our line for someone to take charge of. He then flipped over the body and made a thorough search of it, admiring his impressive marksmanship.

The rest of us stayed in our positions, covering our fields of fire, waiting for Mr. Q to give us the signal to do otherwise. Grimes pulled the body back out of the trail. Mr. Q

pulled the body back farther and signaled the men behind
him to pull it farther back out of the way. Still no words
were spoken within our platoon. As the body was dragged,
being passed back to the next person in the patrol each time,
it left a bloody trail in the mud.

Now here I was, lying in the wet mud with a shot-up,
bloody gook beside me. The blood trail in the mud led clear
to the front of our platoon. Blowing them away was one
thing, but having to lay next to their smelly, shot-up bodies
was another. Other than searching the bodies for documents
and weapons, I didn't want anything else to do with them.

We lay there silently waiting for more Vietcong to appear.
The Vietcong who Grimes had wasted must have been sent
into the camp to make sure the coast was clear before the
rest of them came back. The flies and mosquitoes started
collecting around and on the gook's lifeless body. They
crawled in and out of his eyes, nose, mouth, and gunshot
wounds, gathering mostly around the bloody areas. That
could be me, I kept thinking as I watched my perimeter
carefully. The flies even gathered around the muddy blood
trail. I stared at the dead Vietcong, his eyes and face full
of mud and blood as he lay on his back staring into the sky
above. I tried not to look at him, but with him being right
beside me, that was impossible. I had seen lots of dead
Vietcong before, some blown into pieces. But this one really
bothered me. Personal discomfort, of a different kind. The
mud, mosquitoes, and lying in uncomfortable body positions for hours didn't bother me, but lying next to this shot-
up dude did. He didn't look more than twelve or fourteen
years old to me. Fuck 'em, I thought. If they pack a weapon,
I'll grease them.

Reeves and I continued to cover the rear of our platoon
for a possible enemy attack. Charlie knew we were there
but didn't know how many of us. I couldn't hear a thing
outside our perimeter. Maybe the sound of our gunfire decided Charlie to slip away from the area. The Vietcong were
probably undermanned and underarmed at the time we had
inserted from the chopper. By the looks of the piece of shit
for a weapon the young Vietcong was packin', I wouldn't

doubt it. The contrast between the dead gook and ourselves was the difference between night and day. Our enemy wore cutoff black pajamas, while we wore Levi's jeans and camouflage clothes. We packed Stoners, M-60s, and M-16s, and he packed a Soviet bolt-action rifle. We were highly trained; he was barefoot and fighting for a cause.

My heart was pounding; it was hard to listen for the enemy over my breathing. The sweat ran down my face. In fact, the parts of my body that hadn't made contact with the water or the mud were also soaked, but from sweat. With my blue and gold tee-shirt, my cammo top, my UDT life jacket covering my chest, and my nylon Stoner vest full of ammo and grenades, I was pretty damn hot.

The Vietcong were very unpredictable. What would be their next actions? I wondered. We lay quietly in our positions awhile longer, ready for anything that might happen. Mr. Q finally decided to widen the search for prisoners. If the Americans were around, they were surely gagged and under heavy guard. Any South Vietnamese prisoners around were probably afraid to show themselves, as they might be mistaken for Vietcong. It was a very frustrating situation. The mosquitoes were driving me crazy just lying there; I was glad to be moving again. Quan was asking our Chieu Hoi a lot of questions. Quan found out the ex-Vietcong had led us to the wrong part of the camp on purpose. Mr. Walsh and Strausbaugh were really pissed off at the gook.

We searched the area again and came up with nothing new. To the north of the camp we found a small canal that ran north. One by one we dropped down into the canal and patrolled to the north very quietly, watching both canal banks cautiously. The water in the canal was chest deep with thick green algae floating on the surface. Thick reeds lined the banks, with small trails entering and exiting the canal in different directions. Small openings like windows in the thick brush were used by the Vietcong to check the perimeter of the POW camp. We continued to move along slowly, like a long snake sliding up the canal. The suspicion intensified the farther we patrolled. I felt insecure while patrolling down in the insect-infested, wet, shitty canal. Not from all the insects, but from a possible enemy ambush.

The canal meandered through the thick vegetation. Grimes came across a dead Vietnamese body floating face-down in the algae. Whether it was a Vietcong or South Vietnamese prisoner was unknown. Grimes searched the bobbing body and found nothing. The gook had been shot in the back and hadn't been there too long. Maybe it was a South Vietnamese prisoner trying to escape when the helos inserted us. Each one of us had to push the body to the side, out of our way, to get by it. Each time it was pushed aside, it drifted back to the center of the small canal.

The center of the canal was clear of algae in most places. The Vietcong used the canal as a major trail for traveling around the area. Still searching for the Americans, we moved on. Panella packed the captured Soviet 7.62mm carbine. This weapon was very common with the Vietcong in South Vietnam. It weighed 8.91 pounds and was fifty-two inches long with its bayonet extended. The magazine held five rounds of ammo. It wasn't worth shit without a round in the chamber.

We soon reached a major trail that led out of the canal to our right. The signal was passed back to set up a secure perimeter again. We must have found another part of the POW camp, I thought, as Reeves and I were the last ones to climb out of the canal into the thick vegetation to find a concealed area for us to cover the rear of our patrol. I didn't get to see much of the area behind us as Mr. Q and the searching element of our platoon carefully investigated the area. A wounded South Vietnamese ARVN was found with some serious leg wounds. Doc was tending to him as the search continued. Everyone in our platoon had a designated job to perform. The security element guarded the perimeter, while the searching element explored the area. Again evidence of at least two Americans being there was discovered. Two rusty chains, like that of a swing set, were found. They looked like they could be pulled apart by hand. Small locks were attached to them. Also, two wooden bowls full of rice with two wooden spoons and a short-wave radio were found, along with a couple of American canteens. Special areas separate from the regular prisoner-holding areas were found with the chains empty. Nipa palm woven together was used for a floor in the American holding area. The area had recently been evacuated. Maybe they had monitored us on the short-wave radio.

Our optimistic views of freeing the two Americans turned into frustration as the search continued. Trails and human tracks led in all directions. No American footprints could be found, just the area in which they had been held captive. If American footprints had been discovered, we surely would have followed the trail. Strong disappointment came over everyone in the platoon when we realized we would probably never see the American POWs after thoroughly searching the entire area. Doc was ordered to radio the two Army slicks to stand by for our extraction. The word was passed back for Reeves and me to regroup with the rest of the platoon as we started to patrol toward the extraction site. The wounded ARVN was taken along for extraction. For a moment my frustration turned to relief just knowing we were on our way to the site. Reeves packed out the rusty chains and the short-wave radio.

After reaching and securing the LZ for extraction, Doc radioed for the two slicks. Watching for any signs of enemy movement, we waited quietly. I could hear the two slicks, the racket of the rotor blades filling the stillness of the Vietnamese countryside as they grew closer. They soon dropped out of the sky toward the yellow smoke grenade marking our position. Running through the wet green grass and weeds, I reached the port door of my ride back to camp. The revolving rotor blades picked up speed and our chopper lifted out of the wet swamp, water dripping from the skids. As we gained altitude and turned to the east, I looked back down at the area we had just patrolled through, feeling I had left something behind. I did—two American servicemen at the mercy of the Vietcong.

CHAPTER THIRTY-TWO

It wasn't long before we were back at our camp. Our platoon had been the major strike force of an important operation. Already several platoons of ARVN soldiers had been inserted into the same area to mop up the POW camp. We had our debriefing and began to clean our weapons. About two hours after the platoon returned to camp, Mr. Q passed the word that the ARVNs had collected about thirty South Vietnamese who had been held captive by the Vietcong. Some of them had been prisoners for more than four years. Like the earlier POW op, all the VC and prisoners scattered when our presence was known.

No Americans had been found in the area. I blamed that on the bureaucracy. Maybe if we had inserted a couple of miles away the night before and patrolled to our objective overnight under cover of darkness we would have been more successful. There are a lot of maybes in an operation of this nature. Our point man had been the only man in the platoon to fire his weapon. Juliett Platoon had tried but was unsuccessful. Without very fresh intelligence, recovering the Americans was next to impossible. This was the last we were to hear of them.

A few days later Weber's stomach began to bother him again, so Doc sent him back to the hospital in Binh Thuy. I collected mail for him that came to our platoon. Finally, on October twenty-sixth, Weber was sent back to the States with severe stomach problems. I was glad he had returned to the States. If anything had happened to him in combat, I would have had a hard time handling it. I returned all his mail to the Naval Amphibious Base in Coronado. It looked like I was to spend my R&R by myself now.

My R&R was confirmed for November third, and I decided to go to Australia. I wrote a letter to my brother and informed him of my change of plans. I also wrote a letter to my parents informing them not to write to Weber at this address anymore. During my tour in Nam, I had a lot of support from my family and friends back home. They kept the letters coming my way, which sure helped my morale. I told my parents in my letter to keep their heads up and I'd keep mine down.

Our platoon took turns rotating squads on operations over the next few days. First squad one night, second squad the next—ambushes, listening posts, and just about anything the platoon had intel on to make an operation. Weber was missed by the platoon. He was a good SEAL operator and a good M-60 man. We'd had a lot of good times in the past together.

One night while in UDT/SEAL training our class had a night compass course quite a few miles north of San Diego, and part of it was to be conducted in a residential area named Cardiff by the Sea. Weber and I thought we were smart by getting all the checkpoints from Class 52, which had already gone through the course a couple of weeks earlier. The instructors dropped us off at the starting point. Everyone had instructions and grid coordinates. We were not to meet up with the instructors again until the wee hours of the next morning at the last checkpoint.

We split up into pairs, set our compasses toward the first checkpoint, and began. The instructors drove off in the six-by, probably to have a few beers someplace. After reaching our first checkpoint successfully, Weber and I waited until other class members left the area. We then walked out to a nearby highway. Hitchhiking with our camouflage clothes and web gear turned out to be easier than we thought. After three different rides, we found ourselves at the last checkpoint, only one and a half hours into our "all-night" evolution.

"What now?" Weber asked.

"It's simple," I answered. "All we have to do is climb

up the side of this mountain and hide up in those rocks. We'll have a good view of the checkpoint from up there, and we'll wait for the instructors to show up in the morning with the six-by.'' We climbed through a barbed-wire fence along the highway and maneuvered through the cactus and brush until we reached a good place behind the rocks on the hillside. We had an excellent view of the last checkpoint, a wide turnout along the highway out in the middle of nowhere several miles from the starting point. Weber slept while I kept watch, and I slept while Weber kept watch. It was a very long, boring night. We filled out all our checkpoints on the paper to be handed over to the instructors when we checked in. The night went so slowly we almost felt like we should have gone through the entire course with the rest of our class just for something to do. We knew how to use a compass, in fact we were pretty good at it, having had lots of compass problems in the past.

Finally, still early in the morning before sunrise, the sound of the six-by could be heard coming down the road. It pulled over in the wide turnout. While Weber and I watched from the rocks above, the instructors were milling around the six-by, waiting for members of our class to show up. ''Let's go down now,'' said Weber.

I stopped him, saying, ''We can't be the first ones to check in, let's wait till some of the other pairs show up first.''

After a while one pair showed up, then another. Finally, Weber and I started down a gully to our right to avoid coming out directly across the highway from the instructors. For some reason I was quite a ways out in front of Weber. I crossed through the barbed-wire fence and waited for him on the other side while watching for other members of our class. Weber came running down the hill behind me. Why he forgot about the barbed-wire fence I'll never know. At a full run, he ran right into the strands of wire. He was immediately thrown back up the hill, like being shot out of a slingshot, and landed on his ass. Both of us lay on the ground on opposite sides of the fence, trying not to let the instructors hear us laughing. Luckily, he wasn't hurt.

After we calmed down, we walked down the road to the six-by. Our checkpoints were handed over to the instructors for them to study. Suddenly the shit hit the fan. The instructors had changed one of the checkpoints on us. They wanted to know how we got to this point using the wrong coordinates. We had no answers. After doing push-ups till we couldn't do them anymore, with the instructors yelling at us the whole time, we were told to sit in the back of the six-by until all of our training class had shown up. I just knew this was the end of UDT/SEAL training for Weber and me. The instructors seemed to always be one step ahead of the trainees. The compass course had been altered from Class 52's just to prevent cheating. After the last pair came in, we were trucked back to our barracks at the Naval Amphibious Base in Coronado. To our surprise, nothing more was said to us by the instructors. We never did tell them how we got to the last checkpoint. Good old Weber, he had survived his first tour to Vietnam, even if he did get to go home early.

By November 1970 the South Vietnamese people were soon expected to be taking over their own war. I personally didn't see that happening. I had lost faith in most of the South Vietnamese military because they relied on us Americans too much. I, for one, was getting tired of doing their dirty work for them with very little support from the South Vietnamese military. Of course, maybe it was better that way—at least I was still alive. I could depend on American support groups.

I actually enjoyed the local South Vietnamese people who farmed the land and lived and worked in the smaller villages. Only thing was, you didn't know who your enemy was. I didn't have any use for the Vietnamese in the bigger cities, though. Seemed they were always out to get you. But that seemed to be the same in all countries, not just Vietnam. I felt free in the country, but the cities seemed to gobble me up. Maybe it was just me. The wet, muddy, humid Vietnam country was taking its toll on me and my gear. Most of my clothes reeked of mildew and seemed to be rotting away. Even the Levi's jeans we wore on operations were falling apart. November third couldn't arrive fast enough.

After a boat ride up the Bassac and a helo ride to Saigon, I found myself aboard a Pan Am 707 en route to Sydney, Australia. Even my civilian clothes smelled of mildew. The plane landed in Sydney, but before we disembarked the entire inside of the aircraft had to be sprayed to kill off bugs we might have brought from Vietnam. First thing I did was go to Bondi Beach, get a room in a hotel, and then buy some new clothes. I spent the next seven days hitchhiking around Australia. Why seven days in Vietnam couldn't go by that fast, I'll never know.

R&R expended, I returned to camp at Dung Island on November eleventh, ready to continue protecting the South Vietnamese from Communist aggression. But by then our platoon was getting short. Still rotating squads, Mr. Q was letting different members of our platoon lead the operations. The grass around the perimeter of our camp grew so fast it constantly had to be cut and burned back. One nonoperating day we were helping the Seabees burn back the grass, but the gasoline that Shannon was using caught fire and burned the hell out of him. He was given a shot of morphine and a med-evac helo was called to our camp to take him to the hospital in Binh Thuy with first- and second-degree burns. Everyone was more careful after that.

Shannon was the tallest man in our platoon. He had a great sense of humor and was a great morale booster who always had a smile on his face.

The time I spent in Nam sure made me appreciate the United States more. It was a good experience for me. Vietnam was a land of simple people, simple ways, and simple ideas, not the complicated ways of us Americans. American money and machines were changing the Vietnamese lifestyles in many ways, but the average countryside rice farmer just wanted to grow and harvest his rice in peace. I had a lot of respect not only for the Vietcong, but the basic Vietnamese people in general. They could take something that was, to us, worthless, and make good use of it. Americans could only take the Vietnamese by the hand, show them American ways, try to train them, give them American ideas and tools. But after America was gone, they would return to their old ways.

Trying to free a country from Communist aggression when it wouldn't help itself was very frustrating for me. Yet the North Vietnamese and most Vietcong had a religious cause for fighting the war; the South Vietnamese had the backing of big-bucks America. It takes more than money to win a war. It takes people dedicated to a cause, fighting for what they believe in. The North Vietnamese and Vietcong had a cause. They also had the dedication. At times it was more like fighting a spirit—or a plague—than an enemy. Kill off the enemy and he would be right back, taking over the area you thought you'd pacified.

A united country, that's what North Vietnam wanted, but our platoon continued to operate on a steady basis, trying to stop the North from taking over the South. Any intelligence we collected to help us do that was put to use. I kept the bananas hanging in our hootch, reminders of a no-contact operation. Bringing back bananas and catching rats for our snake had become an obsession with me by then. Many a night when I did sleep, I was awakened by a fuckin' rat jumping off the shelf over my rack and landing on my face or chest. They reminded me of the Vietcong; there was no end to them, they just kept coming. My personal war with them continued. A captured rat would immediately be rushed to the snake cage, where several of us would stand around listening to the rat's bones popping from the constricting snake's body. From the hair standing up on the rat's body to its disappearing down the snake's jaws out of sight, I enjoyed it all.

Late one afternoon the sky turned dark and the wind kicked up. Looking toward the South China Sea, I noticed a tornado coming in the direction of our camp. The closer it came, the larger it grew. Then it was tearing the jungle apart, ripping up everything in its path, and the Bassac began to dance and waves crashed against the shore. Expecting the worst, we ran to secure our weapons and gear. The drum dock began to twist and torque, metal bending in all directions because of the wind and strong wave action. I had visions of plywood hootches spread across the Bassac River like a deck of cards. The twister turned north, in the direction of the Bassac River. Pieces of jungle flew high into the air. Finally reaching the river downstream from our camp, it sucked up water and dissipated. But our dock was left a twisted wreck of metal plates and fifty-five-gallon drums. Debris was scattered everywhere around the camp.

The mosquitoes buzzed, the flies flew, and the sweat dripped from our faces. Man, it could get hot and humid around there. All the cold beer I could drink didn't seem to help. Just sittin' in the shade wasn't enough; a few trips down to the Bassac became mandatory. Trying to sleep on a sweat-soaked mattress at night added to the long sleepless nights. Many a nonoperating hour was spent in our bar with our overworked air conditioner. The monsoon rains that came and went were more and more welcome.

With each day that went by, my stay in Vietnam was getting shorter. Eventually I figured I might have a chance to make it home alive after all. Just being in Vietnam made my life a booby trap. It didn't matter what part of this country I was in. I had already earned the Bronze Star with the Combat V and the Purple Heart. My life was more important than any medal pinned on my chest. Guarded by South Vietnamese, Seabees, and the antipersonnel devices that surrounded the perimeter, I felt secure within our three-acre camp. The camp had become part of me, but with the right weapons, personnel, and training, Charlie could have run through it within minutes if we SEALs had been gone on an operation or up to Binh Thuy.

One day some South Vietnamese SEALs (LDNNs) showed up at our camp to operate with us. For South Vietnamese fighting men, these guys were hard-core. They showed no mercy for our captured Vietcong, and they were excellent at interrogating the enemy.

One peaceful night the LDNNs pulled out two bottles of Bosy Day, an alcoholic drink I think they used to power the motors on their sampans during the day. We began to drink where they slept, inside a cot-lined porta-tent. It was horrible stuff, but I didn't tell them that. Four SEALs and a squad of LDNNs. Coffee mugs of the foul-tasting shit were quickly consumed. Then I went to my hootch and returned with a bottle of V.O., which tasted better, at least to me. A short time later I slid away from the fun to an isolated spot in camp and puked till I could puke no more. Then I returned to the fun again. The fun had turned into a staggering, tangled mess of Vietnamese and Americans hugging each other and holding each other up.

Boy, that Young was something, they must have thought, he can sure hold his booze. I was the only one out of the group that felt basically normal the next morning. Because of the possibility of the camp getting overrun by the Cong, I wanted to keep my head at least halfway screwed on. The night before, watching my buddies and the LDNNs dropping like insects flying into our perimeter lights, hadn't seemed like a really good time to me. But then again, what else was there to do in a three-acre camp far from anything considered normal? At least smoking a little pot now and then didn't make me feel like warmed-over shit the morning after.

CHAPTER THIRTY-THREE

Fourteen hundred hours, 29 November 1970. Vietnam time.

Reeves had taken ill, but even with his high fever, he wanted to join our platoon's last mission. With the hot muggy afternoon sun beating down on it, Mr. Q and Mr. Walsh were in the briefing hootch laying out the mission briefing. Even with the door open, it stayed hot in there.

This was also to be Quan's last operation with Juliett Platoon; he would be assigned to another SEAL platoon after we left. The Vietnam War was never over for Quan.

Even so, there was always something about Quan I didn't care for. I was glad he was always at the other end of the patrol from me.

Some of the guys were lying in their racks catching zzz's, and some guys like Strausbaugh and Shannon were throwing the Frisbee. The heat didn't seem to bother them. Reeves and I went to the village, taking along some C-rations and candy for the kids and papasan. We had made some good South Vietnamese friends since we came in-country, especially in the village.

After a short visit with the villagers, we returned to camp in time for the mission briefing. At 1830 hours twelve SEALs mustered in the briefing hootch. I realized how lucky our platoon had been. The only two SEALs missing were LePage and Weber. The only two SEALs not yet wounded were Mr. Q and Reeves, but damn near all of us were still together. The platoon had gone on operations using everything from helos to Vietcong sampans. Not being wounded seriously or having spent any hospital time, Reeves and I always seemed to be handy while other SEALs were out of action for some reason or another.

Going on two operations back to back had not been uncommon. This operation was to be conducted in the vicinity of Xom Rach Ngat, a small village on Dung Island's northeast shore. We had been in the area a couple of times before, and I didn't like it. I didn't know anyone who did, maybe except for Mr. Walsh and Grimes—they actually enjoyed going into places like that. Thick jungle, the consuming mud sometimes up to your ankles (solid for the Delta), and at other times (the next step) up to and past your ass. It smelled worse as it got churned up while we patrolled through it. The mud was the normal patrolling condition. Then throw in the pungi pits, trip wires, and anything Charlie might have thought up to blow away even one American.

The platoon had been hearing more stories from the South Vietnamese people of Dung Island about the same young gang of Vietcong terrorizing the inhabitants of the island. Even though the platoon had put a dent in their activities earlier in our tour, they were still regrouping and still recruiting gang members, stealing rice, pigs, and chickens, and torturing Vietnamese to put the fear of God into the others on the island. From fresh intelligence, we now knew where they were held up. Twenty of them or more, they moved around the island a lot, not staying in any one place for more than a few days.

The Khem Bang Co Canal would be used to get us close to the insertion point. We would insert on Rach Ngat Canal. For a second, the Last Will and Testament that I had filled out before leaving the States flashed through my mind. But it didn't spook me. I didn't give a damn what the job was, I was going to do it to the best of my ability, and do what I had to, to come home alive.

Rach Ngat Canal was too small for any of our boats, and it entered the Khem Bang Co Canal which splits Con Coc Island from Dung Island. Other than two LAW rockets, no special gear had to be carried. Any extra ammo over the standard load was left up to the individual, so I packed an extra hundred rounds in my Stoner vest immediately after the briefing.

At 2250 hours the platoon met down to what the storm had left of our dock. We boarded the medium at 2300 hours and got under way northwest, up the Bassac. The night was hot and clear. Our perimeter lights and the last quarter of the moon reflected off the muddy Bassac as we sped off into the night. The radar scope's glow reflected off Mr. Q's forehead as he leaned over and looked into it. The breeze coming across the deck of the medium held back the beads of sweat under the thick greasepaint on my face.

The fast, smooth night ride on the Bassac River soon had everyone lost in their own thoughts. At 2324 hours we reached the northwest end of Dung Island. Mr. Q and the MST coxswain kept a close eye out for sandbars or other obstacles in the boat's path. The tide was up, but that didn't mean anything because the Bassac River bottom was always changing. After rounding the northwest end of Dung Island, we headed southeast down the largest of the two channels of the Bassac that flow on either side of the islands. The large supply ships coming upriver from the South China

Sea to supply the Delta usually did so in the daytime because
Charlie had been known to use the area to launch B-40
rocket attacks and had placed mines in the channel several
times in the past.

Without losing any speed, we continued toward the insertion point. At 2340 hours Khem Bang Co Canal appeared
on the radar. The medium slowed way down while Doc
looked for its entrance through the starlight scope. We had
been down the channel many times in the past, and it wasn't
hard to locate on the radar because it was larger than a
canal. We received the signal to load weapons. Nobody
needed that signal twice.

We entered the channel from the main Bassac. The jungle
quickly moved in on both sides of the medium. Everything
immediately grew darker. It was like being swallowed by
a large snake. This was a spot where the Vietcong leaders
stationed one of their men to fire warning shots, but that
night we heard none. That was not normal for the area.
Maybe Charlie was asleep in his mud-log bunker built above
the riverbank back in the jungle a few meters.

Our boat was quiet. Not long after entering the channel
we passed Rach Tau Canal and then Xeo Dong Canal, which
entered the channel from our left. The medium was moving
along just above idle. At that speed we were a good target
for a B-40. I expected the night to open up with white,
blinding flashes and the deafening explosions from a rocket
attack. But our boat's wake lightly lapped the mud and
vegetation along both shores, and that's all I heard outside
the twin muffled 427 Chevy engines. Tilting my head back,
I could see past the canvas top. The stars filled the night
sky through the gap in the triple-canopy jungle. Beads of
sweat popped out of my forehead.

We maneuvered past the entrances of Rach Thay and
Rach Ong Chu canals, getting closer to our jumping-off
point every minute. Light flickered from candles in a few
hootches situated along the north shore of the channel as
we passed Xom Ben Ba village; the curfew hours kept its
occupants indoors. Still no warning shots.

At 2352 hours Mr. Q gave the signal to stand by for a

fake insertion on the south shore. The medium turned ninety degrees to starboard and we nudged the bow up into a small canal. The entire platoon could have inserted in just a few seconds. That's about how long we stayed there. The medium backed out and we continued on down the channel. We reached Rach Ngat Canal a few minutes later. The medium turned ninety degrees to its starboard again and was able to insert us about fifty meters into our insertion canal.

Counting Quan, thirteen of us slipped over the bow on our sides and maneuvered through the chest-deep water to set up an immediate perimeter on both canal banks. A few seconds later the medium backed out of the canal and continued farther down the channel to make a couple of fake insertions and to stand by for our extraction. Doc and Shannon, each packing a PRC-77 radio, made their radio checks by clicking the mike. As I did after most insertions, I wondered if I'd ever see the medium again. The crew's job wasn't an easy one either. I was not only concerned with my life, but the lives of my fellow SEALs and the MST boat crew too.

Reeves and I weren't far apart, covering the channel behind our element. We definitely needed the element of surprise on this operation. About 0030 hours the normal jungle sounds reappeared. Grimes and Quan were given the signal to check out the canal up ahead. The objective on our minds could instantly be altered by the Vietcong at any time. You might not know he's watching until it's too late!

I hugged the muddy canal bank covering my field of fire. The signal was finally given to follow. My body seemed to be glued to the muddy bank as I pulled myself up while trying to keep my weapon dry all the time. If one hadn't seen us insert, he would never know there were thirteen of us patrolling up the canal. We were all quiet, like the current itself. We took our time, not everyone moving at the same time. Cover the man in front, cover the man in back, watch my flanks. These thoughts registered in my mind. Weapon off safe, low silhouette, standard operating procedures.

Paying attention to small, critical details could mean the

success or failure of a mission. Grimes and Quan would move up, check out the canal, then we'd follow. Move up, freeze, listen, move up a little more. After we patrolled like that for a while, security was set up so we could climb up onto the canal bank to our left. One at a time we helped each other quietly out of the insect-infested muddy water. Some leeches were already moving around inside my cammo shirt top, but there was nothing I could do about it until first light.

After we had a hidden perimeter in the nipa palm, we waited quietly for sounds of enemy movement. Most of the water had drained from my clothes and gear while I laid low to the muddy jungle floor. Pungi pits, some covered and some open, awaited a slipping foot around the canal bank. The pattern reminded me of a checkerboard in some places.

I could pick out Reeves's pale, hollow-eyed face hiding in the vegetation not far from my position. I knew he wasn't feeling well, so I kept a close eye on him. Then, one at a time, we got up quietly and moved farther in the direction of the objective, pointing out to the man behind us if we became aware of any obstacles in our path—for more clarity pungi pit, trip wire, or just a jungle vine.

At 0220 hours we had finally reached a point not far from the objective. We all took advantage of the thick vegetation to conceal ourselves while we waited and listened. It had taken us almost two hours to cover just a few hundred meters. At 0222 hours I heard voices and movement of the Vietcong in the distance. After Mr. Q and Mr. Walsh had studied the situation for a while, we crawled closer. The voices and sounds of movement of several Vietcong grew louder the closer we moved in. I could pick out a small fire near two hootches off in the distance. Reeves and I were signaled to take up positions in the nipa palm to cover the element's rear while the rest of the SEALs moved closer to face the hootches on two sides. We couldn't have been more than forty meters away from the target by then.

Mr. Q split our element in half, his group moving to the left and Mr. Walsh's moving toward the right. Up and

moving around this early in the morning, the Vietcong must
have had something planned. The voices of the VC continued with no change, a sign that the platoon hadn't been
detected. I covered the area toward my rear and to Mr.
Walsh's right flank. Reeves covered the area behind him
and to Mr. Q's left flank. Through the nipa palm, far to the
right of where Mr. Walsh was supposed to be, I noticed
some movement. I slowly trained my Stoner in that direction.

For a second I saw the silhouette of a crouched human
moving from right to left. Was it Mr. Walsh? Was it a
Vietcong sneaking up on Mr. Walsh's element? Mr. Walsh
wasn't supposed to be so far to the right. I kept my Stoner
trained in that direction, watching for the movement again.
Again I spotted the silhouette, but just for about two seconds. It seemed to be popping up and down and moving to
the left toward the two hootches. My uncocked Stoner stayed
trained in that direction. I looked at my watch—0234 hours.

My eyes peered into the dark jungle, trying to determine
who it was. I had to be sure of my target before I let go
with a burst of automatic-weapon fire. All of a sudden the
dark night was filled with blinding flashes from detonating
grenades. Tracers filled the air, ricocheting off the limbs
and nipa palm. Still not knowing if the dark figure was Mr.
Walsh or not, I fired my Stoner way to its right. I received
no return fire from the area where I last saw the silhouette.
I stayed very low to the ground to avoid accumulating any
ricocheting bullets while firing to Mr. Walsh's far-right flank
and into the jungle to our rear. Reeves fired his Stoner to
Mr. Q's far left flank and behind him on his side. That
would keep Vietcong from coming to the aid of their comrades from behind us. From out of the dark, tracers came
toward Reeves's position and mine. We returned the fire,
suppressing it, at least for the moment. Mr. Q was shouting
orders to his element. Tracers continued to streak through
the area, some the Vietcong's and some of our own. I don't
know about Reeves, but I felt all alone from my hidden
position in the nipa palm. Splitting a SEAL platoon into
two different elements had created some serious problems

in the past. In the darkness, getting into a fierce firefight with each other was a strong possibility.

Grenades continued to explode near the two hootches. Reeves continued to put out maximum fire into the jungle behind our element. Soon one of the hootches was on fire, then the other one. My night vision deteriorated because of the blinding flashes that lit up the jungle. Tracers continued to crisscross through the night sky. Reeves and I had to hold our position until the rest of the element regrouped or until we were ordered to do so. Finally, the platoon started regrouping close to us. We covered them from our positions.

After a quick situation report and a head count, at 0248 hours Doc called in air support, then Mr. Q signaled Grimes to start patrolling back out the way we had come in. Our extraction route had to be aborted due to the enemy's occupation. With three prisoners and some captured weapons and documents, wasting no time, the platoon followed Grimes through the booby traps and pungi pits. We were still receiving incoming rounds, and enemy tracers cracked over our heads as we climbed down into the canal, crossing to the other side. This was the shortest and fastest way to the extraction site. Even so, the Vietcong were close on our ass.

Everyone made it across the canal except Reeves. Our bodies were still heavily loaded with ammo, our weapons, and grenades, plus the captured enemy and some of their weapons. Then Reeves jumped into the muddy water and started to swim toward our side. The platoon had set up a perimeter and was covering him. Reeves was an excellent swimmer, but if he stopped swimming, he would sink from the weight he was carrying. He finally reached our canal bank, keeping his Stoner above the muddy water the whole time. I watched Reeves try to muster enough strength to pull himself up the canal bank using some vines and bushes. Above him on the canal bank Mr. Walsh was reaching down when the vines and canal bank gave way and Reeves flew back into the water, where the mud and vines pinned him underwater. Tracers were coming from all directions across the canal and from the direction of the burning hootches.

Reeves's excellent swimming couldn't save him this time, but his hand stuck up through the vines and muddy water. Mr. Walsh jumped down into the water and, holding onto some vines with one hand himself, he reached out and made contact with Reeves's hand. I continued to fire across the canal in an attempt to keep the Vietcong down. It seemed like Reeves had been underwater a long time, but Mr. Walsh pulled him out of the water and to the canal bank. Reeves was gasping for air. With no time for thanks, Reeves and Mr. Walsh climbed up onto the canal bank and we were on our way again.

Our air support still hadn't arrived overhead as we patrolled down the canal. The enemy rounds slowed down; maybe Charlie had lost us. We soon found ourselves down in the muddy leech-infested water again, but the going was a little easier down there, and patrolling was much faster, as we had already patrolled in on that canal. The Khem Bang Co Canal was finally reached. Security was immediately set up on both banks of Rach Ngat Canal and the medium was notified to extract us. An occasional tracer passed overhead through the jungle night.

We had put a hell of a dent in Charlie's party and left him in a confused state. The medium lost no time coming to our aid. Doc guided it into our position using his radio. The prisoners were passed on board to the MST crew. Quickly, the platoon climbed over the bow of the medium and below its gunwales. With us, we brought the captured weapons and documents. The medium then backed into the channel, turned to the northwest, and got under way toward the open Bassac. Our weapons were trained at both banks in case the Vietcong had set up on us. I looked at my watch; it was 0314 hours.

After we entered the main Bassac from Khem Bang Co Canal, we unloaded our weapons and the medium got on step, heading back to camp.

We secured the medium to the dock at 0347 in the morning, tired, wet, muddy, and with all personnel safely back at camp.

At the debriefing Mr. Q informed us that Juliett Platoon

had just successfully completed its last operation in Vietnam, unless a priority situation came up. Needless to say, everyone was happy. But for Quan the war continued. I told Mr. Walsh about the dark figure bobbing around the jungle to his right flank. He told me he had to go farther to his right than he thought he would have to go. Once he started sneaking toward the hootches he encountered too many obstacles so he had to bear to his right.

"That sure scared the shit out of me," I told him. I always made sure of my targets and wouldn't shoot unless I was sure of what I was shootin' at. Shooting into the jungle to keep Charlie down was another thing. Even though I couldn't see the invisible little bastards, the shooting had its purpose. At least I knew what my platoon was doing and knew where each man was. I had taken a chance not shooting at the figure I had seen; it could have been a Vietcong sneaking up on Mr. Walsh. But not knowing for sure, I didn't fire my weapon directly at it. I was sure Mr. Walsh could have handled any Vietcong coming from that direction.

Splitting a platoon in half to accomplish a mission can be very dangerous. Carrying it off takes many hours of training and operating together, getting to know each man's habits under all conditions.

CHAPTER THIRTY-FOUR

The morning of 30 November 1970, Juliett Platoon officially shut down its operations. Another SEAL platoon was already in Saigon, fresh from the States and ready to relieve us. Back on Dung Island, the Vietcong knew the men with green faces would be back, but they didn't know where or when. Later that day intelligence sources informed Mr. Q that we had killed twenty Vietcong on our last operation. With our training, weapons, and the element of surprise, we were able to overcome a larger enemy force than ourselves.

We spent the next few days packing weapons and gear, getting ready for the trip home. The upcoming return didn't seem real to me. After a six-month tour to Vietnam, I had many mixed feelings about the Vietnamese people, the Vietcong, and the North Vietnamese. Some of the South Vietnamese people had become my good friends, but I couldn't stand to be around some of the others. As for the Vietcong, I had the utmost respect for them and hated them at the same time.

Reeves still wasn't feeling well. He had a high fever and cold spells. During our six-month tour, everyone in our platoon had been wounded except for Mr. Q and Reeves. Two days before we were to leave camp for the trip home, Reeves was diagnosed as having malaria. A med-evac helo was called to airlift him to the hospital. I stood on top of the thirty-foot machine-gun tower and took pictures of Mr. Q helping to load Reeves onto the chopper. Reeves was wrapped in a poncho liner and his head and face were covered with a wet, cool towel. One way or another, Vietnam had gotten to everyone.

On 11 December 1970 we loaded all the platoon's gear on board the medium for the last ride up the Bassac River to Binh Thuy. We said our good-byes to our Seabee friends who were staying at camp. Grimes put the eight-foot, three-inch python in a large cardboard box and put it on board the medium also. As the medium backed away from the fifty-five-gallon drum dock, I took a good look at the South Vietnamese outpost that had been my home for so long. Some of the worst and best times of my life had been spent in that three-acre camp. I had the feeling I was leaving something behind, that maybe I shouldn't be leaving.

The medium got on step going up the river. I watched until our plywood hootches disappeared behind us on the horizon. Grimes picked out a spot along the triple-canopy

jungle shoreline and the medium slowed down and turned
toward the south shore. Just in case Charlie was in the area,
the weapons on board the medium were made ready. The
bow nudged up against the muddy bank and Grimes stepped
off the bow with the cardboard box and into the thick nipa
palm. Reaching into the box, he picked the snake up by its
head and body, laid it down on the damp ground, and then
we all watched it slide off into the thick jungle. Once again
our boat backed out into the river and headed upstream.

After arriving at Binh Thuy, our gear was transported to
a C-117 aircraft and we flew to Tan Son Nhut Air Force
Base in Saigon. On December thirteenth, after sitting around
Tan Son Nhut Airport for a few hours, our C-118 departed
Saigon at 0445 hours. I expected the Vietcong to throw in
a rocket attack before we took off, but that never happened.

I looked down on Vietnam for what I thought would be
my last time in-country. I felt as if I should still be down
there, working my way across one of those rice paddies,
covering the element's rear or setting up a perimeter.

Juliett Platoon worked as a team, the way we were
trained. One for all and all for one. All the men of Juliett
Platoon have their own stories to tell. Some may be more
accurate, some may not be. This is my story as seen through
my eyes from my position within the platoon.

After brief stops in the Philippines, Japan, Midway Island, and Hawaii, we arrived at the SEAL Team One compound at 0400 hours on 16 December 1970. I put in for a
transfer to Underwater Demolition Team 11 a few days later,
and it was approved. A few months later I deployed to
Vietnam again with that unit.

I owe my getting back to the States alive to the professionalism of the officers and enlisted men of Juliett Platoon.
What a lucky man I am to be alive.

ABOUT THE AUTHOR

Born in Carmel, California, on August 18, 1950, Darryl Young graduated from South Fork High School, Miranda, California, in June 1968. He joined the Navy on February 17, 1969, and while attending Navy boot camp in San Diego, California, volunteered for BUDS (Basic Underwater Demolition/SEAL) training. After completing boot camp, in May of 1969 he received orders to the Naval Amphibious Base, Coronado, California, to start his UDT/SEAL training with Class 53. In November 1969 Darryl Young successfully completed UDT/SEAL training and received orders to SEAL Team One, also at the Naval Amphibious Base in Coronado. He deployed with Juliett Platoon, Detachment Golf, to Vietnam in June 1970, and returned to the States in December 1970, being awarded the bronze star with combat "V" and a Purple Heart. In July 1970 he transferred to Underwater Demolition Team 11 and deployed to the West Pacific a second time for thirteen months.

Honorably discharged December 1, 1972, Darryl Young is currently one-hundred-percent disabled due to avascular necrosis, a rare degenerative bone disease caused by a gradual buildup of nitrogen bubbles in the major joints while deep diving in the Navy. In November 1984 Darryl handcuffed himself to the Federal Building in Boise, Idaho, headquarters of the Idaho State VA, to protest the Veterans Administration's mishandling of his disability claim. According to the VA, Young's is a "landmark case," opening up the VA door to other military divers with symptoms of this rare service-connected diving disease. Young is the first man in the history of the VA to be compensated for avascular necrosis.

Darryl Young is now living in Montana with his wife Sandy, son Jamie, and daughter Jennifer.